The Private Lives
of Britain's
Royal Women

The Private Lives of Britain's Royal Women

UNITY HALL

MICHAEL O'MARA BOOKS LIMITED

First published in Great Britain in 1991 by
Michael O'Mara Books Limited,
9 Lion Yard, Tremadoc Road, London SW4 7NQ

Copyright © Unity Hall 1990, 1991

A CIP catalogue record for this book
is available from the British Library

ISBN 1-85479-083-8

Designed by Simon Bell

Typeset by Florencetype Limited, Kewstoke, Avon
Printed and bound by Richard Clay Limited, Bungay, Suffolk

Contents

Introduction:
The People's Love

ROYAL WOMEN may, like other women, live for love, but if the Monarchy is to survive, the love they must court the most assiduously is the love of the people. To be the recipient of mass affection is a wondrous thing, but it is hard earned. And once earned, the goodwill of the people carries with it a responsibility to conform to certain standards.

The British are demanding of their Royal women. Not only must they be elegant figureheads, but they must be seen to care for others less fortunate than themselves. They are expected to uphold family life. They must never act in a grand manner though the public demands that they are constantly in the spotlight. They should be aloof from the people yet contrive at the same time to appear friendly. They must not seem to be extravagant even while dressing and living in the style that the people expect of Royalty. They must always do their duty and set a good example. Above all, they must give value for the money that the taxpayer provides for them. The British public is quick to recognize those who are lazy, selfish, arrogant, or greedy. It is a delicate balance and one that the Queen and most of the women of her family have sustained brilliantly.

Since Elizabeth II has been on the throne, the Republican element in Britain has dwindled, even though Monarchs, unlike Presidents, are not elected by the people. The people have no choice in the matter, and neither do those who are born to reign. Britain has had bad Kings and corrupt Queens and courtiers in the distant past but not for more than a hundred years. The Queen and those Kings that preceded her have all been decent, honourable people who have earned the nation's respect.

The focus of the people's deepest curiosity and their love and affection is almost always the women of the family. The lion's share of the power to keep the Monarchy alive is held by them through the affection they inspire. The Princess of Wales today excites the greatest interest. If Royalty is the greatest show on earth, the Queen remains the leading lady—but it is Diana who daily steals the show. Yet in their youth, the Queen herself; her mother, Queen Elizabeth; and her sister, Princess Margaret all fired the public's imagination in precisely the same way as the Princess of Wales and the Duchess of York do today. And the nation's respect for the Queen has remained unchanged throughout her reign.

The country's love for its Monarch was demonstrated as never before on the June morning of Queen Elizabeth II's Silver Jubilee in 1977. She stood at her Buckingham Palace bedroom window and looked across the courtyard to the broad, tree-lined Mall. Outside the palace gates were thousands of her subjects, some singing and some still sleeping. Many had been there all night. This vast crowd had come to rejoice and to give their sincere thanks to a good Queen who had served them well for twenty-five years.

But the throng was there for more than that. They had come to present the Monarch with their love.

From his room farther down the palace corridor, the Prince of Wales, her eldest son, stood awestruck, watching the same sight. It was to be a day when the reserved and unemotional British would permit themselves to be unashamedly for their Queen and for their country. The occasion was as emotional and moving for the Queen and her family as it was for those who came to cheer.

Four years later, early one July morning, Prince Charles looked again from his palace bedroom window on his wedding day to see another crowd singing and laughing below. This time there was a new focus for their affection. Lady Diana Spencer had captured not just the heart of the Prince of Wales but the heart of the nation. As Prince Charles turned from the window, his valet noticed that his eyes were filled with tears.

The people had come to bless his bride.

— 1 —

Power and Wealth:
The Royal Aphrodisiacs

ONE OF LIFE'S more imponderable problems for Royalty is knowing whether they are really loved for themselves. Or, they wonder,
does it have nothing to do with their bonny blue eyes? Is the strongest
factor in their chosen partner's decision to say 'I do' the high position
that comes with marriage to a member of the Royal family?

The problem increases when we take into account that love and
marriage don't necessarily go together in the goldfish bowl of Royal
life. Generally speaking, suitability is the first and foremost quality
required in a Royal's spouse; therefore, marriages in Royal circles have
never had a great deal to do with love. On the occasions when true
love is present, it is considered not so much a necessity as a bonus.

As we all know, great power and great wealth are formidable
aphrodisiacs. Cynics say that it is just as easy to fall in love with
someone rich as someone poor. No doubt, given the opportunity, it is
just as easy to fall in love with a Royal as a commoner. In recent years
both Sarah Ferguson and Lady Diana Spencer have discovered the
truth of this. Two women both in the Royal eye by reasons of birth or
circumstances were given the opportunity to become Royal—and
grasped it. Lady Diana Spencer was less of a surprise. She did have the
requisite background. She was couture-made for the job. Sarah
Ferguson's credentials were a touch more off the peg, yet the Queen,
who is no snob, has taken her second son's boisterous wife to her
heart.

It was always in the cards that Diana Spencer would marry into the

1

Royal family. She was ideally placed for it. Her father had been a Royal Equerry to the Queen in Coronation Year, and her maternal grandmother, the Countess of Fermoy, was one of the Queen Mother's closest friends and, up until recently, one of her ladies-in-waiting. Also, Diana's childhood home, Park House in Norfolk, abutted the Queen's Sandringham Estate. She was literally the girl next door, and as a child, Diana and her older sisters, Jane and Sarah, were invited to play with the Royal children and shared many a nursery tea with Princes Andrew and Edward. Later, Prince Charles was briefly involved with her sister Sarah. It came to nothing. However, their brief friendship could have been enough to make Diana see Charles as her sister's ex, rather than as someone for herself.

Anyway, she had a boyfriend. He was a young writer, George Plumptree, the third son of a Kent landowner. They were cosy enough for him to bring his washing round to her flat to be put through the twin tub and the dryer, and he had planned to take her to the ballet on the day her engagement to Charles was announced.

George was around for about a year. But it was, in fact, Andrew about whom Diana dreamed her adolescent dreams. At an early age she had a schoolgirl crush on the Queen's most boisterous son. Charles was so much older than she—thirteen years—that she barely knew him. In her early teens she considered him old, and he saw her as a schoolgirl (which she was). She belonged in Andrew's age group. 'Wouldn't it be funny if I grew up to marry Andrew?' she said to a friend one day. And once, when teased for her lack of boyfriends, she laughed and said, 'I'm saving myself for Prince Andrew.'

In fact, those closest to the Royal family always had it in the back of their minds that Lady Diana would be the perfect mate for Prince Andrew. And when she turned up on the Royal yacht in August 1980, at first she was definitely considered one of 'Andrew's crowd'. She was one of the many friends of the younger Royals, in particular Lady Sarah Armstrong-Jones. The younger group was all much of an age, but now that Diana was nineteen, tall, rounded, and with the blonde hair and blue eyes that have always attracted the Prince of Wales, suddenly Charles didn't appear quite so old. He seemed handsome, romantic, and a great deal more glamorous than his noisy, younger brother.

The flirtatious young Diana decided she wanted the Prince of Wales, and she went all out to get him. The late Stephen Barry, who was the Prince's valet at the time, watched it all. 'He didn't stand a chance,' he said.

Not that Charles took much notice of Lady Diana at first, though it was noted that her eyes followed him everywhere. He liked her enough to invite her to one of the Queen's house parties at Balmoral that September. The staff, who understands the Royals and their habits better than most, had fallen in love with her to a man and was beginning to think that maybe Diana was the one for 'the job'—as marriage to Prince Charles was always called. But then there had been many other occasions when they had thought that the Prince might have found The One and had been proven wrong. As it was, everyone believed Lady Diana was perfect and he'd never do better. The trouble was that the Prince didn't seem to be taking much notice of her.

It was at this point that the two grannies stepped in. The Queen Mother and Lady Fermoy decided that Charles was not seeing what was under his nose. Lady Diana was invited back to Scotland a month later by the Queen Mother to stay at her hunting lodge, Birkhall. Lady Fermoy was also present. The party was to stalk Highland deer, and it was a much smaller, more intimate group than the gatherings the Queen had given next door at Balmoral. Prince Charles was a guest too, Birkhall being one of his favourite places. The Queen Mother has a gift for making homes cosy, and cosy is one of Prince Charles's favourite words. Cosy Birkhall was much more suitable for getting to know someone than the rambling Balmoral. Unfortunately, the Prince still didn't seem to take too much notice of Lady Diana, who sat demure and good as gold, working at her needlepoint and speaking when she was spoken to.

She was passing an important test—managing to appear as if she thought Scotland was the best place in the world, which Prince Charles believes it is. In light of her later obvious dislike of 'boring old Balmoral', as she has been known to refer to the place, this must have taken some doing. Perhaps she knew how many of Prince Charles's romances had foundered when his girlfriends decided that not even marriage to the next King was compensation enough for week after weary week every year at this Scottish Gothic castle in the middle of nowhere.

It was a strange courtship, with all the effort coming from Diana. Prince Charles was hardly gallant. She was driven down to

Highgrove—Prince Charles's country home in Gloucester—four times in the autumn before they became engaged. On each occasion, when she arrived at the half-furnished messy house, Prince Charles was out hunting. Lady Diana amused herself by walking around the gardens until he returned. It was the sort of behaviour that had sent his previous girlfriend, Anna Wallace, into tearing rages. Diana put up with it.

For a nineteen-year-old woman the courtship was downright dull. They would have tea alone together and later eat a light supper, which the valet would cook for them. It generally consisted of spinach from the garden with country eggs, left on a hot plate. They ate off a card table in the unfinished sitting room, and at about 9.30, accompanied by his policeman, the Prince would drive Diana back to her London flat.

They did see each other at Buckingham Palace, and half the fun for Diana must have been getting there. She had a baptism by fire during the courtship when her Kensington flat was under siege as the world began to realize that this was it. She was The One. Beleaguered by the press, the couple had to work out all sorts of subterfuges so they could meet. Prince Charles had not proposed, and maybe he wasn't going to. It would have been harmful to the young Lady Diana's reputation if it were obvious how much time—in private—she was spending with the Prince. Stephen Barry was most often delegated to fetch her, and they had worked out a series of complicated arrangements for escape. Out of the back door, down the fire escape, into a waiting taxi. She would lead a convoy of press cars to her grandmother's flat in Eaton Square or her sister's home in what has been called the Royal housing estate, Kensington Palace, and then nip out of the back door from there. She had a series of coded telephone signals that explained where she was, and once free of her pursuers, she would make a quick call to Stephen Barry to come pick her up. In all this she received no other assistance from the Palace. She had to cope alone as a salutary lesson in exactly what being Royal entails. It was to give her the opportunity to make up her own mind as to whether or not she would be able to deal with the strain.

She never cracked—and she got 'the job'!

Barry told how she would relax in the front passenger seat of the car while he drove, chatting about all sorts of things. She never minded the press's interest in her and coped with it very well. It is interesting to speculate whether the press's interest was, as irritating as it must have been, in a curious way making her position stronger. Even the public, prompted by the media, was beginning to think that she might be the one for the job. To Barry she merely said she didn't mind all the fuss as much as other people seemed to and chatted on about clothes and children while tucking into a bag of sweets.

She also asked him a lot of questions about the Prince's likes and dislikes. She was always buying the Prince small presents, like a blue sweater because Barry said his favourite colour was blue. But she never asked questions about the other women in Prince Charles's life. Perhaps she sensed that even though Barry would have known all the answers, he wasn't likely to give them to her.

It must be said that Diana was as cunning as any young woman bent on conquest of a man. She charmed everyone around the Prince, and she charmed members of the press, letting them know subtly that she didn't mind how much they pursued her. In a way, they were playing her game. She never put a wrong foot forward with either her future relatives or staff, with the result that everyone was rooting for her. Everyone adored Diana. Anyone close to the Prince was willing him to marry her, and great sighs of relief went up when the engagement was announced.

She was, however, to change considerably once the marriage was a fait accompli. . . .

The Prince's thirty-second birthday party in November 1980 could have been a turning point for Diana. She was invited to Sandringham for a long weekend as his birthday companion. They had planned four days together—but not alone. That is not the Royal way. Diana was there with an assorted house party for a pheasant shoot. The weekend was a disaster. There were photographers and reporters from everywhere in the world camped all over the public roads that crisscross Sandringham, all certain this was IT. The hullabaloo was such that it wasn't even possible for Diana to go for a walk with the Prince. Over Sunday lunch a furious Prince Philip said that the only thing to do was for Lady Diana to go back to London. That way everyone would get some peace, and he could get on with his shooting.

Stephen Barry, acting as decoy, took the Prince's Range Rover down the drive and turned into the fields—the press in hot pursuit.

Prince Charles drove Lady Diana in the farm Land Rover in another direction. There they kept a rendezvous with an unmarked police car waiting two miles away. It worked. A depressed Lady Diana was back in the warmth of her Coleherne Court flat while the press still waited in freezing Norfolk.

Still Charles vacillated. Those close to the throne could not understand why. His father was pressuring him. He was thirty-two, and Prince Philip had been saying for some years that it was time his son married or there wouldn't be anyone suitable left. And now here was the eminently suitable Lady Diana Spencer, age nineteen, obviously in love. Indeed, she was someone who had always been vaguely considered as a possible Royal bride, even if it was the younger brother everyone had had in mind.

Diana was young, healthy, dewy, and virginal. Embarrassingly, her uncle, Lord Fermoy, publicly confirmed the intimate fact that she had had no lovers, so there could be no doubt of her sexual purity (though one does wonder how he could have been so certain). Therefore, unlike other women Charles had loved in the past—and according to his valet, he did fall in love quite regularly—there were no ex-lovers to come out of the woodwork. Charles accepted that Diana was certainly the most suitable possible bride he had found yet. But he hesitated to make the commitment. It took a lecture from his parents about tampering with the affections of a nineteen-year-old to force his decision to propose.

There was no doubt that she was in love with him. As Barry said, she was always available when he called; she always fitted in with his plans, did her best to make it look as if she liked opera as much as he did (she couldn't stand it), and obviously adored being with him.

Charles's doubt might have come from that old niggle—was it the thought of the life ahead as Princess of Wales that attracted her or was she really in love with him? For despite all the difficulties that go with being Royal, notably the loss of privacy, the title of Princess of Wales is a glittering prize. And for him there were other anxieties to face. For a man of his sophistication and education she was frighteningly young—green as a spring lettuce. Her education was virtually nil. Also, they had nothing in common. Diana tried very hard in those early days, but she could not stop her beautiful eyes from glazing over at any intellectual conversation. It was unfortunate that she hated horses when she was about to join a family who thinks of little else and that her basic reading was novelettes rather than the sophisticated tomes Charles favours.

Nor was he sure he was in love. Once, when asked if he were in love, he hesitated and then said, 'Yes, whatever that is.' Diana's reply was blithe, 'Of course.'

Diana fell in love with Charles surely enough, but when she did, Charles was still nursing a yen for the difficult and delightful Anna Wallace, who had walked out on him in a spectacular manner. Perhaps that was at the root of all his hesitations. Anna Wallace was the only one of his girlfriends to blow the whistle on him. She walked out in August 1980, coinciding with Lady Diana's appearance on the Royal yacht. In many ways Anna would have suited the Prince more than the young Diana. She was just as good-looking as the Princess of Wales and had an equally sparkling personality, but in addition she shared the Prince's interests. She was as crazy about hunting as he was and enjoyed polo. She was also more sophisticated and knowledgeable than Diana. He was enormously attracted to her. His only anxiety was that the press would rake up something from her past that would preclude her from becoming Princess of Wales. It had happened to him earlier when he thought he had found the perfect woman for the job—Davina Sheffield.

Davina was rich and stylish, though not aristocratic. She was Charles's girlfriend for two years, between 1974 and 1976. She was very like Princess Diana in looks and charm, but rather more grown-up. Charles was undoubtedly in love with her and she with him. She had even gone away for the regulation 'thinking about it' period, in this case to Saigon to look after orphaned Vietnamese children. Then, just as the relationship was coming to fruition, a young man with money on his mind came on the scene. He was James Beard, an Old Harrovian boat designer, and he sold the story of his romance with Davina, describing their life together in what he called a rose-covered cottage. It ruined her chances of marrying the Prince. The future Queen could not have so obvious a past.

Prince Charles was always furious at what he called the press's muckraking when journalists dug into the backgrounds of his girlfriends, but he had to admit privately that their detective work was in some ways a service to him. Any woman, like Lady Diana Spencer, whose private life could stand up to that intense scrutiny, backed by editors and proprietors waving large cheques, was unlikely to cause the Royal family any embarrassment. Had the treacherous Mr. Beard appeared after the wedding, it could have been disastrous for the Monarchy.

Anna Wallace might or might not have survived the muckraking. She certainly had seen and still was seeing other boyfriends while she was escorted by Charles. But she had lunched with the Queen at Windsor, and the Queen, not wishing to be used as an added attraction, never met just a casual girlfriend of Charles. Anna had also been shown around Buckingham Palace and was Charles's guest at his grandmother's eightieth birthday celebrations at Buckingham Palace. It was there that their famous row that ended the friendship took place. Charles left her at the table while he circulated. When he returned, she was furious at what she considered the discourteous way he had treated her. She stormed out. The Prince tried to restore the relationship, but she was generally fed up with the secrecy that had to surround the romance and with the press probing into her private life. None of it was for her.

Her decision left the field clear for Diana.

But Charles still had not declared himself to the patient young Lady Di by Christmas of that year, though it seems certain he had almost made up his mind to do so. Royals cannot get married on the spur of the moment. All their engagements are fixed six months in advance. If Prince Charles were going to marry Lady Diana, he had to make up his mind before he sat down with his 'officials' to decide on his engagements for the second six months of the year. As Stephen Barry put it, if Lady Diana had turned him down he would have had an awful lot of free time for polo in the summer of 1981. But she wasn't going to turn him down.

Diana has always bitten her nails. They must have been down to the quick by Christmas 1980. She spent it with her own family and he with his, but then the call came for her to join the Sandringham house party in January 1981. She arrived at the house in her own Mini Metro with reporters in a pack behind her, much to Prince Philip's fury. She was forced to stay within the confines of the house and spent most of the day drinking coffee with the footmen and waiting for the Prince to come back from the shoot while journalists roved the estate.

This time it was Charles, not Philip, who decided that Diana's presence was ruining everyone's fun. He said to Stephen Barry, 'I can't bring her down here anymore. Highgrove's full of workmen, but we'll just have to go there next weekend.'

Again Barry was dispatched to pick her up at her grandmother's flat in Eaton Square, and they drove down to the Cotswolds on a grey and rainy day. She slept most of the way, a cassette of her favourite music, a Tchaikovsky piano concerto, playing. Stephen Barry and the gardener had worked out a back route into Highgrove, which they took. As a further decoy, Charles was hunting in Leicester-shire. Again Diana sat waiting for him in half-finished, gloomy Highgrove.

This time her patience was rewarded. That night the Prince proposed. Stephen Barry had no doubts that it had happened when she told him as he drove her back to London in the grey early dawn that she was planning a three-week trip to Australia to see her mother and stepfather. 'Ha-ha!' thought Barry, 'that's her thinking-it-over time.' It was the Prince's style to tell people to 'think about it' before making any decision, and marrying him was a pretty serious one to make. Diana undoubtedly knew what her answer was going to be before she even left. And even though her mother gave the news a cool reception—seeing too many similarities between her own first, broken marriage to a much older, powerful man—Diana's three-week trip was whittled down to two. She said yes and flew home to announce her engagement.

Charles was still not acting like a man deeply in love. Diana was the one who did all the phoning from Australia, his mother paid for the engagement ring, and his style with his young fiancée seemed more a deep, protective fondness than passionate love.

She moved into Buckingham Palace immediately after the engage-ment was announced. The Prince carried on with his duties, and she spent a great deal of time alone. And it was while she was trying to amuse herself that something happened that could have caused her early insecurity and unreasonable jealousy of all the Prince's old staff and close friends.

In a drawer of the Prince's desk she found a beautiful and very expensive bracelet. At first she thought it was a surprise present for her. But it was not. Whether or not she ever asked the Prince outright why it was there is not known, but the bracelet certainly never came her way.

Could her determination to clear out all the old guard who had known so much about her future husband's life pre-Diana have begun then? Because clear them out she did, policemen, valet, and eventually even private secretaries.

But mystery bracelet or not, she had no need of the support of these men anymore. They had served their purpose. And there were other changes appearing in Diana. The Royal family, to its dismay, was beginning to realize that she was not quite the demure and pliant young girl she had played. She had a mind of her own, could be extremely stubborn, and, worse, was unpredictable. But she had not allowed this steelier, defiant side of her nature to emerge in the courtship days. Her stepmother, Raine, could have given the Royal family a few tips, since the new Countess of Spencer had seen this other aspect of the demure Diana. No doubt Raine still smarts when she remembers being unwise enough to suggest that Diana wear 'suitable clothes' for a memorial service. As a gesture of defiance, Diana went out and bought the brightest pop clothes she could find—and wore them.

There were moments throughout the engagement when Charles seriously wondered if he might have made a mistake as his fiancée's unpredictability began to show. The most troublesome incident was when she burst into tears at a polo match. The press photographers had been harassing her, and the woman who had been so cooperative with the photographers before the engagement suddenly couldn't stand it a moment longer. Big tears trickled down her face. She was whisked away and popped into bed to rest. But Charles was worried that she wouldn't stand the pressure of being Royal, and no doubt the rest of the family was worried too. The truth of the matter was that her distress was probably caused by nothing more than a touch of premenstrual tension, but of course Royal ladies aren't allowed to suffer from that. At least, not in public.

There was another outbreak, perhaps one that Prince Charles was not aware of. It took place at a gala night at London's Guildhall where the late Princess Grace of Monaco was to read her own poetry.

This was the occasion before the wedding when Lady Diana caused a sensation by appearing in a rather naughty black strapless dress, a dress which had caused the Prince of Wales to raise a slightly censorious eyebrow even before they left the Palace. Princess Grace noticed that the young Lady Di looked totally panicked, perhaps because she realized that the dress had been a mistake. Grace suggested that they go to the royal retiring room where Diana promptly burst into tears. She couldn't stand it, she wailed. She couldn't stand the way people spied on her and invaded her every waking minute. 'What shall I do?' she pleaded.

Princess Grace, who had been along the same difficult road herself, put her arms around the young woman, hugged her and said ruefully, 'Don't worry, dear. It can only get worse.' The remark brought about a watery smile from Diana and got her through the rest of the evening.

The time of engagement was certainly not all roses. And even when they were safely married it took some while for the couple to adjust and come together in an adult and sensible manner. Diana went through a period when she was acting like an unruly teenager, which didn't do a lot for either the marriage or the Monarchy. She now seems to have grasped (which Fergie has not) that the Royal family must not behave like the more stupid type of aristocrat, who behaves badly and gets away with it, nor can its members publicly perform in a Sloane Ranger fashion. The Royal family must be classless, neither ordinary nor grand. The Queen has always understood this. She is dignified without being standoffish. She is regal without being pompous. And she is loved without pandering to the masses. Gradually, Princess Diana is coming to understand these subtleties. Prince Charles has always understood them, and her change in attitude from Sloane to Royal can only help the marriage. He is, of course, no less selfish than his privileged position has inevitably made him, and Diana will have to live with that. He does, however, seem to have found some serious and useful purpose in life.

*

Fergie's marriage to Prince Andrew might never have happened without the intervention of Lady Di. In the early days of her growing friendship with Prince Charles, Diana met Sarah at Cowdray Park, where the Prince was playing polo. Diana needed a cosy girlfriend to keep her company through the interminable polo matches she was obliged to watch—with a smile—in her role as the Prince's possible intended. Sarah's wacky companionship made the polo a lot more fun, and the two women, who already had many friends in common, became close. And Diana, aware of the considerable romantic problems Fergie had at that time, began matchmaking. She also had Prince Andrew's interests in mind, since the Royal family was beginning to be alarmed by the obvious unsuitability of his hit parade of actress and model girlfriends.

Even with Diana's backing, Sarah Ferguson was something of a surprise runner in these particular filly stakes. She was a commoner (some, notably Princess Michael of Kent, say a touch too common), a girl who giggled her way through school and led the usual Sloane Ranger life of dabbling in various socially OK jobs when not having fun and whizzing around the world—when her meagre funds allowed it. Very likeable, good with people, and competent when she wanted to be, she had charm, a sense of fun, and enthusiasm that helped her get away with murder with a series of indulgent employers.

But when she popped up in Royal circles, she was already a lady with a past. Royals aren't quite as obsessed with feminine purity as the media would have us believe, but the past of the hoydenish Sarah with the wonderful red hair could have been considered too recent for comfort. Her affair with one Paddy McNally, a middle-aged widower and father of two teenage boys, had been going on for three years. He had gathered her up at the ski resort of Verbier in Switzerland when he noted that her romance with a ski enthusiast, Kim Smith-Bingham, had ended. In the autumn, Fergie had returned to Verbier to the apartment she and Kim had shared to find Sarah Worsley, a niece of the Duchess of Kent, there. Fergie had been off exploring South America, and naturally she was dismayed that Smith-Bingham hadn't the patience to wait for her return.

Paddy McNally lived 'up the road' in a splendid chalet known as The Castle. He knew Fergie from her winter visits to 'Chelsea-on-Ski', as Verbier is known. He had always enjoyed her company and found her amusing. He took the trouble to get in touch with her when he was in London. Fergie found herself heavily attracted to him.

McNally is wealthy, a businessman involved in motor racing. He has a string of equally rich and somewhat raffish friends, including some aristocrats like the now reformed drug-taking Jamie Blandford, son of the Duke of Marlborough. McNally lived much of the year in the Verbier castle, where the besotted young Sarah became his lover, looked after his boys, and played his hostess throughout the ski season. Her various employers back in London were resigned to her disappearances in a way they might not have been if her father, Prince Charles's polo manager, had not had Royal connections.

The life at Verbier was not at all like that of our own dear Queen, and today Fergie must be aware of a yawning difference between a Balmoral house party and the après-ski days she spent with McNally's hard-living friends. Their social habits ranged from jolly japes like throwing cream cakes at each other to heavy drinking and all-night rowdy parties, as well as other self-indulgences. The Royal family does not give rowdy parties or drink a great deal (though admittedly Andrew can throw a cream cake with the best of them when given the opportunity).

Sarah Ferguson fell very deeply in love with Paddy McNally, but he and his set gave her a hard time. She wanted marriage. He wanted nothing of the sort. He was twenty-two years older than she, an odd-looking fellow with a thin, beaky face, not much hair, and glasses. But though no Adonis, he is a man who is interested in women and is therefore remarkably attractive to them. Fergie spent a lot of time nursing painful jealousy, fighting with him when he paid another woman too much attention. Not unnaturally McNally invited a great many women he fancied to his castle, and Sarah used to try to guard her position with a sort of eager, puppy-dog friendliness. 'Hallo, I'm Sarah,' she would say, hoping that this would make it clear she was the Sarah who was the other half of the McNally twosome. It usually worked. It was called 'the Fergie treatment' by the gang, and one woman who experienced it remembers, 'You got the "stay away" message loud and clear.'

Ingrid Seward, the editor of *Majesty* magazine, the Royal watcher's bible, who knew and liked Fergie, asked her one day why she put up with it.

'Because I love him,' Fergie said with touching simplicity. At other times she would say, 'I know I'm being a fool, but . . .,' and then she would find some reason to convince herself it was right to continue the relationship.

In those days she did a lot of crying on girlfriends' shoulders—most of whom advised her to ditch him. She didn't always take his philandering quietly. Once she emptied a bucket of ice water over his head when she felt he was flirting too obviously with one of the better-looking female visitors.

Verbier was not good for Sarah Ferguson's confidence. She didn't have the finances to compete with the McNally crowd. She was always the worst-dressed of the set—she has little gift for style—and she was always the plumpest in a crowd where slender elegance was all. Like many overweight women she had learned to compensate by making herself the life and soul of the party and by permitting herself to be the butt of others' jokes. She was popular because she made sure everyone was happy—often at her own expense. The Verbier gang that ran with McNally could not be called kind. Sarah learned to make herself amusing to them by clowning—in the same goofy manner that caused pained expressions in the early days of her public appearances as the Duchess of York. But she shone on the ski slopes. There she was a match for anyone—including the men. On the slopes she was happy, athletic, and uncomplicated. It is not surprising that she returns as often as she can to these scenes of glory.

In June 1985, Fergie announced to Paddy McNally that she was spending Ascot week at Windsor as a guest of the Queen. The Princess of Wales had persuaded the Queen to invite her redheaded friend. McNally actually drove Sarah from London to Windsor Castle, helped her with her suitcases, and kissed her good-bye—not knowing that this week would prove to be the beginning of the end for their affair. This small courtesy that he paid his girlfriend was eventually to create much raucous laughter from his bitchy set.

At the Princess of Wales's urging, Andrew, who had known Sarah most of his life, took a second look at her. Two years previously they had met at Floors Castle in Scotland, the home of their mutual friends Lord and Lady Roxborough, who have since separated. Andrew, newly involved in photography, had spent most of that weekend taking pictures of Fergie, fascinated by her wonderful hair. The June Ascot week gave him the opportuity to get to know her even better —and for her to know him.

It must be said that Andrew was not enormously popular with women of his own class and background. He was known as the 'Great I Am' by his contemporaries at Gordonstoun, where he was educated, because he behaved arrogantly and exactly as he wished. Later he behaved exactly as he wished with young ladies, working on the assumption that since he was a Prince they would be flattered by any attention he paid them. 'He thought he could put his hands on their thighs under the table at dinner,' said one who had observed him, 'and of course those who weren't model girls didn't like it.'

In short, pre-Fergie, Andrew was about as subtle as a Sherman tank. One of his methods of impressing himself on a young woman was to force-feed her. Fergie got the same treatment. He endeavoured to make her eat a plate of sticky, fattening, chocolate profiteroles. Fergie was on a diet and eventually made this plain by giving him a playful but powerful right-hander. Legend says this was the moment that Andrew fell in love. He certainly might have been impressed that this was a woman who was taking no nonsense from him. It might also have dawned on him that since they were both excessively extroverted, perhaps they were made for each other.

Sarah was very much on his arm throughout that Ascot week. The media took little notice. This jolly, rather hefty young woman was too far removed from the exotic girls that normally attracted Andrew and spent weekends with him at Buckingham Palace while the rest of the family were away. Not his type, the press decided.

Almost immediately after Ascot ended, Andrew was off on a tour of Canada. Fergie spent her summer, Sloane style, on the island of Ibiza at the villa of friends. She was there for several weeks, with Paddy as her companion. The affair was still going strong. And it continued even after July 13, when Andrew, back from Canada, asked to see her again.

'She was surprised—and flattered,' a friend recalled.

Very soon she and the Prince were more than just good friends. She continued to be flattered, though her friends insist that she never expected anything serious to come of it.

'She was always poor old Fergie,' one said. 'She was the girl who had the love problems. She never saw herself as marrying a Prince and living happily ever after. In fact, she didn't have much confidence that anyone would want to marry her at all.'

Certainly McNally didn't want to though he did care about her. Prince Andrew courted her in a way that her older lover never had. Andrew sent red roses. He arranged candlelit dinners. Every Friday he drove from his naval base at Portland—150 miles—to see her. Either she went to Buckingham Palace to see him or they met up with friends. Andrew, surprisingly, was proving to have hidden depths of romanticism. But Paddy was still a fixture, and Sarah still wanted to marry him. She saw Prince Andrew as nothing more than a dalliance —someone who would never really take her seriously, but who, from her point of view, was helping her through a difficult time.

For Paddy was obdurate that they had no future together. He said he was too old for her. He pointed out that he had two lads and she was too young to take on another woman's children and that she should have her own family and he didn't want to start being a father all over again. He said his business was too demanding for him to be married. One of their mutual friends, Richard Jeffries, whose son was briefly married to Andrew's ex, Koo Stark, said, 'It may sound a little cruel, but Paddy wanted Fergie off his back.'

Jeffries also recalled how when he met Fergie for the first time she instantly announced herself as Paddy's girlfriend. Then she asked him to tell her all about Paddy's wife, who had died of cancer in 1980. 'She was determined to find out all about it. She seemed genuinely concerned about the welfare of the two children, Paddy's sons Sean and Rollo,' Jeffries said. 'There's no doubt about it; Fergie was besotted with Paddy. She was head over heels in love with him.'

In October Fergie had one last try. In Italy, where she and Paddy had gone for the Grand Prix at Imola, she brought up the subject of marriage again. It was not exactly an ultimatum, but not far off.

Paddy chose to say good-bye. Perhaps looking at the situation from his greater experience and age, he appreciated her lack of confidence in herself. He may have seen more clearly than she did that she had a very good chance of marriage to Prince Andrew. After the romance was over McNally said, 'She is a girl in a million. Any man would be lucky to go out with her, let alone marry her. She is a marvellous lady—an outstanding woman.' But nevertheless, he slid gently out of her life. Without him on the scene, her chances would improve. Today, Major Ronald Ferguson, Sarah's father, says, 'He behaved very well.'

And Sarah was beginning to fall in love with Andrew, even though she still had no hopes that there could be any future in the relationship. What she didn't know at that stage of the courtship was that, quoting Andrew before the wedding, 'Sarah was Mummy's choice originally.' Mummy might not have approved that it was already a passionate affair—Andrew is a lusty lover like many of his Hanoverian ancestors, and Sarah doesn't have that red hair for nothing! Both of them now were slowly realizing that they were ideally suited to each other, but even so, Andrew was cautious. They spent weekends together at friends' homes, and in December, just before Christmas, Sarah took herself off to Verbier to collect the clothes and belongings that she had left at Paddy's castle. That relationship was now dead and gone. She came back to find that Andrew had bought her a triple Russian wedding ring of gold, which she wears on her little finger. That should have given her a clue to his intentions, since in Sloane Ranger land a Russian wedding ring is a *serious* gift. And sure enough, in the New Year, at the Queen's house party at Sandringham, Andrew proposed.

It was perhaps too soon for Sarah to say a wholehearted yes, having said the final good-bye to Paddy McNally so recently. She asked for some time to think. But as far as the Royal family members were concerned, they were delighted with the romance. At last the prodigal son had met a woman who was 'suitable,' someone they had known, if only vaguely, since she was a child. There is an old picture of the Queen shepherding a group of children like a mother hen. The only one who isn't Royal is a cheerful child, about age ten, standing right in the front of the picture and beaming broadly. It is the young Sarah. Since she was the Queen's choice and Prince Philip also approved, Fergie, in spite of her hesitation, was invited back to Sandringham, where she was a great success. Not surprising really. With an army officer for a father, she understood rank and ceremony. Her father is also an able courtier, which had taught her how to be amusing—without presuming. Her high spirits did occasionally take over, however. During a game of hide-and-seek at Floors Castle, Andrew had hidden under the table. Sarah, blindfolded, encountered his bottom and pinched it hard. 'Steady on!' yelped the Prince. 'You're not allowed to pinch the Royal bottom—yet!'

It was all going splendidly. The Princess of Wales was delighted that her matchmaking appeared to be succeeding. She asked Sarah and Andrew to Highgrove for the weekend in order to keep up the momentum of the budding romance.

There seemed little doubt that Fergie would accept Andrew in spite of the changes that being Royal would bring to her life. When Andrew proposed for a second time at Floors Castle, they were together for just a few hours. Sarah had caught a plane north on Saturday, and Andrew had a forty-eight-hour pass. This time he went down on both knees in an attempt to make her understand that he really was serious. She accepted but still could not quite believe it. 'She told me that when I woke up the next morning I could tell her it was all a huge joke,' Andrew said. 'I didn't.'

A bemused Fergie flew back to London that Sunday night using the assumed name Miss Anwell. The next day she lunched with Princess Diana at Kensington Palace and told her the news. Diana was delighted.

For Sarah Ferguson it was a dream come true. Poor old Fergie had become a shining winner. She was over the misery of McNally and in love again. What made it even better was that she found herself more and more physically attracted to Andrew—sometimes to the point of causing their friends embarrassment. Neither of them could keep their hands off each other! Both physical people, they would take affectionate swipes at each other. There was a lot of giggling, bear hugging, and disappearing somewhere private. And once the engagement was announced and Sarah moved into Buckingham Palace for the months preceding the wedding, she and Andrew quite openly slept together whenever he was home on leave. They made no attempt whatsoever to hide the fact. This deeply shocked the Palace staff, who felt such behaviour was disrespectful to the Queen. Certainly they had not been aware of any such goings-on when Lady Diana had stayed at the Palace prior to her wedding. But then Prince Charles had always been more discreet than his brother.

This physical attraction between the Duke and Duchess goes on. During their honeymoon on the Royal yacht, the double bed that is normally kept in the hold was brought up to the Queen's rooms, and unlike other Royals, they continue to sleep in a king-sized bed. Even coming up to their third wedding anniversary the sexual pull was as strong as ever. At a solemn public engagement at York Minster—when Andrew thought no one was looking, he seized the moment, grabbed Fergie, pulled her into an alcove and into his arms, and gave her a full-sized passionate kiss. The clergymen and the new

Bishop could not see what had happened. One fortunately (or unfortunately for Andrew!) well-placed photographer did and snapped the proof. It is impossible to imagine Prince Charles seizing such an opportunity to give Diana what can only be described as a smacker.

Pre-Sarah, Andrew had well and truly earned his nickname of Randy Andy. And his own well-publicized sexual adventures no doubt strengthened Fergie's position. It would have been hypocrisy in the extreme had her love affairs put her out of the running when he was so far from being a pure and virginal Prince himself. But, unlike Diana, she was not to be the future Queen. Her past was of much less importance. Also, her previous love affairs, so easily accepted by the Royal family, did at least give the impression that they had entered the twentieth century. It was as if they had finally discovered the existence of premarital sex.

Sarah, who for all her clowning is basically a thoroughly nice woman, does her best to keep up with all those friends of yesteryear, including Paddy McNally. She has not dropped one of her girlfriends, though as time goes on some complain that her manner with them has become grander. But remembering how things were, she would not be human if she did not feel the teeny-weeniest sense of triumph when they all meet for their smart restaurant lunches. Cinderella married the Prince, and now they have to curtsey to her.

*

Diana and Fergie saw their chances and grabbed them. So did Princess Michael of Kent, born Baroness Marie-Christine von Reibnitz, daughter of Baron von Reibnitz, ex-wartime SS officer. The future Princess Michael of Kent was born in Czechoslovakia on January 15, 1945. Victims of the war, she and her mother and brother emigrated to Australia in 1949, when she was a small girl. She grew up to be both remarkably good-looking and ambitious. Australia wasn't big enough to hold her, and she returned to Europe and settled in Britain in 1965. In 1971 she married banker Tom Trowbridge, a most eligible bachelor.

Marie-Christine is a commoner (though one with a vast and impressive amount of titled foreign ancestors) who found that it was possible to marry a Royal if one put one's mind to it. And since she managed it as both a Roman Catholic and a divorcée, it was quite a remarkable feat. But then most things—not all—that this big blonde puts her mind to come to fruition.

She was not always lucky in love, and the climb to becoming a British Princess was a long, hard one. Her parents' marriage had broken after the war. The Baron had gone off to Africa, her mother to Australia, where she eventually remarried. Her new husband was a Czechoslovakian Count. For all the abundance of titles in the family there was little money. In Australia, where Marie-Christine was educated and first started life as a working girl, she did not bring her friends home to the ordinary suburb where she lived. Early on she had realized rich was better. Her home, she feared, might spoil her image with the classy friends she had made. Despite living on the wrong side of the tracks in Sydney, her remarkable brunette (as she was then) good looks, charm, and brilliance at social climbing led her to become part of a set that was basically too rich for her pocket.

If not at the top of the social tree, she was clinging like grim death to the lower branches. She had reached them by the age-old method of becoming involved in charity work. She had style, brains, and a conviction she was made for better things. And perhaps most important, she knew how to promote herself. In Britain she is known as Princess Pushy. She was pretty pushy even as a young woman. When she was invited to a party at which there was a possibility that the press would be present, she would telephone the editors of the social pages and inform them what she would be wearing and whom she would be with.

For a while she worked as a secretary in the Sydney office of the J. Walter Thompson advertising agency, where she was popular with her fellow workers. It was when she was nineteen and after she had left Thompson to set up her own dressmaking business that she fell deeply in love.

He was Ted Albert, the son of an immensely wealthy Australian family who had made its fortune from the sale of sheet music. His father, Alexis, was a good friend of Prince Philip from wartime days, and he was an honorary aide-de-camp to Sir John Northcott, then Governor of New South Wales.

In the fifties, the socialites of Sydney were as snobby as their London and New York counterparts. The Alberts were prominent in Sydney society, and they wanted their three sons to marry well. When

Elsa Albert heard about her son's affair with Marie-Christine von Reibnitz, she also heard that the woman was an immigrant, a dressmaker, a Catholic, and poor to boot.

In spite of the fact that she had never met Marie-Christine, and probably had no idea about her title-littered background, Elsa Albert declared, 'I will not have my son carting around a new Australian!' Ted was told that the affair must end.

It continued for a while in secret, but Sydney was too small a place for people not to gossip. Marie-Christine, faced with the prospect of loving a man who was never going to defy his parents and marry her, was stronger than Sarah Ferguson had been when caught in the same position. Though it caused her great pain, Marie-Christine ended the affair and left Australia for Europe. She was twenty.

It was a pretty humiliating experience for a woman as proud of her background as Marie-Christine, and it could well explain why recognition has been overly important to her ever since.

She flourished in Britain. Her Australian twang was rapidly replaced by a charming European accent, and she became a blonde, studied interior design at the Victoria and Albert Museum in London, saw a great deal of her European relatives, and at age twenty-two became a secretary at Charles Barker, another advertising agency. The job lasted six months, until her very full social life intruded so much that she was let go. Unlike Fergie, whose social life was equally intrusive, Marie-Christine had no Royal connections to give her clout. Not then.

Two years later Marie-Christine met Tom Trowbridge at the kind of social engagement that had caused her to lose her job. They had both flown to Austria for a wild boar hunt. Tom Trowbridge spoke fluent German and had clientele in Austria. He was not only highly eligible but also extremely attractive, and so was she. They seemed made for each other. They married not much more than a year later, and it was on her wedding day that she met her first member of the Royal family, Prince William of Gloucester, ninth in succession to the throne. The Prince, who was an old friend of her husband, was a guest at their September wedding at Chelsea Old Church. Prince William was enchanted by the bride and after the honeymoon began inviting himself round for supper at the Trowbridges' new home. It was obvious that he was attracted by Marie-Christine.

She was equally enchanted to be in the presence of real Royalty, particularly when Prince William invited her and her husband to a shooting party at Barnwell Manor, his family home in Northamptonshire. There fate took a hand. Another guest was Prince Michael of Kent, who also was instantly fascinated by this elegant, seemingly Continental lady, Australia having been well ironed out. Marie-Christine now had two Royal admirers calling round at her Chelsea home and flirting with her while she flirted with them.

Princess Michael told Ingrid Seward, the editor of *Majesty* magazine, that in those days she saw Prince Michael as a charming spare man. 'I used to invite him to dinner parties or when I had extremely eligible European relatives over. I thought, 'This young man is all alone. I'll produce the right girlfriend for him.' I saw myself as a sort of fairy godmother, waving my magic wand.'

Friends of the period say that at the time Marie-Christine was more interested in Prince William, but she, her husband, and the two Princes went around as a foursome. It was to end when Prince William was tragically killed in an airplane crash. He was taking part in the Goodyear Air Race at Halfpenny Green in the Midlands, and he made an elementary piloting error. His plane crashed, killing him and the copilot. He was thirty years old.

Marie-Christine's life was in some turmoil. She and Tom Trowbridge were not getting on, which hardly seems surprising. He was stationed in Bahrain, and she joined him there for a while. But Bahrain was hardly the right setting for Marie-Christine; she would have been better off staying in Sydney. She returned to London, alone, and by 1975 she was in love with Prince Michael. They re-encountered each other at a luncheon party. He had just ended a love affair, and she was in the throes of ending her marriage. She and Tom Trowbridge had by then lived apart for three-and-a-half years. She said, 'For a long time we [she and Michael] cried on each other's shoulders. I saw him, for a year, simply as a friend. Now I'm glad we had that time, because friendship is something you never lose—and when you are in a rocking chair, friendship is what counts.'

Tom Trowbridge returned to England in 1977, and he and Marie-Christine were quietly divorced, by which time it was common knowledge that Mrs. Trowbridge was involved with Prince Michael of Kent. They had got to know each other better when Marie-Christine took to riding in Richmond Park—some distance, one might think, from her Chelsea home, but it was where Princess Michael rode. According to Marie-Christine, 'As luck and Cupid would have it, my beautiful dancing Arab steed fell madly in love with this other rather churlish animal [ridden by Prince Michael] and from miles away would whinny and gallop up to him. Then it was—"Oh, hello, what a surprise. How nice to see you!" ' The morning rides in the park became a regular thing, and eventually they were seen together in Chelsea restaurants and went about together on Prince Michael's motorbike. Princess Michael believed that the helmets they wore hid their identity.

Prince Michael wanted to marry her, and Marie-Christine wanted to marry him. Royalty was where she felt she belonged. But there were two serious impediments to their wedding: she was a Catholic and she was divorced.

Marie-Christine's love story had stormy passages to weather before there could be a happy ending. In fact, it needed only a small twist to history and there might never have been an ending. Perhaps not even a beginning if Michael's mother, Princess Marina of Kent, had been alive. When Michael, her youngest and favourite son, married Marie-Christine Trowbridge, Marina, who died in late August 1978, must have spun in her grave. It seems highly unlikely that the marriage would ever have taken place if she had still been alive, since Marina most definitely would not have approved and would almost certainly have had enough influence on her son to dissuade him. Marie-Christine once complained that her transition into Royalty would have been much easier if she had had a mother-in-law to help her through the protocol. Had her mother-in-law been alive it is unlikely that the problem would ever have arisen.

Marina's own marriage was a model of Royal propriety, and yet at the same time it undoubtedly caused a collective sigh of relief to float round the entire Royal family. She wed the future King George VI's brother, Prince George, and thus they became the parents of the present Kent family. At the time of the wedding, their union was billed as the greatest love story ever told, which possibly it was, though those who knew the facts didn't think it seemed quite so great.

Prince George was handsome, certainly, and talented too in artistic matters, but his taste hadn't entirely been for ladies until

Marina was found. There had been one or two near scandals—black-mailing over letters—and he had a distressing habit of appearing in public wearing makeup. Later was to come quite a bit of chat about an affair with Noël Coward when Coward was in his mid-twenties. Prince George was bisexual. One of his heterosexual affairs was with Poppy Baring—King George VI's first love. Prince George's Hanoverian appetite for sex was so strong that he was not too particular about whether his partner was male or female. He was also an amusing man, fun to be with, and physically brave. He liked fast cars, fast living, and talented people.

His bride, Princess Marina, was stunningly elegant and in her day quite the best-looking member of the Royal family. Before her marriage she was an exiled, penniless Princess with all the arrogance of that breed. Her family, who weren't even Greek, had been summarily ejected from the Greek throne during the First World War when King Constantine, her uncle, was accused of being pro-German. Though he denied this vehemently, he might well have been, since he was of German descent. After the war various members of the Greek Royal family were crowned and uncrowned at dizzying speed. Her family was banished three times before she was seventeen. This was during the same period as their other foreign Royal relations were having similar problems in hanging on to their thrones. It made for a very unsettled life for the crowned heads of Europe, and there must have been much envy of the stability of the British Royal family.

Marina, in the same way as her cousin Prince Philip, who eventually married the present Queen, was just another wandering, exiled Royal when marriage to Prince George became a possibility. She was twenty-eight. When asked why she was not married, she insisted, hand on her heart, that she would marry only for love. And it is likely that she did fall in love with Prince George. He was certainly good-looking and charming. But even if she hadn't been attracted to him, her family would have been unlikely to let her turn down the chance of marrying into the security of the British Royal family.

It was a rapid courtship. Marina, a favourite of his mother, Queen Mary, had known Prince George casually since she was a child and saw him at Royal gatherings. Her brother-in-law was Prince Paul of Yugoslavia, a good friend of Prince George. Prince Paul and his wife, Marina's sister Olga, brought Marina on a visit to London when they

The future King Edward VII
and Queen Alexandra
in 1864, when they were
Prince and Princess
of Wales

The official wedding photograph of King George V and Queen Mary, then the Duke and Duchess of York, who were married in May 1893

The future King George V and Queen Mary with their children in 1906.
Front row, left to right: Princess Mary, Prince Henry, Prince George,
Prince Edward, Prince Albert.
Back row: King George V and Queen Mary, holding Prince John

The future King George VI and Queen Elizabeth at Polesden Lacey in
Surrey, where they spent part of their honeymoon in 1923

Princess Elizabeth, seated between her grandparents, Queen Mary and King George V, returning from morning service at Crathie Church in Scotland in 1935. The Princess's mother, the Duchess of York, faces Queen Mary

Larger than life: the Duke and Duchess of Kent, George and Marina, in a billboard-size photograph at the time of their wedding in 1934

George and Marina, the Duke and Duchess of Kent,
with their three children, Princess Alexandra, Prince Michael
and Prince Edward, at Prince Michael's christening in 1942

Family outing: Queen Elizabeth holds the reins while King George VI
and Princesses Elizabeth and Margaret take to their bicycles
at Sandringham in 1943

Royal bride: on May 6, 1960, Princess Margaret married photographer
Antony Armstrong-Jones, who later accepted the title of Earl of
Snowdon. The marriage officially ended 18 years later

Princess Alexandra and Angus Ogilvy leave Thatched House
Lodge, Richmond with their son James for the christening of their
three-month-old daughter, Marina Victoria Alexandra, in 1966

Anna Wallace, difficult
and delightful, the
girlfriend who walked out
on the heir to the throne

were taking their son back to his English preparatory school. George visited them at Claridge's, the London hotel where they were staying. In the two weeks they spent in London, he escorted Marina around the town. At the end of the stay, she returned to Paris, and George made no arrangements to see her again. Sometime later, when Paul and his wife were again staying at Claridge's with Marina, George reappeared and again acted as escort. This time, before the Yugoslavs left Britain, they invited George to spend a week or two at their beautiful Slovenian home at Bohinj. The Prince said he would think about it. A little later, in the middle of the annual yachting races, Cowes Week, which he was possibly finding a little dull, he made the decision to take up the invitation. He sent a telegram to Yugoslavia, saying that he would arrive by air on August 15, using the Prince of Wales's airplane. Princess Olga hastily imported her unmarried sister, Marina, to Bohinj from Munich, where she had been staying with another sister, Elizabeth. Prince George was surprised to find her there. Perhaps he saw it as fortuitous. She was twenty-eight and he was thirty-two, and Queen Mary was anxious that he find himself a 'suitable' bride. Marina was at the top of her list of possibilities.

Five days later he proposed and was accepted. He sent a messenger to the King and Queen at Balmoral asking for their permission. Not surprisingly, it was readily given. Marina was, like Prince Philip, a member of the Greek Orthodox Church—a religion acceptable to the Church of England. There were no impediments of any kind, and Prince George was made Duke of Kent just prior to his wedding day.

So, was it an 'arranged and suitable' wedding? It sounds like it, but it is one that vindicates Queen Victoria's theory that marriages begin in the bedroom. The couple appeared to be passionately in love. A near contemporary recalled them locked together, dancing at the Embassy Club in London in the twenties in a way 'that certainly suggested they fancied each other'. Yet George said to a friend before the wedding, 'She is the one woman with whom I could be happy to spend the rest of my life. We laugh at the same sort of thing. She beats me at most games and doesn't give a damn how fast I drive her when I take her out in the car.' Not much love and passion in those words, but the couple produced three children: Edward, the present Duke of Kent; Princess Alexandra; and Prince Michael.

George was a lucky man to have Marina. She was trained for the job of being Royal and did it well. Her life was never easy. After her unsettled childhood was redeemed by the security of marriage to George, she could have expected a happy future. But her husband was killed in a wartime plane crash while serving in the Royal Air Force. Her youngest child, Prince Michael, who is now married to the controversial Princess Michael, was only seven weeks old when his father's plane plunged into a mist-covered Scottish hillside on a flight to Iceland. George was the only member of the Royal family to die on active service, and after his death the British public never ceased to admire Marina for the courageous way that she faced a lonely future. She was thirty-five when her husband was killed and a beautiful woman. Not surprisingly there were men in her life, but such was her discretion that few people knew. The most surprising of these lovers was Danny Kaye, the brilliant entertainer who died aged seventy-four in 1987. It was an odd combination, the outgoing Jewish-American show business personality and the widowed Duchess, who could be more regal—and much stuffier—than her mother-in-law, Queen Mary.

Marina was the most suitable of Royal brides, a genuine Princess and a firm believer in Royalty's proper place in the scheme of things. She was, in the manner of European Royalty, a great believer in Royalty marrying Royalty. Keeping the family in the family, as it were. And she saw nothing wrong with arranged marriages. Like most of her European cousins, and as Queen Mary had been before her, she was a Royal of the old school. She was aware that her children had the bluest blood of all the young Royals of the day. They had an impeccable background. She was a Princess of Greece, and her husband, George, was the only child of King George V and Queen Mary to marry a Royal. Both were untainted by commoner's blood. On the other hand, Princess Elizabeth was heir to the throne but was only half Royal since her mother, Queen Elizabeth, was merely the daughter of an Earl. George's brother, Harry of Gloucester, had married Alice Montagu Douglas Scott, daughter of the Duke of Buccleuch. Buccleuch might have been extremely rich, but he wasn't a Royal Duke. Marina, a crashing snob, referred to the Duchess of Gloucester and Queen Elizabeth as 'those common little Scottish girls.' It was true her children had the best pedigree in the family, a fact that was remarked upon many years later by Princess Michael of Kent. It was an unwise remark and one that did not endear her to the Queen, who took it as a slight upon the Queen Mother.

When it came to her own children, Marina firmly believed that if they must marry outside the magic circle into which she herself had been born, it should be to an aristocrat of impeccable background, someone whose religion and education were suitable for the dynasty into which she had been fortunate enough to marry. Most preferable would be a European Prince or Princess with the same type of background in which she had been raised.

It is perhaps as well that she did not live to see Marina Ogilvy, her namesake granddaughter, become pregnant by a young, working-class photographer with whom she had been living. When her pregnancy became public knowledge, she at first insisted she would not marry. Eventually she did—wearing black. Their romance was the sensation of 1989. For such a scandal to have occurred within her own family would have seriously distressed Princes Marina.

It was perhaps Marina's strong views on a suitable marriage that forced Angus Ogilvy to court her only daughter, the delightful Princess Alexandra, for eight long years before the marriage at last took place in 1963. Princess Alexandra, probably the most loved within the family of all Royals, is a thoroughly nice person. Kathleen Dodds, who was her headmistress at Heathfield, where the Princess was educated, recalled how she had no idea how to behave in school. 'When a matron said, "Alexandra, you forgot to clear your shelves," ' Miss Dodds said, 'she was apt to fling her arms round the astonished matron's neck and cry, "Oh, darling Matron! I am so sorry!" ' A big girl, she had a loud, carrying voice, which was not muted even for prayers. It was Miss Dodds's contention that God must have found Alexandra's supplications very revealing—not least because of the nicknames she had for her Royal relatives!

'In the dormitory she was pure hell,' said Miss Dodds. 'One night I was working late in my study when thumps, thuds, and bangs from overhead made the great bronze chandelier start to swing. Next day I sent for the head of the dormitory. It was Alexandra. In answer to my accusation that she had nearly brought the chandelier down on my head she looked up at the ceiling and then said, "Oh, it's only a small chandelier. I thought it was like the huge ones they have at Windsor" ' But the thing that Miss Dodds remembered best about her

Royal pupil was that she was one of the most popular girls in the school. No one disliked her, and she disliked no one.

She once nursed a schoolgirl crush on Prince Philip, and certainly Marina would have preferred someone of similar rank for her daughter. Her greatest ambition was that Alexandra would marry either Harald of Norway or Crown Prince Constantine of Greece, but Alexandra rebelled against a 'suitable' marriage. She was twenty-one, she had been educated at Heathfield, and the schoolfriends she had made there would most certainly not be expected to marry someone who was chosen for them. Alexandra was determined to have a normal life. While she was still a teenager she told her friends and family that when she married, 'He must be rich. He must be madly in love with me—and he must be tall.' Since Alexandra had grown to be 5'10", the 'tall' was understandable. So was the 'rich', since a contemporary of hers at Heathfield recalled that she was always dressed in second-hand clothes. Most had once belonged to Princess Elizabeth and Princess Margaret, until Alexandra grew too tall and the clothes didn't fit anymore. Princess Margaret's were the worst problem. 'I'm so huge and she's so small, I'll never get into them,' Alexandra would wail.

Angus Ogilvy, her future husband, was certainly tall. He was also madly in love with her. Rich he wasn't, and isn't, but happily it has never seemed to matter.

He wasn't Marina's idea of a suitable husband at all, and she was forever wheeling Alexandra off to Greece to mingle with the family, particularly Prince Constantine. But the more Alexandra and Constantine were pushed together, the less interested the girl was. The pressure was great, but Alexandra stood up to it. Having tasted an ordinary life both at school and in the company of friends of her older brother, Eddie, she certainly had no desire to wake up and find herself Queen of Greece one morning. She did not speak the language, nor did she like the country all that much. Alexandra is the quintessential Englishwoman and the most natural of all the Royal family. Once, on one of her early public engagements (she joined the 'Royal firm' and began work at sixteen), she dropped her cup and saucer—and bent to pick up the pieces herself. For her pains she received a quiet lecture from her mother, who said she should have left that task to someone else. But she had her own methods of saving situations. Once when touring Australia she managed to sit on the Governor of Queensland's hat. Having realized what she had done, she picked up the squashed hat and waved it triumphantly to the crowd, which roaringly applauded.

It was at a party given by the Queen's great friend Lady Zia Wernher at Luton Hoo that Alexandra met Angus Ogilvy and was immediately attracted to him. He led a bachelor life and was both handsome and intellectual. They had met briefly before when Alexandra was home from school and Ogilvy had visited the Kents' home, Coppins, to advise Princess Marina about a tour of Malaya she was to make. He had served there with the Scots Guards. Alexandra had remembered him, and now that she was grown up Ogilvy took a second look.

It was a long, drawn-out courtship. They went out together frequently, and she came to know his wide circle of friends. He escorted her back to Kensington Palace every night in a taxi. She stayed with his family at Airlie Castle in Scotland. The Queen Mother encouraged the romance. He would be invited to lunch or dinner by her at Royal Lodge. Angus Ogilvy's family, the Airlies, were family friends. Constantine was family but less of a friend, and Queen Elizabeth has never had a great deal of time for foreign Royalty.

Angus Ogilvy might have proposed a great deal earlier if he had not been anxious about the difficulties of marrying into the Royal family. Since his family had had a long history of service to the Monarchy, he had no illusions about what it would entail. Princess Alexandra was expected to undertake a heavy programme of Royal duties, and he had no wish to be any part of them. He was an independent man who earned his own living, and he probably didn't care for the idea of his wife receiving money from the Civil List. So he hesitated.

As far as Marina was concerned, Angus was merely the second son of the Earl of Airlie. He was also eight years Alexandra's senior and not particularly rich. Nor would he ever succeed to a title unless the Queen gave him one. Marina did not approve.

It was the Queen Mother who clinched the match. She invited the young couple to be houseguests at Birkhall, just as much later she would invite Lady Diana Spencer. Angus proposed and was accepted. And it was agreed that they would both carry on with their own careers, as long as the Queen approved. Alexandra herself went to see the Queen to ask permission to marry, which was instantly given. The Queen also offered to give Angus an Earldom. Politely, and with Alexandra's full approval, Ogilvy said no. He could see no reason why he should be given a peerage simply because he had married a Princess. Nor would he take a grace-and-favour residence. He wanted his own home.

For Marina, this must have been the final, devastating blow. It meant that her grandchildren by her daughter would have no titles either, since within the Royal family titles descend through the male line and even then not indefinitely. Marina, however, could hardly voice too many objections to her daughter's choice of husband since the Queen had given her approval. Angus's grandmother had been lady-in-waiting to Queen Mary, his father was at one time lord-in-waiting to King George V, and his elder brother, Earl of Airlie, is the Queen's Lord Chamberlain. There was no question of the Queen refusing her permission for the wedding. The British Royal family is simply not as grand as their foreign relations, nor as paranoid about their position and titles, undoubtedly because they are so secure.

Marina, the Greek Princess, was not happy about her eldest son Eddie's choice of bride, either. Katharine Worsley, the woman he fell in love with when he was just twenty-one, was not Royal. However, she was charming, kind, extremely pretty, and two years older than Eddie—a respectable, well-brought up woman from a good, solid English country family. An impeccable background but not particularly impressive by Marina's standards. If she thought the Duke of Buccleuch and the Earl of Strathmore common, heaven knows what her opinion of the Worsleys could have been, though by normal standards they too would be considered grand. Katharine's father, Sir William Worsley, was Lord Lieutenant of Yorkshire's North Riding, and the family lived at Hovingham Hall, a fine late-eighteenth-century manor house set on four thousand acres near York.

In 1957, when Katharine was twenty-three, the young Duke of Kent was serving with the Royal Scots Greys at Catterick Camp in Yorkshire, and Sir William was given to inviting officers from the camp to Sunday lunch at his home. It was at one of these roast-beef-and-Yorkshire-pudding lunches that Katherine met her future husband. She was thrilled to meet him and had hoped to do so since she saw a newspaper picture of him at the Coronation. He was seventeen and a sword-bearer. She cut out the picture and kept it. When they did meet, it was love at first sight for them both; two gentle people, neither extroverted nor limelight seekers, they found they had much in common and wanted to marry.

It is possible that the Duke could not believe his luck in finding such a charming woman. In those days he was considered a bit of a joke by the British. His facial features unfortunately caused him to be known as the chinless wonder. He was also something of a Hooray Henry playboy. The Kents had no money to speak of. Apart from the title, Eddie did not appear to be much of a catch, but he had a good brain. Fluent in languages, he won the modern languages prize at Sandhurst and was in the top ten at Camberley Staff College. And still Marina harboured ambitions for him to marry a foreign Princess. No doubt a foreign Princess would have snapped him up for a safe seat at the British Royal table. But Eddie wanted Katharine.

Aware of his mother's ambitions, he did not tell her that he was courting the quiet blonde Yorkshire lass. The first that Marina knew of the budding romance was when he told her he was going to ask to be excused from the Royal family's Boxing Day festivities and attend those at Hovingham Hall instead.

Marina was appalled. She said he would do no such thing, nor could he mention it to the Queen, because the Queen would never agree.

Marina was wrong. The Queen did agree.

But Eddie's mother did not give in easily. She checked out the woman's background and could find nothing wrong other than a lamentable lack of Royal blood. And to make matters worse, when Eddie proposed, she had the effrontery to hesitate. Katharine Worsley was not unnaturally concerned by the thought of the pressures that would come from marrying into the Royal family. Her ambition had been a much simpler one. She wanted to be a teacher. She had studied music at Oxford and went to London to work in a kindergarten. In York she worked at St. Stephen's Orphanage, where she cooked, washed nappies, polished floors, and taught. She loved the life and today has gone back to doing much the same kind of meaningful work within the community. The Worsley family motto is, 'Do good to as many persons as possible.' She lived by it then, and she lives by it now.

Hoping that the problem would go away, Marina insisted that her son and Katharine have a trial separation. It lasted two years. Katharine went to Canada to stay with a brother while she thought things over. It was an unhappy time of her life. Her heart was three thousand miles away, in Germany, where the young Duke had been sent with his regiment. His sister, Alexandra, acted as a go-between, relaying news to both of them. When the 'thinking about it' separation was over, nothing had changed. Katharine and Eddie still wanted to marry. When they finally met again at Kensington Palace and Eddie saw Katharine waiting for him at the bottom of the stairs, so eager was he to greet her that he dashed down, tripped, and broke his ankle.

They were able to marry a year later in York Minster in June 1961. They had one powerful ally. The Queen Mother had been saying for months that Katharine was just the right girl for Eddie, and when he told the Queen that he and Katharine Worsley were in love, her permission for the marriage was given without hesitation. Many years later she would reluctantly agree to Eddie's brother Michael's request to marry a divorced, Catholic woman, but when Eddie approached her back in 1958 she was delighted that the young Duke had found someone who made him happy.

Their marriage has been a happy one, marred only by a nervous breakdown suffered by the Duchess in 1977, when, in her forties, she suffered a miscarriage in her seventh month. Though she already had three children, she had wanted to increase her family. The loss caused severe depression that did not go away; eventually she was back in the hospital again, and a string of illnesses followed. For a while it was thought that she would never recover her health. But by finding solace in work with others worse off than herself, she gradually returned to normal. She works tirelessly for the Samaritans and regularly visits a hospice for dying children, where she is much loved. Her long illness aged both her and the Duke, but he was a tower of strength throughout the years it took his wife to regain her health. The marriage is as strong as ever, and he still calls her 'beloved one'.

Marina, with her firm views on who her children should marry, was perhaps the last of her kind. The Queen has never insisted on aristocratic partners for her own children. With three down and one to go, both her daughter and second son have married commoners, and Prince Edward shows no signs of running with an aristocratic crowd. When he brings girls home to the family get-togethers at Balmoral or Sandringham, they are from what the Queen would consider the right kind of background, as were those his brother and sister chose. And it does help, of course, if they are interested in the family passion — horses. In the Queen's eyes anyone potty about horses can't be all bad.

It was a passion for horses that led Princess Anne and her husband, Mark Phillips, to fall in love. And it was probably that passion that held them together, though on a very loose rein, before their fifteen-year marriage finally ended. Anne was only eighteen and barely out of school when they first met. Their first encounter came about through the Queen Mother, who seems to have an uncanny knack for match-making. It was 1968, the year the British equestrian team had won the gold medal in the Mexico Olympics. Mark Phillips, a young reserve, did not get to ride, but as a member of the team he arrived home with a medal.

On their return from Mexico, Whitbread's, a large British brewing company known for supporting equestrian sports, threw a party for the gold medallists in their cellars in London. The Queen Mother was the guest of honour, and she took along her horse-mad granddaughter. Mark Phillips was invited to make up the numbers and escort Princess Anne at a small dinner party afterward.

At that time, that was that. No bells rang. Anne began grooming herself for her first public duties in 1969. She lost weight and found herself a professional makeup artist and beautician to advise her. She learned how to deal with her hair herself — she has always thought hairdressers a waste of time. Mark Phillips went back to the Royal Military Academy, Sandhurst, where he was still an officer cadet.

Anne had a perfectly miserable teenage period. She was not particularly pretty, and she had no confidence in herself, which made her surly in self-defence. She scowled at the world through that thick mane of hair that her mother said made her look like a sheepdog. Her hair is her best feature, but in those days she used it as a shield against the none-too-friendly world. She had difficulty finding her own fashion style. Somehow, like Fergie, she rarely managed to get it right.

Charles was no help in smoothing her transition to becoming an adult. He had chosen a much older, intellectual set of friends who didn't interest her. Her little brothers were too young and boisterous to be companions and, patience not being one of her virtues, drove her mad.

She did try to have some fun. Someone told her that the Royal College of Arts gave good parties with great bands, so she invited herself along. Alas, no one danced with her—perhaps out of shyness or maybe it was simply the usual rebellious student behaviour. She was forced to dance with her detective. It hurt and gave her confidence another battering. Her father, seeing how glum she was, in desperation asked his polo-playing friends if she could be invited to some of their children's parties.

But then she discovered the world of three-day eventing, something at which she could really shine and where her being a Princess meant nothing to the horse she was riding. It was through this most horsey of sports that she encountered Mark Phillips again.

But there was someone else in her life before Mark became important to her—a young commodities broker named Sandy Harper. He too came from a horse-mad background. The son of a lieutenant colonel, he was a keen polo player. Anne fell in love with him, and the Palace thought they would marry. Throughout 1969 they were together a great deal. It was Harper who took her to see *Hair*, the daring musical by the standards of the day, where she danced on the stage with the cast at the end of the evening (some of them naked, which shocked elderly aristocrats and caused them to protest that this was no way for Royalty to behave). Harper seemed to be courting her, when suddenly he ended the romance and, rather too quickly for Anne's comfort, married a model.

Perhaps he was scared by the prospect of joining the Royal firm, but Anne was devastated until Mark came into her life again. He and she found themselves competitors in the same horse trials. Some say that for her it was a rebound relationship, and maybe it was—but at least it was a relationship of some kind. They were drawn together because of their mutual love of horses; they couldn't help but keep meeting as they were always to be found at the same equestrian events.

As they became friendlier and wanted to see more of each other, it was not difficult to arrange meetings and be at the same house parties without the press becoming too aware of what was happening. In any case, the press was certain for a long time that Anne's prospective husband was Richard Meade—perhaps the finest horseman Britain has ever produced. The only thing that gave them doubts was that he was twelve years older than Anne. But in 1971, the penny was beginning to drop, and Anne and Mark had to be a little more cautious. Even so, in October of that year she invited him to Buckingham Palace to attend the silver wedding anniversary celebrations of the Queen and Prince Philip. The next month she was a guest at his parents' home at Great Somerford in Wiltshire. She spent most of the pre-Christmas week with Mark, and he was invited to Sandringham for the New Year house party and was there for two weekends. This did bring the press out in force, and when Mark left to join his regiment in Germany the Princess went riding without him. She grinned at photographers and reporters and said, 'I'm on my own today. Isn't it a pity?' It was a remarkably civil remark from Anne to a group of journalists. Any conversation with the press is usually of a much saltier nature, and by this sudden attack of geniality they should have guessed that something was up.

But still, she probably managed the nearest thing to a courtship of any of her immediate family. There were six wonderful weekends in Yorkshire when Mark was stationed at Catterick Camp that received hardly any publicity at all. The Princess enjoyed hunting, hunt balls, and long moorland rides with Mark as her only companion. And one of the army officers' wives was surprised when her husband said casually, 'My dear, I rather think that Princess Anne would like to stay with us for the weekend.'

It was an average, upper-class, quiet kind of courtship. Ordinary, one might say. But then whereas Prince Charles's idea of bliss is to be 'cosy', Princess Anne would go for being 'ordinary' every time. She is not one to do things in a flamboyant way. *Down-to-earth* is the adjective most often applied to her, and down-to-earth she is.

The press, therefore, only became really excited about her and Mark when, after a few days' leave, he returned to his regiment in Germany, sailing to the Hook of Holland. Anne drove the young lieutenant, as he was then, to the docks, and it was there that a car-park attendant saw her kissing him good-bye and passed on the news to the waiting reporters.

It had been a proper, really-meaning-it kiss, not one of your pecks on the cheek, and speculation was instantly at fever pitch. Royals rarely kiss in public. But the Palace stoutly denied there was any romance. Although Anne was obviously in love with this handsome, pleasant young man, it wasn't until 1973 that the Palace came clean. In fairness, it couldn't come clean earlier since Mark hadn't yet said anything positive. It was not until after the Badminton Horse Trials in April of that year that he proposed. Having got that most important event of the year out of the way, he no doubt felt he could concentrate on other things.

In all this time had Anne been wondering if he would or if he wouldn't ask her? It seems that she had. Though with her temperament she would rather die than actually admit it, she did go so far as to say she believed he had no intention of getting married. She said he had made no secret of the fact: 'He kept telling me he was a confirmed bachelor, and I thought at least one knows where one stands.' But she also said defiantly, 'It's been a complete myth over the years that the only thing I wanted to do when I left school was get married. It couldn't have been further from the truth.'

But she did want to marry Mark. His proposal was somewhat spur of the moment and took her by surprise. And some say he surprised himself too. He did admit, 'If two people love each other it's just something they feel. When it comes to getting engaged, it is just something they feel they want to do. There's no question about it.' Having taken the plunge he then did everything correctly. He asked the Duke of Edinburgh for his daughter's hand, having flown especially from Germany to do so. Both the Duke and the Queen declared themselves satisfied by their daughter's choice. Mark Phillips had remained cool and collected throughout all the press attention, and, of course, he was positively brilliant with horses. But Philip felt he was dull. After leaving Marlborough, one of the top British schools, his educational qualifications were not good enough to get him into Sandhurst. He had to spend six months in the ranks as a private soldier before he was admitted. Prince Charles, who liked his new brother-in-law to be, warned him not to put up with too much from Anne, advice that Mark tried to take; for a while he could tame her temper.

With his fiancée's help, Mark undertook a crash course in Royal

behaviour. He bought her a beautiful sapphire-and-diamond engagement ring, which she first wore at the family engagement luncheon.
That lunch should have given Mark a warning of things to come.
Anne had to leave early to catch a helicopter to watch a group of
handicapped children at a riding-for-the-disabled school.

It was the first of hundreds of occasions when Anne's job was to
intrude into their marriage, sometimes with negative results. From the
beginning Mark was uneasy about joining his wife on her Royal duties,
but for a while he did travel with her to South America, Australia,
New Zealand, and Canada. There were more engagements back in
Britain. He did his best for a while but hated standing around behind
her like a spare part and was so bored that they both decided it would
be better if she soldiered on alone.

Soon it was not so much a matter of being alone simply when
working as never being together at all. It does make one wonder if
what was to happen to them (see Chapter 6) vindicates Princess
Marina's view that when you are Royal, an arranged marriage is the
best marriage.

— 2 —

Marriage
and Mistresses

To some extent the marriage between Lady Diana Spencer and Prince Charles was an arranged one cooked up by two formidable old ladies—the Queen Mother, Prince Charles's maternal granny, and the Countess of Fermoy, Diana's maternal granny.

Royals have a history of arranged marriages, and it is because of this that divorce, in the past, has so rarely raised its unsettling presence in their exalted ranks. It is only in recent times, since Royalty has become more middle class and less aristocratic in its habits, that its members have married for that untrustworthy emotion called love. Queen Victoria's attitude toward marriages was that they were made in the bedroom. She believed that if a couple was 'suitable,' they should marry and it would be all right on the wedding night. Up until the time of the First World War Royal marriages were arranged basically for political reasons, and everyone involved knew exactly what was expected of him or her. When the Hanoverians took the British throne, one of the many rules that George I brought with him from Germany was that a Royal Prince must marry a woman of Royal rank. If a Prince had chosen to enter into what is called a morganatic marriage—meaning to wed an ordinary aristocrat or (heaven forbid!) a true commoner—the marriage would not officially exist; the wife and children would have no position and would not even be acknowledged.

Suitable Royal partners were hard to find, a situation that was exacerbated in Britain, since Catholic Princes and Princesses were definitely not in the running. Then the rules were partly changed when King George V decided that Royal blood was no longer a necessity when it came to the marriages of his younger children. He gave permission for them to choose their partners from the families of the first three ranks of the nobility—Dukes, Marquesses, and Earls—though Catholics still wouldn't do. This new thinking led to the present Queen Mother becoming the first commoner to marry a King's son in more than two hundred years.

Previously, this insistence on Protestant Royalty marrying within the faith created a great deal of interbreeding. It brought about a situation where most Royalty was of German background and descended from Queen Victoria. This caused horrendous family problems for the British Royals throughout two world wars with Germany, when the vast, sprawling family descending from Victoria and Albert was split asunder, cousin against cousin.

Yet arranged marriages had a history of working. And when they didn't, couples simply led separate lives, as did Princess Anne and Mark Phillips before their legal separation. Not that it was ever that simple for Royal women. Catherine the Great's lover, Count Orlov, may have knocked out the brains of her husband, Peter III, with a footstool, but in Britain there is still an old law that says that it is unlawful for any man other than her husband to have carnal relations with a woman of Royal blood.

No such rule ever existed for Royal men, many of whom have had mistresses—usually married women, whose husbands amazingly never seemed to object. Fidelity was not a virtue expected of Royal men at the beginning of the nineteenth century. The beautiful and elegant Queen Alexandra bravely endured constant adultery by her husband, King Edward VII. Perhaps realizing he would never change, she even gave his mistresses little presents—one was a beautiful jewelled presentation spyglass given to Alice Keppel. With astonishing generosity, she sent for Mrs. Keppel, her husband's last amour, to be present at his deathbed on May 6, 1910.

Alice Keppel was Alexandra's cross to bear (as, indeed, the King must have been Mr. Keppel's, though he did refer to him quite cheerfully as 'Kingy'). The Royal love affair was common knowledge. 'King's Cross,' Mrs. Keppel once directed a cab driver to a London main-line station. 'Not with you, ma'am,' said the driver gallantly.

She was a regular visitor to Sandringham, and once a year, leaving the Queen and Mr. Keppel behind, she and the King went away for six weeks to Biarritz on the southern Atlantic coast of France, where they lived as man and wife. But she was so discreet, kind, and tactful as well as truly beautiful that even the resentful Queen could not help but like her.

Alexandra's was a marriage arranged by Queen Victoria, though at first the Queen had her doubts about the suitability of the union. Alexandra was Danish, the daughter of Prince and Princess Christian of Denmark. The Christians were a disorganized and unsophisticated couple who had little financial stability. They were, however, good parents and had given their nine children much in the way of love and security—but little, unfortunately, in the way of culture and education. It has to be said that the stunningly beautiful Alexandra was not very bright intellectually, and she was also rather deaf—which perhaps was the reason for her mental slowness.

Such was her charm, however, that her lack of education was not immediately obvious. At first Queen Victoria was more concerned about Alexandra's family background than the fact that she could be stultifyingly boring. The prim Queen was convinced that the Danish Court was decadent. An added disadvantage was the political trouble between Germany and Denmark. It looked very much as if the two countries would go to war over a border dispute. Victoria was completely pro-German in her loyalties and wished to do nothing that would give the impression of any sympathy toward Denmark. But as the need to find her eldest son a wife became more pressing, these considerations were put aside when Victoria received a letter from her daughter, Vicky, the Crown Princess of Prussia.

It read: 'I send you now a photograph of Prince Christian's lovely daughter. I have seen several people who have seen her of late—and who give such accounts of her beauty, her charm, her amiability, her frank manner, and many excellent qualities. I thought it right to tell you all this in Bertie's [the Prince of Wales] interests, though I as a Prussian cannot wish Bertie should ever marry her. I know her nurse who tells me she is strong in health and has never ailed anything.. . . I must say on the photograph that I think her lovely and just the style Bertie admires, but I repeat an alliance with Denmark would be a misfortune for us here.'

Political unrest between Germany and Denmark or not, and even though the Queen wrote, 'It is a pity she is who she is,' the photograph did the trick. Even the Queen's husband, Prince Albert, exclaimed, 'I would marry her at once!'

It was fortunate that Princess Alexandra was not only stunningly beautiful but also had been blessed with a warm and loving personality. Other Royal foreign families were hopeful of snaring her for their unmarried sons, but the British Prince of Wales was undoubtedly the best catch of all. It was on a match with him that Alexandra's hard-up parents pinned their hopes.

Because of her remarkable beauty, Bertie, the Prince of Wales, was attracted to Alexandra from their first meeting—but he was reluctant to commit himself because he was in the middle of the first of his many secret affairs. The lady in question was Nelly Clifden, an actress. When the affair was discovered by his parents, he immediately ended it and expressed his contrition for what had occurred. Weeks later his father, the Prince Consort, who had been horrified by his son's liaison, died of typhoid fever. Victoria blamed her husband's sudden death on the Nelly Clifden affair (actually it was caused by the appalling state of the drains at Windsor Castle), and she never forgave the Prince of Wales. But because her beloved Albert had wanted their eldest son to marry Alexandra, she was more determined than ever that the wedding should take place.

The seventeen-year-old Alexandra herself never voiced an opinion about the man that both her family and his had chosen as her husband. All that can be said is that at least she seemed to have no objections to a planned future that would eventually lead to her being crowned Queen of England.

As for Bertie, there were only seven suitable Royal brides for him in Europe. He was indeed fortunate that one of them had the charm and beauty of Alexandra. Three days after their betrothal he wrote to his mother, 'I frankly avow to you that I did not think it possible to love a person as much as I love her.'

And at the time he meant it.

But was Alexandra, still only eighteen on her wedding day, in love with him? Vicky, Victoria's daughter who had begun it all by extolling Alexandra's virtues, paid her brother and his bride a visit after the Royal wedding on March 10, 1863. She wrote to her mother, 'Darling

Alix looks charming and lovely and they both seem so comfortable and at home together. Love has certainly shed its sunshine on these two dear young hearts and lends its unmistakable brightness to both their countenances.'

Marriage to Bertie most certainly improved the quality of Alexandra's life. Perhaps love came along with gratitude for a secure future, though the Prince of Wales was a dashing sort of chap, and it would not be surprising if she were attracted by him. Most women were. As the Princess of Wales, Alexandra for the first time in her life had money to spend and was expected to wear beautiful clothes. Like her successor, Princess Diana, she always had the gift of style—when times were hard in her youth she was perfectly able to make her own dresses and hats to professional standard. She soon found herself a leader of fashion. She was also acclaimed as the queen of society. Everyone was charmed by this child Princess, by her beautiful smile, her winning grace, and her noble innocence—as the fulsome Victorians described her. In her day, her effect was as great—if not greater—than that of the present Princess of Wales.

Many other arranged Royal marriages were enormously successful. Queen Mary, as the young Princess May of Teck, was at first the intended bride of Queen Alexandra's eldest son, Prince Albert Victor, Duke of Clarence, or Eddy, as he was called. Victoria was still Monarch, which made Eddy second in line to the throne. Eddy was dissolute, ignorant, lazy, and interested in nothing but pleasure. There was even a persistent rumour that he was the evil, unapprehended Jack the Ripper, infamous slayer of prostitutes in London's East End. All that could be said for him was that he had a certain charm. Charming or not, he would have made a perfectly dreadful King, and it was providential for the British Monarchy that he conveniently died of pneumonia at Sandringham on January 14, 1892, aged twenty-eight.

Princess May of Teck was intelligent, well-educated, and a woman, as she described herself, with *besoin de plaire* (the need to please). She was a strong character, and her fiancé's death, only months after their betrothal, was the best possible thing that could have happened to her. She certainly did not love Prince Eddy. Indeed, she was beginning to wonder if perhaps she was about to take on too much of a problem when the freezing winter cold of Norfolk removed her degenerate fiancé from her life.

The so abruptly halted marriage caused the sympathy of the British nation to pour upon this pretty Princess, suddenly bereft of her future husband and with the crown of England snatched from her. But like Queen Victoria and certainly May's ambitious mother, the Duchess of Teck, whose disappointment had no bounds, the public knew what the answer was. In her heart, May herself was aware of what was in everyone's mind but was embarrassed by the very thought of it. The consensus was that May should marry Prince George, Eddy's common-sense, bluff younger brother, who was now heir to the throne. And that is exactly what she did on May 13, 1893, only sixteen months after the Duke of Clarence had breathed his last, surrounded by his sobbing family.

The marriage may have appeared heartless and self-seeking, but it is correct to say that being Royal is a profession. Princess May, though sensitive enough to feel that marrying her fiancé's brother must give the impression that she had never cared for his brother—which indeed she had not—nevertheless followed her profession. She married the man who would make her his Queen, beating a half dozen or so European contestants for the prize. In spite of grand addresses and titles, her childhood had been woefully poverty stricken. Her family had been constantly in debt, her mother never failing to exasperate Queen Victoria in one way or another. Marriage to the future King put all that behind her.

And the marriage worked. She had married a good man. In 1911, after she and George had been together for seventeen years, he wrote to her, 'We suit each other admirably & I thank God every day that he should have brought us together, especially under the tragic circumstances of poor Eddy's death, & people only said I married you out of pity & sympathy.

'That shows how little the world really knows what it is talking about.'

Even if the marriage had not been a success, neither Queen Mary nor her husband, King George V, would have considered ending it. Royalty was their profession, and Royalty did not divorce. Queen Mary was the most royal Royal in many generations. She believed in her job and did it superbly well. Fifty years ago she overheard a young member of the Royal family complaining of aching feet and yet another visit to a hospital.

'We,' said Queen Mary frostily, 'are the Royal family. Our days are never too long, our feet never ache, and we love hospitals.'

Queen Victoria's reaction was much the same when she was told she was Queen. Aged eighteen, she said with the utmost simplicity, 'I will be good.' And she was.

Her marriage to her German cousin Prince Albert had been plotted by their mutual grandmother, the Dowager Duchess of Coburg. When he was three years old Prince Albert was constantly told by his nanny that one day 'the little English May flower' would be his wife. It apparently never occurred to him that his married life would take any other direction.

Years later, when the unmarried Victoria had come to the throne, the young Queen announced she did not wish to marry her cousin Albert, even though her relatives were urging the match for ambitious reasons and her Ministers for political ones. As Queen she was in a position to do as she pleased. She made it clear that she liked and admired Albert very much, but had no intentions of marrying him. In fact, in April 1839, after she had been Queen for two years, she said firmly that she had no intentions of ever marrying at all, a statement that caused some consternation in the Court, since had she died childless the British throne would go to her cousin, the King of Hanover.

And then in the autumn of 1839, Albert visited Victoria in Britain, and the twenty-year-old Queen fell in love. Love hit her like a thunderbolt. Albert, she decided, was beautiful with his 'exquisite nose,' 'his beautiful figure, broad in the shoulders,' and his 'fine waist.' She even swooned over his moustache. Three days after his arrival, she sent for him, receiving him in private, and asked if he would consent to marry her—even though, she pointed out, she was quite unworthy of him. Albert agreed. He would be very happy to do so, he said politely if a little unenthusiastically, for unfortunately he was not in love with Victoria. He was, however, extremely conscious of the high position in Britain that marriage to the Queen would bring him.

Though before the wedding day dawned the Queen went through the heart searching that every bride suffers over whether she was doing the right thing, the marriage was a success. Albert was relentlessly serious-minded, but regardless, Victoria adored him to the day he died; after he did, at the early age of forty-two, she mourned him for the rest of her life. He did his duty, gave her nine children, and was a good and devoted husband and consort, though, to both his and Victoria's dismay, the British never really took to him. He looked too foreign, his accent was foreign, and though he was brilliant and able, he was a bit of a prig and a bore. In turn, he thought the British far too frivolous.

History was to repeat itself a century later when Princess Elizabeth fell in love with Prince Philip of Greece. But there is absolutely no doubt that the young Princess Elizabeth was captivated by him when she was no more than thirteen years old, barely out of the nursery. She never was and certainly never will be interested in another man. But in those early days, what were his feelings towards her? As Victoria and Albert's did, the marriage has worked. Like Albert before him, Philip has worked hard for Britain and achieved many things for his adopted country. But the British have never really taken to Philip any more than they took to Albert.

There are similarities between Victoria's love story and that of the present Queen, since both their husbands were bereft of a real role in their adopted countries. Yet for these foreign Princes the game was worth the golden candelabra. All Prince Philip had when he married the British heir presumptive was his naval pay—no other money. He owned no home; when he came courting he camped out on a camp bed at Uncle Dickie Mountbatten's London house, and he had even had to relinquish his Princely title in order to become British. He married as plain Lieutenant Mountbatten.

There is an irony about Elizabeth's total commitment to Prince Philip. Had George V not changed the rules, Princess Elizabeth would have been obliged to marry Royalty, and Prince Philip would have been the only real possibility for her. When she was of marriageable age there were no other suitable HRHs available besides Prince Philip. And for her it would have been simply a bonus that he was an exceedingly attractive man. The marriage would have been con-sidered suitable, since he was a Royal Highness—HRH Prince Philip of Greece—while his basic upbringing was British. His mother was a Mountbatten, great-granddaughter of Queen Victoria, and had been known as the prettiest Princess in Europe. She married the dash-ing—and penniless—Prince Andrew of Greece. Five children later, when she and her husband parted after a sink-or-swim life in the dangerous waters of European Royalty, Philip was taken to live in Britain by his Mountbatten uncles and sent off to Cheam, an English preparatory school. In many ways he was just as English as the English.

There were mutterings that Elizabeth could marry Charles, the Prince Regent of Belgium, but the snag was that he was forty-one, more than twenty years older than she, and a Catholic. He wouldn't have done at all. As it happened, George V's rethinking on Royal marriage had given her a much wider choice of suitors, but the choice proved unnecessary. The young Princess fell in love with Philip hook, line, and sinker.

The additional irony was that her parents would have preferred she marry an aristocratic Englishman. Her father, George VI, distrusted the idea of marriage to Philip, undoubtedly scenting the eagerness with which the ambitious Mountbatten family was plotting the marriage of their nephew to the future Queen.

Prince Albert was only in the nursery when it was impressed on him that the role of consort to the British throne could be his, and Prince Philip was not much older. In 1939, when he was only just out of Dartmouth Naval College and aged eighteen, he said to Harold Tom Baillie-Grohman, commander of his first ship, the *Ramillies*, 'My Uncle Dickie [the Earl of Mountbatten] has ideas for me; he thinks I could marry the Princess Elizabeth.'

His startled commander asked the young midshipman, 'Are you really fond of her?'

'Oh, yes, very,' said Philip. 'I write to her every week.'

His commander was so astonished by this revelation that he rushed off to write it down so as to be sure that he recorded the information correctly. Years later the young Prince Philip's somewhat indiscreet remark surfaced in the by then vice admiral's memoirs, which, though unpublished, are kept in naval history records.

As it happened, Philip had every chance in the world of marrying Princess Elizabeth, since someone other than Uncle Dickie had exactly the same ambition—the princess herself.

Marion Crawford, who was governess to Elizabeth and her sister, Princess Margaret Rose, and was called 'Crawfie,' told the story of Philip's appearance in the British Royal family's life in her book *The Little Princesses*. It was a simple book that told in a gentle, if rather breathless, manner the story of the Queen and her sister's upbringing. It caused deep resentment in the Royal family, and Crawfie was no longer persona grata with them after its publication. But the book is fascinating because Crawfie was *there*, and what she wrote is pure history.

The fateful meeting between Elizabeth and Philip took place on a rainy day in August 1939, just before the outbreak of war. The venue was Dartmouth Naval College, where George VI had been a student himself. The King had decided to hold an inspection at the college from the Royal yacht, the *Victoria and Albert*, before he and his family went to Balmoral for the summer. The little Princesses, ages thirteen and nine, were on the yacht with their parents.

Prince Philip of Greece was a Dartmouth cadet, and at that time Lord Louis Mountbatten, Philip's Uncle Dickie, was the King's aide-de-camp. The Royal family, along with Mountbatten, planned to attend Sunday morning church service at the college. Two boys at the school had developed mumps, and it was decided it would be wiser if the Princesses did not attend the service. Instead they were taken to the house of the officer in charge of the college to play with his children and were given a clockwork railway to amuse them.

'We played for ages,' wrote Crawfie, 'and after a time a fair-haired boy rather like a Viking, with a sharp face and piercing blue eyes came in. He was good looking, though rather off-hand in his manner. He said 'How do you do' to Lilibet, and for a while they knelt side by side playing with the trains. He soon got bored with that. We had ginger crackers and lemonade in which he joined, and then he said, 'Let's go to the tennis courts and have some real fun jumping the nets.'

'Off they went. At the tennis courts I thought he showed off a good deal, but the little girls were much impressed.'

The young Philip, undoubtedly wheeled into Elizabeth's view by Uncle Dickie, did a fair amount of showing off throughout the visit. Princess Elizabeth never took her eyes off him, but he paid her scant attention. He was too busy teasing a rather plump little Margaret.

It has always been said that he and Elizabeth began corresponding after Philip spent a wartime Christmas at Windsor in 1943. According to Vice Admiral Baillie-Grohman, it was much earlier. She and Philip had been writing to each other for nearly four years. But according to Crawfie, seeing Philip in the flesh thrilled the seventeen-year-old

Princess that Christmas and she positively glowed. She was in love, and her state of mind was not to alter. The future Queen showed a stubborn determination in her devotion to Prince Philip. While he was on active service, she was doing her bit for the war effort, knitting him socks. Probably rather uncomfortable socks since knitting was never one of her skills. They were darned by Eileen Parker, the wife of Commander Michael Parker, who was the sailor Prince's closest friend and who was to become his private secretary after the war. All the while, letters were winging back and forth between Elizabeth and Philip, sent through the ordinary post.

But did Philip love her, or was the position that went with the marriage uppermost in his mind? Certainly while he was serving in the navy in Britain there was never a sign of another woman. Eileen Parker, who served in the wartime WRNS stationed at Rosyth along with both Philip and her husband-to-be, said, 'It was inconceivable that such an eligible young officer didn't have a sweetheart some-where, but nobody ever came close enough to him to find out who it might be. I was not the only one to feel that when personal relation-ships were under discussion, Prince Philip was holding something back—as if he knew he was "special" in some way and expected to be treated as such.'

A cynic would say that he did not want a whisper of scandal to mar his chances. A romantic would say that he simply wasn't interested in anyone else.

If Elizabeth had a rival, it was another Royal woman—Philip's cousin, the darkly dramatic Princess Alexandra of Greece. At the beginning of the war, Alexandra had been living in Italy. She was forced to leave hurriedly following the afternoon of October 28, 1940, when Italy invaded Greece. She took the last diplomatic train back to Athens, along with other Royal relatives and members of the Greek embassy. Italy's action also altered Prince Philip's situation. Prior to Greece's being involved in the war, Philip, the subject of a neutral country, had not been permitted by the Royal navy to serve in a war zone. Greece's willy-nilly involvement in the war meant that Prince Philip was no longer a neutral. He was immediately permitted to serve in a war zone and was sent to the battleship HMS *Valiant* in the eastern Mediterranean. This could have been bad news for Princess Elizabeth, as from then on the young naval officer certainly saw a great deal of cousin Alexandra whenever his wartime duties permitted.

Alexandra wrote fulsomely in her memoirs of Prince Philip: 'Suddenly Philip turned up in Athens, gay, debonair, confident.. . . Philip would come bounding up the hundred steps [to her mother's rented home] ready for fun—for record playing and dancing—with a whole new group of friends.'

Could it be that Alexandra had a crush on her glamorous cousin? The Greek Royal family eventually had to flee to Alexandria in Egypt. There Philip bobbed up again. Was her crush reciprocated? She was an attractive young woman of nearly twenty. His pen pal Elizabeth was fifteen and far away in England. Alexandra remembered his arrival in detail. 'One morning when Mummie and I were at breakfast we heard a familiar whistle and outside our window Philip and David [Milford-Haven, later to be Philip's best man] shouted to us with whoops of glee. . . . For the first time I found my two cousins handsome and attractive beaux. . . . I like David's lazy smile and Philip's broad grin, and was unhappy at leaving them behind when Mummie and I were ordered to move to the comparative safety of Cairo.'

But Philip turned up again in Cairo, where he and Alexandra swam, talked, went out for meals, and explored the city. And when the Greek Royal family was sent to South Africa for safety, there was Philip at the dock to see them off. And, surprise, surprise, there he was again in Cape Town, fresh off a troop ship, which had been going in the same direction. In spite of the war, fate—or his own efforts —certainly kept throwing him and Alexandra together. By September 1941 she was ensconced in London, living first at the Ritz with her mother and then in an apartment in Grosvenor Square. Philip was also back in Britain and was to spend the next two years there. He and Alexandra went nightclubbing and met at Coppins, the Buckingham-shire home of their mutual cousin Princess Marina.

Undoubtedly Alexandra was peeved when she discovered that Philip and the young Princess were in communication. She discovered this in South Africa as Philip was writing a letter when, as she said, she wanted to chat. She asked who the letter was for. 'Lilibet', he told her.

'Who?' she asked.

'Princess Elizabeth in England,' he said.

Alexandra's reaction was to decide that Elizabeth was only a baby and that, knowing her cousin, perhaps he was merely angling for invitations when he was back in England. It obviously did not occur to her that the letter was one of many and that Philip had his eye on the Princess, even if she was 'just a baby.'

Certainly Alexandra appeared to have her eye on him for a while. But she was to marry Peter of Yugoslavia and become his Queen, though most of their married life was spent in exile. When he lost the throne and times became hard, she wrote her memoirs of cousin Philip. In them—perhaps unintentionally or mistakenly, or both— she gives the impression that they were more than just good friends.

About the time of Alexandra's wedding, the British Royal family was beginning to notice that Philip and Elizabeth were more than just good friends too. The Princess was nineteen and her state of mind obvious. Queen Mary told her friend Lady Airlie, 'They have been in love for the last eighteen months. In fact, longer, I think. I believe she fell in love with him the first time he went down to Windsor, but the King and Queen feel she is too young to be engaged yet.'

At the end of the war Princess Elizabeth defiantly placed Philip's photograph on her mantlepiece. When told this was somewhat indiscreet, she exchanged it for one in which his handsome features were masked by a bushy beard, but unfortunately this proved poor camouflage. The King still did not approve.

It is possible that Elizabeth inherited her stubbornness from her father. He too could be obdurate. He was annoyed by the way in which his foreign relatives were pushing for the marriage. As always, the lesser Royals of Europe had their eyes on a position with the most stable and well-regarded Monarchy of all. The British have always been the crème de la crème on the Royal stage—the stars, one might say, of the whole show. Marriage into the British Royal family for the often exiled and usually penniless Princes and Princesses of Europe means both financial and political safety. The British haven't dethroned a Monarch since they beheaded Charles I in 1649.

The Queen was equally distrustful of the Mountbatten family and their ambitions. A lady with a long memory, she hadn't forgotten that Lord Mountbatten, Uncle Dickie, had been close to Edward VIII and had even offered to be the ex-King's best man at his marriage to Wallis Simpson after the Abdication. The King had no personal objection to

Philip, but whenever the subject of Elizabeth's betrothal to him was raised by his relatives, or by Elizabeth herself, he found reasons for stalling.

Some were emotional. He did not wish to lose his beloved elder daughter so early and break up the happy family unit that gave him so much support. The other more valid reasons were political. The Greek Royal family members were not popular figures in Britain at that time; nor was the Greek regime, and Philip was sixth in line to the Greek throne. Also there was the problem of Philip's Germanic origins and connections. Though he had fought a brave war for the Allies, his four sisters had all married Germans. One brother-in-law died with his family in a plane crash. Two brothers-in-law had been very much on the German side—one deeply involved in the Nazi movement, another a Luftwaffe pilot. 'Future Queen's Brother-in-Law Bombed Britain' would have made a tasty headline for the press. The husband of the fourth sister ran Salem School, the German prototype for Gordonstoun, where Philip and his three sons were educated.

The groom's parents were a touch recherché to say the least. His mother had founded her own religious order on a Greek island and wore flowing robes and a veil. This, though hardly the norm, was not reprehensible in any way. Much more difficult to deal with was the fact that until the time of his death in 1944, Philip's father, Prince Andrew, had lived a Champagne Charlie life in Monte Carlo with a wealthy French widow, Madame Andrée de la Bigne; she owned a small yacht on which they lived for a while. What is astonishing is that much of this rather untidy family background was not revealed to what was by then an indifferent public until many years later. But the facts must have given the Establishment the shivers and been adequate reason for the King to hesitate about giving permission for the marriage.

Philip's saving grace was the brave war he had fought; though he commanded a British navy ship, he was still an alien, however. If he wanted to get further in the navy, and, more important, if he wanted to marry the Heir Presumptive, he would need to take British citizenship and find a new name. Schleswig-Holstein-Sonderburg-Glucksburg was the nearest he had to one, and that would not look good on a cheque, let alone a Royal marriage certificate. It would also take up an awful lot of room on a British passport.

To Uncle Dickie's delight, his family name, Mountbatten, was finally chosen, but Philip's naturalization was delayed because of political problems between Greece and Britain. And nothing was going to make the main problem go away: how would the xenophobic British react to their future Queen's marrying a foreign Prince? In fact, the results of a newspaper poll revealed that 40 percent of them thought it a very poor idea indeed—a fact that must have given Princess Elizabeth the shivers too.

While all of this was going on, Philip and Elizabeth were endeavouring to get to know each other. Most of their courtship was conducted in public with a group of other young people. She and Philip could never slip out for a meal on their own, though they could wander in the Home Park at Windsor, where members of the family, also taking the air, were forever finding them hand in hand and deep in conversation. Princess Marina, solidly on her cousin Philip's side, invited them to Coppins when no one else was there. She believed Philip's flirting days were over and did her best to influence the King that the marriage was a good idea. At Coppins they could be by themselves. In the Palace, if they were locked alone in her own sitting room for too long it would have been noted and caused raised eyebrows among the staff. Even in the homes of other people who might have accommodated them, the ubiquitous detectives were always not far away. And, of course, there was Margaret, who rarely gave them a moment to themselves when Philip came courting at the Palace.

As Crawfie, the invaluable biographer, said, 'It was always a threesome, unless I took a hand and did something about it by removing Margaret on some pretext or other. I felt the constant presence of the little sister, who was far from undemanding, and liked to have a good bit of attention herself, was not helping the romance much.'

And Crawfie said without any equivocation that Philip loved Elizabeth very much: 'One could not see the young people together without realizing what they felt for each other.'

But why shouldn't Philip have loved her? The young Princess was a great deal prettier than her photographs ever suggested. Her skin was truly like porcelain, her eyes were a beautiful blue, and her figure was rounded and womanly. But more important than any of that, she had, and has, a warm, kind, and gentle nature. The sense of duty in one so young was both touching and appealing.

All the while the King was doing his best to distract his daughter from her single-minded determination to marry Philip. Young and eligible aristocrats were invited to Windsor, Sandringham, and Balmoral. Queen Mary (who thought Philip the perfect match) used to refer to them sarcastically as the 'bodyguard.' The King was wasting his time. Elizabeth never showed the slightest interest in any one of them. She continued to behave like any young girl in love, waiting eagerly for the telephone to ring and living for the days when Philip would be on leave and able to visit her.

In the autumn of 1946 he was invited to Balmoral for a month. The news caused much excitement among journalists, who speculated that this was to be a time of trial for Philip. If it were, it appeared that he did not pass whatever test the King put to him. After what must have been a frustrating time for both him and the young Princess, surrounded as they were by other guests, the Palace issued a statement denying rumours that there was any engagement between the couple. It was a curious thing to do, since the King and the Queen both knew this to be denying the truth. On that holiday Philip had taken matters into his own hands. He proposed to the Princess while out on the moors at Balmoral. Elizabeth was only twenty, but she too then took matters into her own hands and accepted. The young couple presented the news to her father as a fait accompli, and yet he still insisted that it must not be made public, hence the Palace denial.

The King still had hopes that separation might change his daughter's mind. Vain hopes they turned out to be. The Princess was separated from Philip for nearly four months while she and her family toured South Africa, and even after their return the King still made the couple wait another two months before the engagement was formally announced. Elizabeth never complained. She accepted all her father's reasons for waiting, but she was quite determined to marry Philip. And on November 20, 1947, she did. She was joined in holy matrimony with her Prince at Westminster Abbey. The nation, happily, was delighted. So was Dickie Mountbatten, who had pulled it off, and so also was Queen Mary, who had been Philip's staunch supporter throughout.

Afterward the King wrote to his daughter, 'I am so glad you wrote and told Mummy that you think the long wait before your engagement and the long time before the wedding was for the best. I was afraid you had thought I was being hard-hearted about it.. . . I can see you are sublimely happy with Philip which is right but don't forget us is the wish of Your ever loving and devoted Papa.'

One of the arguments the King and Queen used when Princess Elizabeth begged for her engagement to be announced was that her mother had waited two years before she made the decision to marry, and look how well that had worked out. The argument was absolutely valid. The young Lady Elizabeth Bowes-Lyon's marriage to the Duke of York was by any yardstick amazingly successful. He adored her. He could not have lived without her, and as the world witnessed, it was she who gave him the backbone to become a much-loved, wartime King. But it must be said that his need was greater than hers. She has been a widow now since 1952. In that time she has made as great a success of her role of Queen Mother as she did as Queen, managing to overshadow her daughter in the public's affection. As her staff knows, the Queen Mother is not the fragile, fluffy, dear old lady in funny clothes that she may appear to be. 'She's as tough as old boots.' one staff member said with affection, 'but we all love her dearly.'

And that's the way it has always been: toughness beautifully combined with the most beguiling charm and genuine warmth and kindness.

It is said that she and the future King met for the first time at a children's party in 1905, when she was five and he was nine. It was held by the Countess of Leicester. Characteristically the little Elizabeth gave him the crystallized cherries from the top of her sugar cake.

They were not to meet again until the summer of 1920, when she and Albert, Duke of York, were both guests at a small dance. He was immediately captivated. Lady Elizabeth, daughter of the Earl of Strathmore, was one of a large, boisterous family completely different from his own, where the children had been repressed and fearful of their parents. He was attracted by everything about her: her wonderfully easygoing manner and her gaiety and abundant charm made him determined to marry her. He began a relentless courtship, something quite out of character for this shy young Prince. But after the first of his three proposals, Elizabeth kept him waiting for two years before she said yes. His brother, the Prince of Wales, interceded on Albert's behalf, but still she said no. The eventual excuse for all this shilly-shallying was that she knew marrying into Royalty meant good-bye to personal freedom forever.

The question is, when she finally said yes did she marry him for love or for position? She could not have been unaware that marriage into the Royal family was a golden opportunity, though to be fair she could not even have guessed that one day she would be Queen. There are those who believe she also came to realize that becoming the Duchess of York was a role that she could do something with. Even as a child she had the gift of charm and the talent to make people not only comfortable but happier as well. She was born tactful and diplomatic. She was also born both strong and capable. She was a natural superstar, and where better to set a superstar than in the Royal family, where there was all the opportunity in the world to shine?

There is a selflessness about the Queen Mother, and it may be that in the end she married the Duke of York because she realized that though she did not need him, he needed her. In fact, this was her own summing up of the situation.

'It was my duty to marry Bertie and I fell in love with him after,' she said simply years later.

Bertie, as he was known in the family, was a difficult man. His temper was appalling. He would fly into wild rages over the simplest upset. He could not bear things not to go his way, and throughout his unfortunate youth they rarely did. In later years, when he had learned more control, he would grind out his temper on his bath sponges, shredding them into yellow pieces. There was a considerable turnover of bath sponges in Buckingham Palace!

When Elizabeth Bowes-Lyon become aware of him, he had a seriously bad stammer, his health was never good, he was desperately shy, he was not at all bright (at Naval College he managed to graduate at the bottom of the class, much to the chagrin of the King), and he drank far too much. But there was a credit side. He was handsome, athletic, good at sports—he played and won the doubles at Wimbledon—a whiz on the dance floor, but more important, he was basically a good, decent man who always tried to do the right thing.

On the face of it, viewed as a man and not a Royal Prince, he wasn't much of a catch, though naturally his family didn't see it that way. If the young Lady Elizabeth Bowes-Lyon hesitated, perhaps it was because she did not at first spot the goodness in the man, for which she could hardly be blamed. She was only twenty and had a string of beaux who were captivated by her famous charm, honeyed voice, and womanly, rounded figure. The description 'all woman' could have been coined for Elizabeth Bowes-Lyon. As a suitor, apart from being the King's son, Bertie hadn't a great deal going for him. When he proposed, Lady Elizabeth might well have pointed out, as one young lady did when Prince Charles tentatively suggested marriage, that she already had a title of her own, thanks.

Author Penelope Mortimer, in her unfriendly biography of the Queen Mother, suggests that the young Lady Elizabeth was in love with another. She points the finger at the dashing and handsome Captain James Stuart. The Honorable Captain James was a neighbour, a family friend, a hero of the First World War, and also Bertie's first Equerry. Maybe Ms. Mortimer's novelist's imagination was working overtime; maybe her writer's intuition was spot-on. Another love, and an unrequited one, would certainly explain the two years that Elizabeth made Bertie wait. But alas the evidence is thin except that Elizabeth kept saying no to her Royal suitor. Since everyone knew Bertie was besotted by her, his humiliation must have been great as Elizabeth danced her way through the early twenties while everyone remarked on the pretty little Strathmore girl. At one time it was even seriously thought that she would marry the Prince of Wales and certainly he was fond of her. But that was long before Mrs. Simpson.

Bertie's best ally was his mother. Queen Mary was determined that her awkward son would have Elizabeth and began to cultivate the Strathmores, which put considerable pressure on Elizabeth. Her own mother might well have pressured her as well. The Countess of Strathmore liked Bertie and prophetically told a friend, 'I hope he will find a nice wife who will make him happy. . . . He is a man who will be made or marred by his wife.' It seems that she too was on Bertie's side, for she began to invite him to more and more of the house parties that the Strathmores enjoyed at their two country homes.

He had been invited to their Hertfordshire house, St. Paul's Walden, in January 1921 and had made up his mind to propose yet again. On Sunday morning he persuaded Elizabeth to skip church. While the other guests were on their knees at prayer, he, so to speak, was on his, begging her to marry him. This time she accepted.

The official engagement picture shows she was not exactly madly in love with him at that time. She is standing a full six inches away from him, hands protectively clasped behind her back, her expression a touch grim. No radiance to be seen. But the official word was that she had married him for love, not position. Society of the day accepted that the long delay in saying yes was because she was afraid of the responsibility that marriage to a Royal could bring—but in the end she could not do without her Bertie.

His parents, King George V and Queen Mary, were delighted. In fact, word has it that it was Queen Mary who removed James Stuart from Elizabeth's ken by arranging for him to be replaced as Bertie's Equerry and sending the unfortunate young man off to the oil fields of Oklahoma. When he returned, he married Lady Rachel Cavendish in 1923, the same year that the Court announced Bertie's engagement to Elizabeth.

It certainly would not be beyond Queen Mary to manipulate the situation to her own ends. And it was not the first time she had involved herself in Bertie's affairs. Before he became so besotted with Elizabeth, Bertie had fallen in love with Poppy Baring, the daughter of the immensely wealthy Baring family. They had a fine house on the Isle of Wight, where they entertained lavishly. The Royal Princes would sail across in their yachts for the hospitality, and Bertie, aged twenty-four, went overboard for the vivacious daughter of the house. He even proposed. Hearing this news, Queen Mary sent him a telegram that said tersely, 'On no account will we permit your marriage—Mama.'

Love did not conquer all. The romance ended.

Neither Queen Mary nor King George V were outgoing people, but the new Duchess of York could do no wrong as far as they were concerned. She alone could break rules as she did when she arrived flustered and late for dinner. The King and Queen, punctual to a fault, were already seated.

She stammered her apologies, and the King said gallantly, 'No, no, my dear. You are not late: it is we who are early.'

Once a member of the household commented on her tardiness and was astonished when the King, who truly believed that punctuality was the politeness of Princes and who fell into wrath if his sons were so much as a minute late, leaped to her defence. 'If she were not sometimes late she would be perfect, and that would be horrible,' he said.

In return, she was always comfortable and easy with the King. 'Unlike his own children, I was never afraid of him,' she said after his death, 'and in twelve years of having me as a daughter-in-law he never spoke one unkind or abrupt word to me.'

Her own husband could be pretty formidable when in a rage, but undoubtedly she did come to love him. There are those who say she moulded him into the man she wanted. They were the happiest of the Royal families, content with the company of their two daughters and each other. If the courting was not a love story, the marriage was, and it remained so until the King's death in 1952. Without her he could never have coped with the train of events that led to this mild, private man becoming King. It is well known that the Queen Mother never forgave Edward VIII for abdicating the throne to marry Wallis Simpson. She still believes that the strain of so unexpectedly becoming King caused her husband's premature death. Perhaps the judgement is unfair. His health was never good. He was a heavy smoker all his life yet lung cancer was only one of the various diseases that led to his death.

Every year on the anniversary of his death his widow quietly takes herself to the Royal Lodge in Windsor Great Park. This was their favourite home and one that they shared before Bertie became King. She remains there quietly for a week in a home that is still full of things he loved. The magnificent garden is exactly how they created it together as a young married couple. She has not changed so much as a plant. When one dies, another of the same family replaces it. Nor has she changed the decor of the house. When redecorating has to be done, it is in the same colours that she and her husband chose when Royal Lodge was first theirs. In the salon there are still the four 'secret doors'. They were called this by the little Princesses because they are painted exactly the same soft green (known as Sandringham green by the family) as the walls and vanish into the background, particularly at night when the room is softly lit. The portrait of the Prince Regent over the arched Gothic fireplace remains as a reminder that the house was once his country residence and a favourite retreat. The King's desk is exactly as he left it; nothing has been moved. There is a patio with pink and white paving outside the long windows where the Queen Mother keeps a long, swinging garden chair. She and Bertie used to relax there, enjoying the view of their garden and looking at Great Windsor Park without being observed themselves.

That is where she is to be found every year on February 6, remembering him. Though she was still a comparatively young woman when he died, there has never been another man in her life. She misses Bertie to this day.

— 3 —

Love Battles Royal

 T HE ROSY privileges of being born Royal have hidden thorns. And the sharpest of these is the loss of personal freedom to marry anyone, anywhere in the world, regardless of circumstances.

Mrs. Tom Trowbridge, the ladylove of one of the Queen's favourite cousins, Prince Michael of Kent, found herself deeply disappointed because for her there was no possibility of enjoying all the pomp and pageantry of a Royal wedding. Indeed, for a short while it looked as if she would not be able to marry into the Royal family at all, though in her case not all of the difficulties were caused by the British Establishment's archaic rules and regulations.

Princess Michael of Kent was still very much married to her banker husband, Tom Trowbridge, when she and Prince Michael fell in love, and the Prince knew perfectly well that he had a problem when he and Marie-Christine decided they wanted to marry. Under the Royal Marriage Act of 1772 they would need the Queen's permission, which, since Prince Michael was over twenty-five, was unlikely to present any problems. The problem was that Marie-Christine was seeking a divorce, and, as a Roman Catholic, she was also seeking an annulment. Their request to marry was going to put Her Majesty in an awkward position, not only for constitutional reasons but for personal ones as well. At heart, the Queen dislikes the whole idea of divorce and is dismayed that it has struck even those closest to her.

Perhaps Marie-Christine knew the Queen's views on divorce. She was certainly doing her best to pull out all the stops to get herself an annulment from the Catholic Church. She explained that she felt her conscience would trouble her less if her marriage were annulled. She also thought that it would make the Queen more favourably disposed toward her. Obtaining an annulment from the Catholic Church is a complicated procedure. Testimony is needed from friends and relatives, and usually the applicant's spouse is called to give evidence. Frequently, when the spouse refuses to appear, the application cannot be dealt with.

The grounds for annulment that Marie-Christine presented to the Vatican were that Tom Trowbridge did not wish to have children and the Vatican accepted her statement, even though Tom Trowbridge was never asked to give evidence. He told English journalist Fiona Macdonald Hull when she called on him in New York, 'I knew about it [the annulment] and I wasn't involved in any way. It was a Roman Catholic thing and I don't know how Roman Catholics go about these things. I have no idea how they got around it or what they did. I wasn't consulted and I didn't have to make any statement. In fact I didn't know it was happening until someone phoned me up and told me. I was certainly not told officially. . . . I don't know what grounds they used or how they went about it. I consider my marriage ended in divorce and by no other means.'

Most curious.

Marie-Christine herself was vocal about the hearings. She said to Ingrid Seward, the editor of *Majesty* magazine, 'You have to discuss very personal things. . . . and it's not easy to do and that's why a lot of people don't even try to get an annulment, because they have to discuss things you would barely discuss with your doctor.'

Marie-Christine must have steeled herself to discuss these personal things. She was granted her annulment in 1978 and instantly reverted to her maiden name—Baroness von Reibnitz.

The whole sequence of events was most extraordinary. Marie-Christine has been known to describe herself as 'not a particularly good Catholic,' and yet she refused to relinquish her religion. Had she done so it would have made her transition to a British Princess a great deal smoother. The eighteenth-century Act of Succession excluded any member of the Catholic Church and anyone who married a Catholic from the Royal succession. The act is not as prejudiced and insulting to Catholics as it sounds. Since the British Monarch is head of the Church of England, the Monarch obviously cannot also be a Catholic. Marie-Christine's attitude, however, was a bit odd, as she had happily married Tom Trowbridge in a Church of England ceremony and at a C of E church. Her decision to stick to her religion enraged Princess Margaret, who had had her own problems with divorce. Margaret, who is one of the most religious members of the family, dropped a speedy note to her cousin Michael's new fiancée, saying that she would never again speak to her unless she became a member of the Church of England. Marie-Christine declined to obey. Royal watchers have noted that there is little communication, if any, between them even today.

Originally Prince Michael took his ladylove to the Royal family's favourite uncle, Lord Mountbatten, for advice. Uncle Dickie thought about it and asked which would do the family the most harm—if Marie-Christine and Michael simply lived together in sin or if they wed. His considered verdict was that it was better to wed. Ever a snob, he felt that Marie-Christine, with her long and complicated Middle European pedigree, would have made a perfectly suitable British Princess if she had not been divorced and Catholic. 'After all', he said, 'she is not a shop girl. She comes from a good family.'

Uncle Dickie was taken with the flamboyant young woman, though warning bells did start to ring. At dinner at his home one night when she was holding court, he slid a note across the table to his private secretary, John Barratt. It said, 'If that woman doesn't stop talking I shall scream'.

But even so he did his best to help her. He made Michael write to the Queen and pushed him to discuss the situation with his brother, the Duke of Kent, and his sister, Princess Alexandra—none of which Michael had had the courage to do. Mountbatten himself lobbied the Queen at any opportunity he had. But he did advise Marie-Christine to scrap her religion. She wouldn't do it, not even for Uncle Dickie and even though it meant that her husband would lose his place in the line of succession to the throne. Perhaps since he was sixteenth she didn't think it mattered too much.

The resulting complications made for a lot of drama and a lot of newspaper headlines.

The Queen's permission was given. Surprisingly, Marie-Christine was to be granted the title of Her Royal Highness on her marriage. It is not an automatic honour, and Court circles felt that under the circumstances it was one that would not be given. They foresaw a repeat of the Duke of Windsor situation, where the former King automatically kept his HRH, but the Establishment would never grant his American bride more than the courtesy title of Her Grace the Duchess. Undoubtedly the Queen wanted none of the bitterness and anger that that decision of long ago had caused.

The pity of it was that the marriage would have to be abroad. Prince Michael, as a member of the Royal family, was not permitted to wed in a registry office or a British Catholic church, and he certainly couldn't marry a divorcée in a C of E ceremony. Marie-Christine may not have realized that the Church of England is actually more sticky on the question of divorce than the Catholics. As far as the C of E was concerned, she had been married in an Anglican ceremony in Britain and divorced in a British law court. The Church of England was not interested in her Catholic annulment. By their rules she had been legally married. She and her husband went to see Dr. Donald Coggan, the Archbishop of Canterbury, and Mountbatten busied himself trying to fix things. He also talked to the Archbishop of Canterbury *and* the Catholic Apostolic Delegate, *and* he dined with Cardinal Hume, the head of the Roman Catholic Church in Britain. At the end of the day he was convinced that at least he had secured for Marie-Christine the dispensation to marry in a Catholic church abroad.

But he hadn't. Marie-Christine had already ordered her wedding gown, booked the Vienna Boys' Choir, arranged for the high mass to be celebrated in the Schottenkirche, a church in the aristocratic quarter of Vienna, and made out the guest list. She had to think again when she found that the Vatican was digging in its holy heels. She had been unwise enough to give the Vatican the ammunition to stop her church wedding. At a news conference after the Queen had given her permission for the marriage, a reporter asked about the religious upbringing of any children she and Michael might have.

'I think it is a matter of who is the head of the family,' she said, 'and in this case the head of the family happens to be an Anglican. . . . With this new ecumenical spirit I think it is Christians versus the rest and it does not matter which club you belong to.'

The Vatican did not agree. She could marry a Protestant, but if she did she must honestly promise to bring up her children as Catholics. If she did that, besides angering her new relatives, she would be cutting her children from the line of succession. This was Mountbatten's principal argument when he tried to persuade her to change her religion. He felt that she had no right to disadvantage her children. But the hard fact remained that unless she made the promise to bring their children up in her faith, she and Michael could not be married in a Catholic church.

And so all the wedding plans were hastily changed. Marie-Christine was married in the Vienna town hall. She spent her wedding night away from her husband, since the next day she was to be permitted a small mass in the oratory attached to the Schottenkirche. No music was allowed. There was room for only a limited number of guests, which included the Duke of Kent and his daughter, Lady Helen Windsor. The Duchess, no admirer of Marie-Christine, was not present. Princess Alexandra and her husband were there, along with Princess Anne. The oratory was so small that it looked overcrowded. It was a humiliating start to the marriage. The marriage also left Prince Michael at odds with his own church for marrying a divorced woman. The Catholic Church did not consider that Marie-Christine was married at all.

It took the death of a Pope, the enthronement of another, and five years of endless badgering of the Vatican by Princess Michael, not one to take defeat lightly, before the Catholic Church relented.

'She never stopped lobbying someone or other,' said her private secretary of the time, John Barratt. 'She was determined that the Catholic Church would finally recognize her wedding.'

She wore down the Vatican. In July 1983 the Pope announced his recognition of the marriage. He sanctioned a dispensation, which permitted Marie-Christine and Prince Michael to renew their vows in church. Marie-Christine had won. Her only disappointment was that the ceremony was conducted by Monsignor Brown, not Cardinal Hume and not even the Apostolic Delegate, Archbishop Heim. Nor was the wedding a grand occasion at Westminster Cathedral. It took place in a private chapel in the Archbishop's house. The Catholic Church's excuse for finally having capitulated was that Prince Michael had allowed his wife opportunity to influence the religious upbringing of the children. And that he had certainly done. Every other week little Lord Frederick and Lady Gabriella are taken to a Catholic Mass. Three of Frederick's godparents are Catholics, and Princess Michael put him down for the only house at Eton that has a Catholic house-master. Marie-Christine was having her cake and eating it.

All of this created a precedent with which the Queen is now burdened. Nine years after Prince and Princess Michael married, the Duke and Duchess of Kent's son, George, Earl of St. Andrews, asked the Queen for permission to marry a young Canadian woman, Sylvana Tomaselli. The Earl was at Downing College, Cambridge, studying for a postgraduate degree in social anthropology, when they met and fell in love—a pair of earnest, unworldly, studious people who appear to be made for each other. A history research fellow at Newnham College, she is an extremely attractive, dark-haired woman who is also academically brilliant. Prior to meeting the Earl, she had edited an extensive tome on rape, which had sold very well. Sylvana has been described as an egghead. But then so is George.

Normally the Queen would have been delighted to have given permission for one of her relatives to marry a Canadian woman. She would regard it as a union that would strengthen ties with her beloved Commonwealth. Unfortunately, there were a few snags where Sylvana was concerned. Her parents, Austrian Max Tomaselli, a civil engineer, and her mother, Madame Josiane Derners, a Frenchwoman, were divorced. The Royal family would have taken that in its stride. As we know, they are quite blasé about the marital status of the in-laws these days. Unfortunately Sylvana herself was also divorced. She had been married briefly to a dropout student, now a Barbados cruise operator, named John Paul Jones, and the marriage had ended seven years before, when she was twenty-two. She was nearly five years older than the twenty-four-year-old Earl. The final blow for the Royal family was that she was a Catholic. As a Royal courtier said resign-edly, 'All that can be said in her favour, remembering the last time [Princess Michael] is that at least she isn't making a fuss about getting an annulment or trying to fix herself a white wedding.' The Queen must have breathed a sigh of relief at this news.

The couple, who had met in the history library at the university, had already been living together in a small terraced house in Cambridge for eighteen months. The neighbours, who had not rea-lized they were in the presence of a real live HRH, had assumed they were already married. It was, one must admit, all a bit much for the Queen to swallow. Her only consolation must have been that though

Ms. Tomaselli would eventually become the Duchess of Kent, there would be no problems over her becoming an HRH. The Royal Highness title dies with the first son of a Royal Duke. The son that was born to them a year later will be known as Lord Downpatrick, and he has a lovely godmother—Princess Diana.

Like his Uncle Michael before him, the marriage meant that George would be obliged to lose his place in the line of succession. His uncle had been sixteenth. He was seventeenth, even less of a loss for love. On this occasion there were no arguments about their children, if any, being brought up in the Anglican faith. The new Countess is a lapsed Catholic and presumably not bothered about which religion her children are taught.

But the Earl and his brainy, rather sexy-looking bride, with her long, casually combed hair, would not be permitted to marry in church in England or Wales. They settled on a much less complicated solution to the problem than Marie-Christine did. They chose to marry at Leith Registry Office in Scotland in January 1988. The reasons were practical. Leith has the largest marriage room of the Edinburgh registry offices, has lots of parking space, and is close to the Palace of Holyroodhouse. Once the Queen had got over the shock, she had agreed the couple could have their wedding breakfast at the Palace, her official Scottish residence. But protocol would not permit her to attend, and no senior Royal would be present.

There were only twenty-two guests at the wedding, including the entire Kent family, and it was all a bit of a washout. The £24 ceremony took fifteen minutes. The Duchess of Kent and her daughter, Lady Helen Windsor, arrived in the same black-and-red outfits they had worn for Christmas at Windsor—where, incidentally, Sylvana had not been invited even though her fiancé was present. The bride wore a blue velvet polka dot suit that cost more than she could afford and made her look a touch plump. She topped it with an unbecoming tricorn hat. When the official photographs were taken, either the Royals had forgotten Sylvana's pint-sized dad or he was too shy to push into the pictures. Eventually, the photographers pulled him into the group, dragging him from behind the Duke of Kent's ramrod-straight back. No wonder George was heard to breathe a sigh of relief from behind his blond beard and say, 'Thank God that's all over.' And the new Countess undoubtedly echoed the sentiment.

The Duchess of Kent, who is probably the most gentle and kindest of all the Royal family, must have been sad for her son and for his bride. She would have remembered the grandeur of her own wedding. She was married in a ceremony conducted by both the Archbishop of Canterbury and the Archbishop of York and attended by every member of the Royal family, almost every other European monarch, and three thousand other guests. Fifteen million people watched the service on TV. Outside, thousands of well-wishers waited in torrential rain to cheer the newlyweds.

It may not be much consolation, but at least the St. Andrews' wedding will go down in history. It was the first ever Royal registry-office marriage in Britain and the first Royal wedding to take place in Scotland since that of King James I in the seventeenth century.

*

But these small hiccups pale before the antics of Princess Alexandra's daughter, Marina, twenty-sixth in line to the throne, who in the autumn of 1989 created one of the biggest scandals the Royal family has ever had to endure.

While her mother has always been an exemplary member of the Royal family, Princess Alexandra's only daughter has always been something of a nonconformist. After leaving school with not an academic qualification to her name, she rejected the Royal way of life. She tried to disappear into the crowd and found herself happier with a different, less privileged social class than her own. An outgoing girl who likes to be called Mo, she auditioned as a singer with a rock band. She worked in a London store for eight months to raise the money to join Operation Raleigh in Central America and did so well that they offered her a job without her mentioning that her cousin and godfather, Prince Charles, was one of the founders of the organization. She also worked for £80 a week as a trainee instructor for an Outward Bound School. She stayed for two years helping with drop-out youngsters who had been involved in drugs and crime and got along with them splendidly.

In those days her parents and the Royal family were proud of her.

One of her problems is that her taste in men has usually been down-market. Marina, it seems, likes 'a bit of the rough'. Young aristocrats or public school boys seem to remind her too much of the upper-class social background she so despises. Before meeting her husband-to-be, Paul Mowatt, she had various working-class boy-friends, one of whom, a painter and decorater called Phil Filton, betrayed her when the news of her pregnancy became public. She had picked up Mr. Filton in a crowded London pub and taken him home to her bed in the family's apartment at St. James's Palace. Her parents were out of London at the time. The torrid affair lasted six days until, alarmed by her suggestions that they set up home together, the young Mr. Filton confessed to being already married.

Marina's subsequent meeting with Paul Mowatt, a leather-clad young freelance photographer, three years older than her and with a background of local comprehensive education and suburban upbring-ing, moved her into a higher gear of rebellion against her Royal background.

It was in September 1987. They met at a dinner party and found that they had much to talk about. It is hard to believe but he insists that for the first few weeks of their relationship he had not the slightest idea who she was. A year later they rented a studio flat and began living together.

From the time she left home and moved in with Mowatt, Marina seemed to suffer a personality change. She has a real talent for music and yet threw away her hard-won place at the prestigious Guildhall School of Music to live with Mowatt, saying that she wanted to become an engineer in a recording studio. The plan has now chan-ged—she says she wants to compose and record her own experimental music.

Once with Mowatt, she was moving further away from her family and in the process, it seemed, beginning both to dislike and reject them. Resentments, perhaps buried since childhood, were beginning to bubble uncomfortably near the surface. She certainly gave the appearance of being more comfortable in the mock-Tudor thirties semi in Kingston-upon-Thames belonging to Mowatt's mother than in the palaces and country mansions where she was brought up. Mrs. Mowatt, an Ulster woman in her fifties and divorced from her trumpet-player husband, quickly formed a close rapport with her son's new girlfriend.

Marina said: 'Paul's mother has been more of a mother to me in the last few months that I have known her than in all the 23 years with mine. She has been completely supportive and has said she will help us with anything she can. I think the world of her. She is a good person and very loyal.'

Yet there was a moment when the Mowatt family began to have doubts themselves. After Phil Filton's revelations appeared, David Mowatt, Paul's father, said, in a burst of perception, that Marina had set out to embarrass her parents and was using Paul as an emotional weapon. He could well have been right, but nevertheless, he changed his mind sufficiently to attend the wedding.

The world first became aware of Mowatt when he was involved in a fracas at a garage. There was an argument over change, and in the resulting row a plate glass sheet was broken and the police called.

It was soon after this incident that Marina, who had been living with Mowatt for some months, discovered she was pregnant. Her immediate reaction was that she wanted the baby but she and Paul would not marry as she did not wish 'to walk up the aisle with a big fat pregnant tummy.' In this day and age this might have been a perfectly reasonable decision for an ordinary girl. For a second cousin of the Queen, it sounded more like a piece of wilful defiance.

Her baby would not have been the first to have been born on the wrong side of the blanket. The Royal family have weathered many illegitimate children but more in the days when it was simpler to hush up such indiscretion. The unmarried King William IV had ten children by his morganatic lover Mrs. Dorothea Jordan and in 1830 he gave titles to all ten. More recently the Earl of Harewood, also a cousin of the Queen, produced an illegitimate son. But not unnaturally Marina's parents did not wish her to become such a historical statistic.

She and her boyfriend went to confront Princess Alexandra and Sir Angus Ogilvy with the news, reputedly asking at the same time for £100,000 from her trust fund to buy themselves a home. She was only twenty-three, naive for her age, sharp-faced and spiky-haired, and going through the teenage rebellion phase rather late in the day.

Her parents reacted as most responsible parents react to the news of an unwed daughter's pregnancy and by a man of whom they do not approve. They were furious. Their disappointment in their daughter was heightened by the effect that Marina's behaviour would have on the Royal family. According to Marina, her mother told her icily,

69

'You have two options. Either you get it aborted straightaway in Harley Street on Monday or we arrange for you to get married this week by special licence.'

At first Marina was prepared to do neither. What she was prepared to do was to sell her squalid story to *Today* newspaper for a rumoured quarter of a million pounds. A great deal of spilling of bile went on. Marina held nothing back in her attack on her parents as she gave a blow-by-blow account of a furious family row. She even accused her mother of trying to trick her into an abortion and said that Alexandra's mouth 'turned up in a kind of angry snarl' when she and Mowatt refused both 'the shotgun wedding and abortion' ultimatums. The result was that her parents cut off her £280-a-month allowance and kicked her out of the family home. Sir Angus, Marina reported, was drinking heavily and she was afraid that he might hit her. She claimed that her parents had said that Paul would be arrested if he went anywhere near the Ogilvy home, and that detectives were following them wherever they went. She declared herself to be afraid to go home for fear of being held against her will.

October 9 1989 was not a happy day for the Ogilvy family. Alexandra and her husband were appalled by the headlines— 'PRINCESS ALEXANDRA'S DAUGHTER IS CUT OFF BY HER FAMILY. ROYAL BABY SENSATION'—and even more appalled by their daughter's hysterical accusations. Within hours they made an official statement saying that there were several inaccuracies in the newspaper report, and adding that they still loved their daughter and they had not cut her off.

Their embarrassment was compounded by the fact that Marina had written to the Queen for advice and support. The Queen did not reply. This did make for some tasty headlines, but since Marina had made it clear she was determined to have the baby and would marry only when she chose, what exactly she expected the Queen to do is not clear. Perhaps order her parents to give her the £100,000 she wanted. But her six-page letter to 'Dear Cousin Lilibet', which she herself delivered by hand to Buckingham Palace, kept the story on the front pages.

'This,' said Marina, 'is the dark side of the Royal family we are experiencing now. The other side of the postcard is just for tourists.'

All good dramatic stuff and fairly typical of anyone's wayward daughter, but for a member of the Royal family to behave so badly was unthinkable. Other people's wayward daughters are not splashed all over the front pages of the world's press. She was doing it her way with a total incomprehension of anyone else's point of view. It then emerged that the girl had spent some time in the Priory—an imposing mansion in West London which expensively and luxuriously houses sufferers from drug addiction, alcoholism and mental disorders such as anorexia nervosa.

With this new revelation all became more understandable and indeed very sad. Yet Marina, protesting that there was nothing wrong with her and no doubt egged on by the media and perhaps others with an axe to grind, eventually went on television to beg her parents to get in touch with her.

'I want you to stand by me and love me,' she sobbed. 'I am your child and I want you to understand that this is what I want. I love my child, and in the years to come I hope you will do so as well.'

And then she told the viewers how she longed for her mother to 'just pick up the phone.'

It was difficult for Alexandra to comply since *Today* had spirited the young couple off to North Yorkshire. The Ogilvys, along with everyone else except the journalists guarding her, had no idea where their daughter was.

It was an impossible situation for Princess Alexandra and her husband, bound as they were by their Royal straitjacket. All they could do was to make a public statement, saying that they loved their daughter very much. They made it clear that she would always be welcomed back to her home and that they felt deeply for her at a difficult time.

But Marina continued to pile public humiliation upon public humiliation on her family and one does wonder why. What could they have done to create such bitterness in their rebel daughter? Eventually Marina did phone home and is said to have made a tearful apology for the scandal she had created, but her remorse was short-lived. The humiliation went on, with Marina continuing to act as if she were under some compulsion to score off her parents in any way possible.

Suddenly a wedding was arranged. Putting a brave face on the situation, her parents attended the ceremony at St. Andrew's Church in Ham, Surrey, near Mowatt's mother's home. The bride wore black—more defiance. Her mother, beautifully dressed as always, smiled happily and said it was a lovely wedding, but looked decidedly out of place among the 30 or so punk-style guests. So did Marina's sister-in-law, Julia Ogilvy, and her brother, James. There was no choir, no bells, no bridesmaids and no flowers. Not even confetti. Paul Mowatt's father, who plays in a brass band in Munich, came over for the wedding, but the two sets of parents, not surprisingly, had little in common. A difficult time was had by all. Such an uneasy meeting of the Establishment and the radical was never going to be comfortable. In various interviews the bridegroom's family said that the Ogilvys gave them the impression that the Mowatts were beneath them. Since the Royal family are not snobs, any lack of enthusiasm on the part of Marina's parents would have come from the fact that they had grave doubts as to whether this upstairs/downstairs marriage could ever work.

But Angus kissed his wayward daughter, posed for photographs with her and gave her away. Other members of the Royal family were conspicuously absent. No-one represented the Queen. Marina's parents had prepared a small reception with a wedding cake at Thatched House Lodge. The newlyweds never turned up. They and their friends went off to their own party at the Duke of York's Barracks in Chelsea.

Paul Mowatt's mother insisted that the Ogilvys had been invited to the party at the barracks but had declined, saying there was insufficient security. This, said Mrs. Mowatt, was not true. There couldn't have been any more security.

'I wonder how many there were at their party?' she added spitefully. 'Ours was lovely.'

With the champagne cooling, the food untouched, the cake uncut, and the bride and groom absent, there can be little doubt that the Ogilvy's party was deeply depressing.

'We'd booked our party first,' said Paul defiantly, 'and we couldn't let our guests down. Everybody was invited and if certain people didn't want to attend, we can't be held responsible.'

As he began his speech at the wedding reception, Mowatt turned to look at the places which had been set for Marina's parents and said sarcastically: 'Thank you very much for your kind words, Sir Angus.'

He then followed up with another jibe directed at his new father-in-law.

'I borrowed an old speech from Angus,' he said. 'Actually, I had to buy it from him. Money's a bit tight these days.'

This appeared to be a reference to the Mowatts' claim that the Ogilvys never paid anything towards the £10,000 reception.

Many of the problems were caused by misunderstandings and the Mowatts' lack of knowledge of the procedures which Royalty must follow. Security problems they should have appreciated, but how could this ordinary family possibly understand the complexities of the Royal Marriage Act? If Marina had waited until the baby was born before marrying, as an illegitimate, her child would have lost its place in line to the throne. Maybe that was of no importance to Marina, but her own family felt that she had no right to disadvantage her child. The Mowatts complained that Sir Angus gave the impression that he was under pressure to telephone the Queen with the date of the wedding—which, indeed, he would have been. Marina had first decided to marry in a registry office, but members of the Royal family are not permitted to do this in England. The plans had to be hastily switched to a church ceremony. Was this more defiance by Marina who, having been brought up Royal and having witnessed the problems of her Uncle Michael of Kent, must have surely understood what was possible and what was not? To most of us—and indeed to Marina herself—all of these restrictions appear archaic, as maybe they are. But they are also the law of the land and have to be obeyed.

Their baby, a girl they called Zenouska, was born by caesarean section at the end of May 1990 at a local National Health hospital and the couple were able to keep the birth a secret for eight days. Fifteen days later the Ogilvys met their first grandchild, and the first pictures were sold for an undisclosed (but undoubtedly hefty) sum to *Hello* magazine.

Though Mr. and Mrs. Mowatt have now settled down to a quiet suburban life, taking it in turns to feed the baby, it is unlikely that there will be any happy ending to this story of a Royal rebel. She has most certainly cooked her goose with the Queen and her relatives. Princess Alexandra is much loved within the family and it has been painful for them to see the suffering she has been caused. The Queen, who normally stands by her relatives through thick and thin, made no secret of her displeasure. Traditionally Her Majesty gives her consent to a marriage within the family with a handwritten, vellum document addressed to 'my trusty and well-beloved cousin'. This written permission from the Monarch is necessary before any clergyman can perform the wedding ceremony.

For more than 200 years every bride or groom from the Royal family has been given this document and so indeed was Marina—but with a difference.

After calling a special meeting with the Privy Council to authorize the wedding (as she is obliged to do under the rules of the Royal Marriages Act of 1772), the Queen gave her consent to the wedding. Buckingham Palace, however, when sending the vellum to the Crown Office in the Lord Chancellor's department for the final inscription, gave instructions that the words 'my trusty and well-beloved cousin' should be deleted.

For the Queen to have given this order—and it could only have come from her—proves that Marina's behaviour had deeply distressed her. It was inconceivable that any member of the Royal family, having from birth enjoyed the privileges that such a position bestows, should have stooped to selling the story of a family rift, with every bitter detail revealed, to a newspaper.

Her parents may in time forgive her, but her relatives never will. Sadly, one day she will wake up, grown up and full of regrets. Princess Alexandra and Sir Angus's only consolation is that their son, James, who married the charming, beautiful and definitely suitable Julia Rawlinson, has turned out fine. They have every reason to be proud of him. Perhaps, in time, Marina will give them reason to be proud of her.

— 4 —
Till Death
Us Do Part

*R*OYAL WIVES are not like wives. They toil not, neither do they spin, and some of them, notably Diana, can give the lilies of the field a run for their money when it comes to raiment. But then neither do they have to rustle up the supper, wash the dishes, or change the baby's nappy. Their duties are to look good in public, carry out sufficient engagements to justify their Civil List allowance, uphold the dignity of the Crown, and make themselves useful to the many charities that clamour for their patronage. The only truly wifely role is motherhood—essential for the continuation of the line. Marrying a Prince or a Royal Duke could be compared to becoming a cross between a career woman and a brood mare.

Most of the Sovereign's subjects would not have it any other way. The thought of the Queen with a duster in her hand or Princess Diana giving the kitchen floor a mop ruins the mystique of Royalty. Royal women are permitted only to play at being housewives. Playing at chores does not diminish the dignity. We are enchanted to know that the Queen visits her uninhabited cottages on the Balmoral Estate, taking a picnic with tea in a thermos and—when she and her lady-in-waiting have eaten—doing the washing-up herself. This is just about as far as her loyal subjects wish Her Majesty to go in being like one of us. The Queen has managed throughout her long reign to make the Monarchy a symbol that people can identify with and yet still respect. But too much ordinary behaviour, any attempt to be like the rest of us, would spoil this carefully nurtured image.

The Queen is even different when it comes to her marriage. Hers *had* to work. It was unthinkable that it should fail. In a modern era when one in four marriages ends in divorce, there was never any possibility of the Queen packing it in or of Philip exchanging her for a younger model. When she was about seven and still in the nursery, she said to her governess, 'When I get married, Crawfie, I shall make my husband as happy as Mummy has made Papa.' All the forty-odd years that she and Prince Philip have been together she has tried to do just that and has worked faithfully to make the marriage successful. She has achieved her goal mostly by her own efforts, and it was no mean achievement, since her Royal career has always been so demanding. Somehow she has contrived throughout her married life to keep Her Majesty the Queen and Philip's wife in two separate compartments.

Her achievement is all the greater since the man she fell in love with and was so determined to marry is no pipe-and-slippers husband. He is difficult, temperamental, and arrogant, but at the same time he has always been the Queen's greatest supporter. He is the oak and she the willow, bending to accommodate his temperament. In the early days of their marriage he was able to make her less solemn and more lighthearted, and over the years she has managed to bring out a gentler, more compassionate side in him. But it has not been easy.

It wasn't long after their wedding that Philip became fully aware of just what he had taken on. Their honeymoon was a fiasco. They spent the beginning of it at Broadlands, Lord Mountbatten's Hampshire home, and the world came to gape. There were hordes of people clambering over tombstones in the churchyard to try to get a glimpse of the newlyweds in church, and above all the press cameras were everywhere. Elizabeth does not like press cameras, but she is used to them and has been since she was a child. Prince Philip was not. The press enraged him and unfortunately has continued to enrage him ever since. His life would have been less choleric if he had tried harder to come to terms with this aspect of his job.

For Elizabeth, a grave young girl with a tender heart, the early days must have been difficult, and she handled them with an instinctive wisdom and understanding of the male ego far beyond her years. Philip is a bossy man and likes his own way. He is not the type to walk three paces behind anyone. He is highly competitive. Any game he plays he has to win. He likes to be top dog. But he had to accept that top dog is his wife's position and always would be—in public. Elizabeth, from day one, let him be boss in private. She may have gritted her teeth when the minute they became engaged he decided he wanted to shift all the furniture around in *her* private apartments at Buckingham Palace, but she let him do it. After they were married, he had the biggest say in furnishing Windlesham Manor, their first home. Most of the furnishings came out of storage at Buckingham Palace or were wedding presents. There was little expense involved except for the running of the house, and Philip was determined to pay for that like any normal husband. It proved simply impossible on his naval pay. Windlesham Manor was therefore desperately short staffed, certainly by Princess Elizabeth's standards, and Philip was trying to get around the problem by getting the detectives to 'muck in.'

But detectives do not care too much for being used as kitchen maids, and in the end the Princess intervened. She borrowed two footmen from Buckingham Palace and paid for them herself. There had to be a limit to doing things Philip's way!

This was unusual. Normally things *are* done his way, and he has always been boss in the home. All their married life the Queen has done all she could to avoid bruising his macho ego. The dining tables in the private apartments of their various homes are round so that there is no question of precedence with the Queen sitting, as protocol would demand even privately, at the head of the table. To all the children's requests she would say, 'Ask Papa.' Before making any decisions she will always say to friends, 'I'll see what Philip thinks.' He makes the family decisions. She once said, 'It's a waste of time trying to change a man's character. You have to accept him as he is.' That she has certainly done.

But before the children arrived and while the King was alive there were few problems. Philip wanted to go back to sea, and Elizabeth, realizing that stuck in a desk job her husband would be bad-tempered and discontented, agreed that he should, though undoubtedly she would much rather have had him at home.

She unselfishly put him first in her order of priorities. He has always come before the children. When Prince Charles was a tiny baby, Philip, enjoying the gung-ho naval life and working hard for promotion, was made second in command of HMS *Chequers*. The ship was based at Malta, and the Princess decided to join him there, perhaps to keep a wifely eye on him. The King agreed she could go, but Prince Charles was to be left at home. The few weeks that she spent in Malta, living in Lord Mountbatten's villa above the harbour, proved to be one of the happiest times of her life. She still talks wistfully of the days 'when I was a naval wife.' And though she was a service wife who arrived with a ton of luggage and her own personal maid, she did have her hair done at the local hairdresser's, had tea with the other naval wives, and went dancing with her husband at the Hotel Phoenicia. She was even able to swim and sunbathe with him on the beach like any other ordinary couple.

These were all new experiences. She was freer than she had ever been before (or indeed has been since). It is easy to understand why Princess Anne was conceived in the warmth and sunshine of Malta.

Elizabeth flew home to prepare for Princess Anne's birth, and she and her husband were separated again until he returned to London just in time for the baby's arrival. August 15, 1950, the day Anne was born, was a highlight in Prince Philip's life. Not only had he a daughter, but also he was promoted to Lieutenant Commander and given the command of his own ship, HMS *Magpie*. Being Commander gave him so much pleasure and he used *Magpie* for so many courtesy visits to kings, cousins, and countries around the Med that *Magpie* became known in the navy as Edinburgh's private yacht. Elizabeth returned again to Malta after she had finished breast-feeding Anne, this time leaving two children behind.

Both Elizabeth and Philip knew that the time would come when the heavy responsibilities of the throne would descend on their shoulders, but since the King was still only in his early fifties there should have been a long, carefree time ahead. There wasn't. Soon after Anne's birth there was renewed concern about the King's health. Elizabeth had to take over more and more of his duties, and she needed Philip's help. The Lieutenant Commander was put on indefinite leave and in July 1951 had to say good-bye to his beloved *Magpie*. Elizabeth had a cross, sulky husband on her hands and when the King died an even crosser and sulkier one. It was 1952, and the Princess and her husband were on an official tour of Kenya when her father died. His health had been fragile before she and Philip left England, and a sealed dossier, to be opened in the event of his death, and a Royal

Standard—the flag flown only in the presence of the Monarch—had been put in among the baggage.

When the news came through, Michael Parker, Prince Philip's private secretary, was the first to hear it. He decided the best person to tell the Princess must be her husband. Parker managed to extract Philip from inside the Sagana Hunting Lodge, where they were staying, and told him what had happened. He then left him with the sad task of telling Her Majesty. Afterward, Parker told his wife, Eileen, that Prince Philip looked at that moment as if the whole world had fallen on his shoulders. 'I never felt so sorry for anyone in my life,' he added.

Through the first few weeks Philip was stalwart at the new Queen's side, until he began to appreciate just how much his life had changed. The Queen had enough to worry about without her husband being difficult and bemoaning his loss of freedom. One would like to think that she pointed out to him that he had had all the benefits of joining the Royal family, and now the time had come to pay for them. The chances are she did no such thing. Her philosophy was, 'There's nothing worse than to fence a man in and stop him from doing what he wants.'

She has never for one moment fenced Philip in. When they moved to Buckingham Palace and he complained that he felt like a lodger, she let him set about bringing the huge building more up to date. He altered the kitchens, modernizing everything possible. He tried to change the age-old chain of command where the Queen tells her page, who tells her footman, who tells a lesser footman, and so on down the line until Her Majesty gets her cup of tea or whatever it was she wanted in the first place. In that he failed. The old way of doing things was far too ingrained in the system and the staff. The Queen must have winced when her husband began putting false ceilings over beautiful old cornices, and the Ministry of Works was decidedly alarmed. She bore with the intercom system he had installed and the aromas from the electric frying pan he set up in his dressing room so he could make himself a quick, if rather smelly, breakfast. But she did put her foot down when he helped himself to some paintings for his study. He had picked upon part of the State collection from the State apartments. 'You'll get us shot!' she told him. 'They belong to the nation.' The Queen insisted that he put them back where they had been. He did as he was told. Philip bosses, sometimes bullies, and often ignores people, but he has never been able to boss, bully, or ignore his wife. The verdict of the staff throughout all these changes was that he was a 'bloomin' nuisance.' The courtiers felt the same.

It was a delicate path that the Queen was treading. Philip had his own way about anything that did not impinge on her role. She would protest only when he attempted something that broke the rules of Royal protocol. She was meticulous in not allowing him to interfere in matters of State. Churchill, her Prime Minister, encouraged her in this, since the Establishment, well aware of his ambitious Mountbatten background, did not trust her husband. And as much as she loved him, the young Queen might have been aware that if he were permitted to involve himself too deeply in her duties, he could overpower her. He could also have been a handicap. As a young man he had a great many rough edges. Subtlety was not and never has been his style.

Nevertheless, the Queen issued a Royal warrant that gave him 'place, preeminence, and precedence' after her.

Her indulgence of him comes about for the simple reason that she loves him, but this indulgence did once paradoxically cause rumours of a marital rift. Philip was to open the Melbourne Olympics in 1956, and the Queen permitted him to take the Royal yacht part of the way. The chance to be back at sea was too much to resist for Philip and his private secretary, Michael Parker.

It wasn't long before they had been able to lengthen the voyage and go round the world. The excuse was that they would visit all the tiny little red dots of islands on the map that in those days made up the British Empire. Philip explained it as a 'showing the flag' expedition, which no doubt caused the Queen a wry smile as she waved him off. They went off for four months, and they sailed forty thousand miles. Also on board were some of Philip's friends and, to add a bit of credence, some naturalists. Philip missed out on Christmas at Sandringham with his children, the Suez Canal crisis, and a change of Prime Minister. But the journey was a great success from a public relations point of view. All those little British islands normally too small to be included on a Royal tour gave the husband of Her Majesty the Queen a tumultuous welcome.

But four months having fun away from the family, which if the truth be told, is what Philip was doing, is a long time. Not unnaturally people back in Britain were beginning to wonder if something had gone seriously wrong with the marriage. As the voyage looked like it was coming to an end, Philip decided to extend it. Hastily it was arranged for the Queen to fly out to be reunited with her husband in Gilbraltar. The whole thing was beginning to border on farce. It was then that the *Baltimore Sun* decided to print the rumours circulating in Britain about the state of the Queen's marriage. Alarmed, her private secretary was unwise enough to issue a statement saying, 'It is quite untrue that there is a rift between the Queen and the Duke of Edinburgh.'

The statement gave the British press the excuse to print exactly what these rumours were. Previously they had been holding back. The headlines dismayed the Queen but merely made Philip angry—as people are always angry when caught in the wrong. The trip had been a foolish indulgence. At a Guildhall lunch, which by tradition always follows a Royal tour, Philip did his best in his speech to justify his long absence.

He said, 'I believe there are some things for which it is worthwhile making personal sacrifices and I believe the British Commonwealth is one of those things and I, for one, am prepared to sacrifice a good deal if by doing so I can advance its well-being by even a small degree.'

The sanctimonious hypocrisy of that statement must have caused his wife yet another wry smile.

In spite of the gossip, it was unlikely there was a rift at the time. More likely the couple needed a little breathing space from each other, and the Queen realized that if her bored husband wasn't let off the hook for a while, there *would* be not a rift but a chasm.

There was another aspect to the end of the round-the world jaunt. It was then that Commander Michael Parker's wife divorced him, and he resigned and went back to Australia, leaving Philip without his best friend. In retrospect, the Queen must have come to realize that this was the best thing that could possibly have happened. The boisterous Mike Parker had not been the best of influences on the Prince. Old shipmates, both knowing a little too much about the other, they were buddy-buddy, egging each other on into situations that were not suitable for the consort of the Queen. Elizabeth put up with Philip's 'funny friends,' roistering chaps who were mostly introduced to him by Michael Parker. These friends were slowly cut out of Philip's life after Parker left, but it is unlikely that the Queen ever said they had to go.

Her tolerance has been the main factor in the continuing success of the marriage. She is able to be so tolerant because over the years she has learned to develop a deep, inner calm. This helps her cope with the often stultifying boredom of her job, and she is able to draw on it in times of crisis. She and Philip do have their rows, and the Palace staff is well aware when one is in progress and goes about on tiptoe. She stands up to him when he is in one of his tempers, and she is not opposed to showing her own anger. One of their worst quarrels was over Prince Edward when he quit the Royal Marines. Philip was furious with his son and gave the boy hell. The Queen felt he was being too tough and was equally furious with her husband. Prince Edward made his decision in the middle of one of their holidays, and for a couple of days out on the moors it was obvious that the Queen and the Duke were barely speaking.

The Queen also can be quick to voice her feelings when her husband does something she thinks demeans the dignity of the Crown. He is pretty hot on protecting this dignity himself, but he can't resist the sharp, unkind crack if the opportunity to make one comes along, such as the day when a photographer fell out of a tree and the Duke remarked happily that he hoped he'd broken his bloody neck. The Queen undoubtedly gave him hell when on a State visit to China he was stupid enough to refer to their hosts as slitty-eyed and then was furious when the remark was reported. In Philip's opinion the embarrassment to the Crown wasn't his fault. It was the press's fault for printing his comment. It was no doubt left to his wife to point out that he shouldn't have made the remark in the first place.

A State visit requires the presence of the Monarch's spouse, and therefore they were in China together. But if one were to add up the number of days that the Queen and her husband have been apart over the years, it would be surprising to see exactly how rarely they are together. In London he is frequently out to dinner, speechifying, which he does extremely well. The Queen is quite content to dine alone or, these days, with the Duchess of York. She is used to dining alone and enjoys the time to herself. Her footman pours her a dry martini with a lot of ice. Her meal—no pudding when she is alone—is served on a hot plate, and as the ice melts the martini lasts her through the meal.

Philip is often abroad. His travels began in the 1950s, when it was said that the Queen's advisers suggested that she let him go away as much as he liked. His abrasiveness was at its worst, and there was anxiety that he could do the Monarchy harm. Travel fascinates him, and there was always somewhere to go. He has always quietly visited his relations in Germany, though the Queen rarely accompanies him, and he is just as likely to bob up in South America or anywhere that his considerable charity work will take him, particularly if the fare is paid.

As a young man his absences were remarked upon. Today, with the focus on the younger Royals, little notice is taken of his travels. The separations seem to have no effect on the marriage, but then the Queen is not the average wife. She is extremely busy—much busier than her husband. She need never be alone, except by her own choice, and she has her own interests away from her work. If Philip is away, she is unlikely to be sitting alone, fretting, miserable, and bored until he comes back.

Only at holiday times are they truly together. When the Court moves to Balmoral or Sandringham these are the happiest days of the year for the Queen. The family members are all together, she has her husband with her, and out on the moors there is no question of his walking behind. He is out in front with the guns, while it is she who strides along behind, picking up dead birds.

On their long holidays—and every weekend at Windsor—they revert to the life of wealthy country people, filling the house with guests, dressing for dinner, and enjoying all the country house pastimes beloved by the English upper class: riding, shooting, fishing, working jigsaw puzzles, doing petit point, playing cards, watching films in their private cinemas (never TV if guests are about), and playing what used to be called parlour games. Their favourite is The Game, a form of charades. It is not only Princess Margaret in the family who has dramatic talent; the Queen is a mean mimic herself.

She and Philip are as close today as they have ever been. Age and arthritis have quelled his restlessness if not improved his temper. But she understands him. Those who work for them report that they laugh a lot together, and there is nothing that holds a marriage together better than that.

*

The new Duchess of York is, of course, Royal only by marriage, and there are those who say that arrogance is beginning to afflict her. Certainly, she seems to be having difficulty in grasping that Royalty must set a good example and give value for money.

Yet there is nothing wrong with her marriage. Her husband calls her 'a real woman' and shows every sign of adoring her. She in turn adores him and mothers him a little. She often refers to him as 'my boy.' He describes her hair as 'glorious Titian,' and three months after their wedding in 1986 he begged her, 'Promise me you'll never change.' He also begged, 'Never, never cut your hair.' He also says, 'Married life is rather wonderful,' and he describes his Duchess as 'vivacious, cheerful, outgoing, vibrant . . . radiating warmth and a sense of fun.'

He loves the woman!

But she is not averse to putting him down, and like all passionate people, they fight. In the early days of the marriage, she would fight with him in public. She lost her temper with him on a ski lift on one of their many skiing holidays. There had been a slight contretemps with a television reporter. She said to her husband anxiously, 'Andrew, I hope that "News at Ten" chappie was all right. I hope he doesn't think it was me who knocked him over.'

Prince Andrew sighed deeply, but since the Royal family's hearts lift if one of the press suffers a mishap, he made no comment on the reporter's state of health. The sigh was for his wife's ignorance.

'Why do you worry about them?' he asked, then added in patient tones, 'Anyway, it wasn't "News at Ten," it was Michael Cole from the BBC.'

Fergie was irritated. She informed her husband that though he might have forgotten it, she was new to the business of being Royal. 'Why do you keep embarrassing me and pointing it out in front of other people when I get things wrong?' she asked crossly. 'It is not very charitable. Why don't you wait until we are on our own?' Then she added, seemingly unaware that they were very much not on their own, 'Unlike some people, I haven't been doing this for twenty-seven years.

84

I'm going to make mistakes and get things wrong. You might as well accept that and help me. Sometimes you're as bad as your father.'

But having said her piece and got it off her ample chest, Fergie then leaned toward her husband, pinched him playfully on both cheeks, and gave him a kiss.

It was a classic marital exchange that could have taken place in any home in the land, particularly the grumble about being like his father. But to be ticked off is a comparatively new experience for Prince Andrew, who most certainly can be arrogant. But it seems that his wife is determined to prick his pomposity. That can only be for the good. There was a time when her husband behaved like Princess Margaret—one minute he wanted to be one of the gang and the next he suddenly would become more Royal than the entire family put together. On one of his matey days he approached a higher-ranking fellow officer in the mess and said, 'Hi, I'm Andrew. You can call me Andy if you like.'

'Thanks,' snapped the officer. 'And you can call me Sir.'

If Sarah can stop him from making gaffes like that, and mercifully she will, she deserves a vote of thanks from the rest of the Royal family. He is inclined to be self-important, and she knows it. Remembering how his contemporaries referred to him as the Great I Am she is fighting a relentless battle to make him say 'we' instead of 'I' whenever he makes public utterances.

Just as her mother-in-law did, she has taken on a problem, but she is tackling it in a different way from the Queen. Where the Queen kept her cool most of the time and turned a blind eye when Philip was playing up, Fergie, the modern wife, makes her point with some force. And it seems to work. Curiously, she seems to have a habit of making her point on Swiss ski lifts. Two years after the incident with the TV reporter, Andrew upset her again. And again she gave him a piece of her mind on their way to the slippery slopes.

This time no one overheard the reason for Fergie's displeasure, though it was obvious she was giving him a terrible telling off. Swearing too, said an awestruck reporter. When they returned from the piste, Andrew beat it to the nearest florist in Klosters, where he bought every yellow rose in the shop. They cost him £40. But Fergie had not yet forgiven him. She stalked off with her friend, Lulu Blacker, and after looking in a dress-shop window, the two women disappeared into the local grocery store. Andrew followed them perhaps not realizing the shop was a co-op, a most unlikely place to find a Prince of the Realm. Once inside he had to hang about for a minute or two contemplating the dairy counter before he got the opportunity to hand over his peace offering. She accepted the roses frostily and marched off to the nearest tea room, carrying them in a way that suggested he needn't have bothered. Andrew, not sure of his welcome, hovered, looking lost before finding the courage to join her — when no doubt all was forgiven over tea and fattening pastries.

It is unusual for Fergie to sulk, so his crime must have been serious. Her normal practice is to say, 'Oh, Andrew! You are silly, but I do love you!' before flinging her arms around him.

But their passionate rows, which likely are ended by a session of passion in bed, are surprisingly public. The British find it rather endearing. After all, Fergie is the one with whom they can identify. The couple also amused the Canadians on their tour there in late summer 1989. They didn't seem to know whether to look at the crowds who had come to greet them or look at each other. Much of the time they looked at each other. It was, said one reporter, 'a touching tour,' since even on official occasions they couldn't resist holding hands. They also slipped off for a couple of days on their own. 'We went to a log cabin. We were completely alone.' Fergie confided to a reporter. 'It was great. And there were two squirrels which looked like chipmunks which came and ate all our nuts. They were our only companions. We had a lovely time. There were our police officers around but they weren't with us. We have great fun together. We have a wonderful *joie de vivre*. I suppose we act as a catalyst for each other.'

We learned this less-than-riveting gush in a series of interviews that the Duchess gave to the *Daily Express*. Royals do not normally give interviews unless it is to talk about their pet charity. In this instance the charity was beginning at home. It was publication week for two children's books that Fergie had written, and she wanted some promotion. She is a woman who knows the value of publicity and admitted later, quite openly, that she had deliberately delayed the news of her second pregnancy for that very week to bring even more attention to her books. The announcement of another newcomer to the House of York was made by the Palace with brilliant timing just about the time Fergie arrived for a Foyles literary luncheon to promote her books, of course.

The *Daily Express* had paid a Grand Duchess's ransom—more than £100,000—for the exclusive interviews, and they were decidedly miffed. In spite of the size of the cheque Fergie had not thought to tell them that she was pregnant. In fact, she had categorically said she wasn't. The day before the announcement of the new baby, the *Express* had unwittingly stated: 'The new slimline Duchess has worked hard to get herself into the great shape she is now in and she is definitely going to hang on to it for a little while longer.' She did telephone the talented Philippa Kennedy, who interviewed her, and apologized for telling 'white lies.' More like big black ones. It was a dirty trick—particularly as what she did say wasn't exactly value for money.

We did learn that when Fergie gets home she kicks off her high heels, takes off her suit, and puts on something comfortable before clearing out cupboards 'just like other people,' as she put it, 'with Beatrice playing around at my feet.' She explained she just likes to be normal; she doesn't like any fuss or bother and wants everyone to be happy and relaxed. If the staff members want a night off, they should feel free to take it. Fergie will don the apron and do the cooking—that is, as long as Andrew doesn't want anything more complicated than steak and chips or an omelette.

Fancy that!

One thing that Fergie has learned quickly from her husband is the value of money. He, like the rest of the Royal family, was brought up to be exceedingly cautious with it. Not to put too fine a point on it, most of the Royal family are stingy. Princess Diana is not. She is a spender and not just on herself. She is forever buying little gifts for her friends and her staff. Fergie is more careful. Though she and Andrew are not exactly on the bread line, they do admittedly have less money than the Prince and Princess of Wales. Until the publishing company Fergie worked for ran into problems she chose to go on working, using Buckingham Palace as her business address. Years ago it would have been unthinkable for any Royal woman to involve herself in any money-making activities. But everything changes. There is no doubt that Fergie's books about Budgie the helicopter and his adventures (in spite of bad reviews) will coin her a fortune—though she herself admits they would not have been published if anyone else had written them. Some of the proceeds are said to be going to charities, but cynics suspect that sum is not likely to be excessive.

There was what appeared to be a fund-raising operation which caused splutters of rage from Fergie's critics. In August 1990, *Hello* magazine published 46 pages of pictures (plus front and back cover) of the Duke and Duchess with their two girls, Beatrice and Eugenie. The pictures were taken by Prince Andrew's photographer friend, Gene Nocon. For the purpose of the feature the Yorks even staged a birthday tea, complete with cake, for Beatrice, some weeks before her birthday.

As *Hello* said on their cover, 'The Duke and Duchess of York grant us the most personal of interviews and for the first time ever throw open the doors of their home and invite us to share their intimate family moments.' Amazingly, that is exactly what they did, creating Royal precedents which those close to the Queen felt were both vulgar and improper.

It seems unlikely that they posed out of the goodness of their hearts. Though it has never been confirmed, the journalist grapevine spread the word that they were paid £250,000. That sounds about right for 75 full colour royal pictures, including two of the Duchess changing baby Eugenie's nappy (with not a nanny in sight). These particular shots moved one of her critics to say that the feature resembled nothing more than a Nappisan advertisement!

The pictures caused such a furore that not long afterwards another rumour, maybe planted, maybe not, began to circulate, suggesting that the Yorks had not received a penny from *Hello*. They had, it was said, agreed to pose for the pictures out of friendship for Gene Nocon.

Whether they were paid or not is largely irrelevant. To be so exhaustively photographed for the benefit of one magazine is not normal behaviour for any member of the Royal family.

Happily, not all the family behaves the same way. Charles has never cashed in on his position (apart from borrowing the odd airplane from rich friends like Armand Hammer). And he and Diana give enormous sums to charity without ever mentioning it. Charles has never kept a single penny from anything that he has had published. All proceeds go to charity.

Class will out.

Though their attitudes differ about money, Fergie and Diana do

Balcony scene: the Queen holding Prince Edward, with the Queen
Mother, Prince Philip, and the young Prince Andrew in the
foreground, at Buckingham Palace

Grandstand view: the Queen and Prince Philip enjoying a day
in the country in 1968

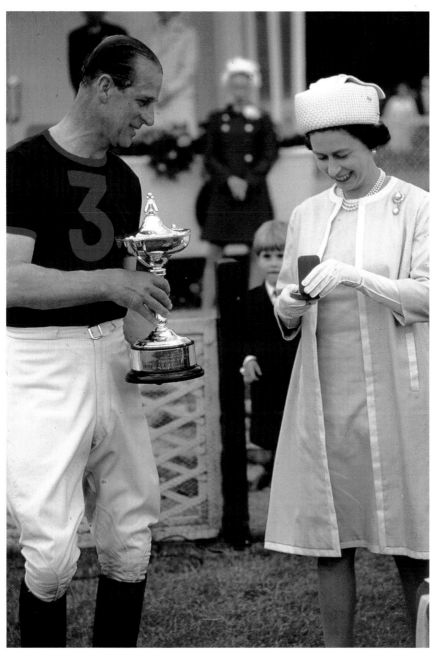

Presentation time: the Queen and Prince Philip after a polo match in 1970

The Royal family in the grounds of Balmoral, 1979. Left to right:
Princess Anne holding the hand of her son Peter, Prince Andrew, the
Queen, Prince Charles, Prince Edward and Prince Philip

Princess Anne in a reflective moment with Captain Mark Phillips in 1982. They parted in 1989

Black tie and satin: the Prince and Princess of Wales in Australia on their fourth wedding anniversary in 1985

The Duke and Duchess of
Kent dancing at the
Grosvenor House Ball in 1988

Prince and Princess
Michael of Kent in 1989

Eye-to-eye: the Duke and Duchess of York in Australia, 1988

Suntan and smiles: Princess Margaret and Roddy Llewelyn in 1989

have one thing in common. Both have friends they want to keep, and both have husbands who are bored rigid by these same friends. They have now come to terms with the problem and see their girlfriends at lunchtime, when their husbands are otherwise engaged. In the early days of Fergie's marriage, some of her more dramatic arguments with Andrew were caused by her determination not to lose her old chums. Unfortunately, like Prince Charles, her husband has little in common with most of them, and his expression becomes decidedly disagreeable when Fergie and friends begin to chat about the naughty things they did when they were schoolgirls. She did try carting him around to lunches and dinners with her Sloane Ranger friends, but he was so bored he just sat there drumming on the table with his pudding spoon. Another experiment soon abandoned.

One does feel that right was on his side when less than three months after the wedding he arranged a romantic candle-lit dinner with his bride at the Waterside Inn, at Bray on the River Thames. The Waterside Inn is a hostelry of no mean distinction, and it is easy to understand that he was somewhat put out when, having driven a hundred miles or so from his naval base in Dorset, Fergie turned up with her old flatmate, Carolyn Beckwith-Smith, and a host of photographers and reporters who had got wind of the dinner. He was very cross indeed and, without worrying about appearances, stalked off and drove straight back to the base.

When the couple paid a visit to Holland for the opening of a new Dutch flood barrier in October 1986, they had obviously had a blazing row and didn't care who knew it. They were not speaking when they arrived half an hour late for the plane. They did not speak throughout the flight, and Andrew still had a face like thunder when they landed. He tried to turn his back on the waiting photographers, but Fergie wasn't letting him get away with that. She grabbed his wrist and hauled him into focus as if to say, 'Stop being such an idiot.'

But she says he is her rock—the most incredible husband, the one who gets her through. 'I think I'm very fortunate,' she said simply. 'I really am. Every day I say how lucky I am, especially marrying Andrew. He's a great guy. A wonderful man. There are so many qualities you can't just sit down and pick out one or two. He is the most caring, loving man you could ever wish to have. Our marriage is a partnership. It's teamwork. Certainly I learn from him and I think he learns from me.'

It is true that he is supportive. He did his best to be present whenever she had medical tests before the birth of their first baby. When her father managed to get himself involved in an embarrassing and sleazy scandal, Andrew asked for a fortnight's leave to give Fergie his support. When fashion editors deride her dress sense, he tells her to take no notice and assures her that he likes her the way she is. This has given her the courage to say, 'I'm just going to be me. To begin with I made a dreadful mistake of taking in everything the fashion people wrote — but I don't really want to change. I'm quite happy with myself.'

If she sticks to her somewhat disorganized manner of dress this could become her own individual style, in the way that the Queen Mother's pearly queen (or Granny Cinderella) style has become indelibly part of her image.

Fergie spent most of her time when she was first married living at Buckingham Palace, a very good address indeed but one that Princess Diana couldn't wait to lose. She was miserable there. Fergie liked it well enough. There was talk that she and Andrew would take over the old Clock Tower apartment in Kensington Palace, but while she was waiting for what's known as the Sunninghill Southfork, her own home in Great Windsor Park, to be completed, Sarah was content to stay with the folks on the Mall — and will probably continue to stay there since the five-acre, £5,000,000 residence with a fifty-foot terrace will be considered a country home.

Taking Fergie's temperament into account, she probably thinks it's a bit of a lark to live at the Palace. It's handy for Sloane land, has a swimming pool, food to order, no need to cook, and plenty of room, even if it's not an ideal place for entertaining. She also gets on well with the Queen, who these days is always coming out with 'one of my young friends was telling me the other day . . .,' the young friend being either Lady Sarah Armstrong-Jones or Fergie, who is completely unselfconscious with her mother-in-law. She chatters on gaily, keeping the Queen up to date in a way that few of her own family (and certainly not Diana) have ever been able to do. It is said Fergie regards the Queen as a friend, while Diana regards her as a mother-in-law. Fergie also won more brownie points than Diana has ever managed to clock up by learning to fly and by taking up Prince Philip's sport of open-carriage racing. These two achievements impressed the Queen and her husband more than if she had won the Nobel Peace Prize. With the royal family, action comes before intellectualism every time.

The depth of the Queen's affection for her daughter-in-law was revealed when Fergie's father, Major Ronald Ferguson, was caught patronizing the Wigmore Club, a high-class brothel masquerading as a health club. Astonishingly, for a man whose daughter had married into the Royal family and who has a young, attractive wife, the Major was an habitué of a massage parlour on Marylebone Lane, London, where, according to redheaded Julia and blondes Lorraine and Kim, who worked at the parlour, money changed hands for sexual services —something the Major never denied. He might have still been an habitué had the owner of the shop opposite not become exasperated because limos owned by the rich and famous who were calling at the club were making parking for others impossible. The shop owner rang the *Sunday People* newspaper, which sent along a photographer. Surprise, surprise, there going in and out of the club's discreet green door was Major Ferguson. After that it didn't take long for one of the female employees to spill the beans about the Major's sexual fads and fancies.

When the story broke, the Duchess of York must have felt that her world had collapsed. The Royal family does not care to be involved with scandals. Her father was Prince Charles's polo manager, and he had known the Royal family for years (though not as intimately as he was wont to suggest). He was jokingly known as polo-stick-in-waiting. Yet in an incredible display of stupidity and arrogance he had enrolled in the club under his own name and gone in and out of the place carrying his monogrammed briefcase for all to see. The press had got him bang to rights. The evidence was indisputable. There was no excuse, nothing to be said in his defence. A plea of insanity would be about the only thing that would have any ring of credibility.

What should have happened next was the Major's being sent on his way so that he could no longer tarnish the image of the Royal family. But it didn't work out like that. Ferguson had the brass nerve to protest that the press had crucified him. He defiantly refused to resign either his post as Charles's polo manager or his job with the Guards' Polo Club. In a display of most ungentlemanly behaviour, he used his own vote to vote himself back into the job. The Guards' Polo

Club, however, showing more sense of propriety than Prince Charles, eventually got rid of him. But his relationship with the Royal family was to remain more or less unchanged. A disbelieving British public saw the Queen shake his hand at a polo meeting. The nation had its mouth wide open in astonishment when it realized that the galloping Major had got away with it.

Princess Diana was probably the most shocked of the family and the most disapproving. For a long time she avoided speaking to him—which was embarrassing, since he continues to work for her husband. If he had not been Fergie's father, it would have been good-bye time for Ferguson, though the Queen did try to isolate him. Her first ruling was that the Royal family should have nothing to do with him. But where did that leave his heavily pregnant daughter? It left her on the carpet before the Queen, close to tears and making it clear that she would not desert her father whatever he had done. The Queen, however, stood by her decision, but since their relationship is still as close, it would appear that Her Majesty admired her daughter-in-law's guts and loyalty.

Of course Ferguson had established the fact he is no gentleman by patronizing the club in the first place. Once caught, he then confirmed it by not quietly disappearing a long, long way away to run a polo club on the other side of the world. Life would have been a lot less embarrassing for his daughter had he done what is known in Britain as 'the decent thing'. But he made no attempt to do the decent thing and was quite determined he wasn't going to. Today there are those who believe he has managed to convince the Royal family that the press was, of course, telling lies and that he only went to the 'health' club to tone up his perpetual tan. It is probably easier for all those concerned—particularly his daughter, who loves him dearly—to believe him.

In spite of the scandals and the commercialization, Fergie remains one of the Queen's favourites, probably because they have things in common. By inclination both are country women, and there are similarities between the Duchess's marriage and the Queen's. Both have temperamental husbands who can be boorish, and the Queen knows very well what it is like to be married to a young naval officer who is away on duty a great deal of the time. That was the pattern of her own marriage when it first began. The Queen always put being with her husband before the children. Sarah has begun in the same way. There was enormous criticism when she left her new baby behind to join Andrew in Australia— particularly when she stayed away an extra two weeks. She travelled 26,470 miles to be with her husband and at the same time missed a great deal of Princess Beatrice's first growing days. The poor woman made things worse when she was asked her daughter's age on a radio phone-in programme—and got it wrong. The criticism upset her, but she would not back down. 'I think it's more important right now to be with my husband than with my baby. I want to be a good sailor's wife—that's the most important thing in my life at the moment,' she is said to have announced defiantly.

She made a telling remark on that Australian trip for the bicentennial celebrations when she was on the warship *Success*. She cheerfully confided to one of Andrew's shipmates, a young naval rating, 'I've been told that sailors' wives don't want their children around when their husbands are on shore leave. I've also been advised to scatter Smarties around the garden to keep the children busy so you can get some time alone together.' She then grinned and said, 'That sounds like a good plan to me.'

She said that she knew when she married Andrew that there would be separations, but 'I am in full support of his career. I think it's important that the wife always does remember that and is always there smiling and has got to get on with her own life. I accept that loneliness is part of the job.'

That may well be, but she has been known to moan about Andrew's absences at sea, which must raise a hollow laugh from other naval wives. She refers to him as 'my weekly boarder' because from Monday to Friday he is supposed to be away at his base. As a Lieutenant, Andrew is entitled to thirty-six days' annual leave, but he also gets time off from duty for public engagements. In January 1989 he had only one booked for the year—a film première in February. He and his wife still manage to see a great deal of each other, and he doesn't seem to spend all that much time with his ship. In 1988 he took six weeks' holiday (besides the many odd days off), and his wife had twenty-seven weeks' holiday, plus time off for having baby Beatrice.

This ceaseless round of pleasure did rather dent their public image, and again this upset Fergie. Unlike Princess Anne, she is not comfortable unless she is popular. She has always been popular. At school, at work, and socially the cry was always 'good old Fergie.' To find that large numbers of the great British public were losing regard for her was a shocking and painful experience. She complained that she couldn't win and that the public had turned against her as they had turned against Princess Michael of Kent. But it didn't stop her from indulging in those antics, such as free-loading and taking holiday after holiday, that were making her unpopular. She managed an amazing amount of holidays—usually at someone else's expense—all clocked up by the press before she finally got wiser. She managed one stay in Marrakesh that received no publicity at all. But since most of the time she lives at Buckingham Palace (in Prince Charles's old apartment on the second floor), perhaps she feels she needs to get away. Buckingham Palace is a good address but not much of a home, and every Friday, when the Queen leaves for Windsor, the place dies. Andrew used to stay there weekends in his bachelor days, but it caused great resentment from the staff, which had to keep the Palace open and running just for him and his girlfriends. Staying there during weekends, even with Andrew, would be lonely. Any chance to get away—particularly if Andrew can escape as well—is snatched.

While they were waiting for Sunninghill Park—their £5,000,000 house in Great Windsor Park—to be built, they used the mansion home of King Hussein of Jordan, Castlewood, as their country residence. It was offered to them rent-free and this arrangement was to become an embarrassment to the Royal family. At the time of Iraq's invasion of Kuwait, King Hussein deeply involved himself as an intermediary between the West and the Iraqis but his stance was basically pro-Iraqi. Obviously it would have been unwise for the Yorks to stay on as his guests.

It was fortunate that Sunninghill was completed at the beginning of October 1990 and the Yorks were able to move out of Castlewood.

Once installed in their new mansion, nicknamed Southyork, they threw a hugely expensive party. At this party all their staff, including policemen, wore masks. The theme was a jungle one, with stuffed animals peering out of the decorations. None of the senior members of the Royal family was there.

Once again Fergie's timing was terrible. She spent the morning of the day of the housewarming party at a memorial service for her stepfather, Hector Barrantes, who had died a few weeks previously. The evening was spent in her new home, entertaining the likes of Elton John, Pamela Stephenson, David Frost and Billy Connelly.

It was a tasteless juxtaposition of two events. But unfortunately the Yorks seem to have a complete blind spot about what is seemly or tactful and go cheerfully blundering on.

Andrew once said with a touch of petulance, 'Why can't people understand that we have a right to be together? I'm away from Sarah far more than the average husband.'

But not, of course, far more than the average naval husband. And though Andrew's intention has been to make the navy his career, Fergie dropped a dark hint that all this might change when she said, 'I don't want the long separations going on forever.'

People in love, of course, are always the same. They want to be together all the time. And Fergie may grumble about the separations, but she has managed to sneak a surprising amount of time with her husband. When she visited Australia in 1988, Andrew stayed aboard his ship, the *Edinburgh*, while his wife travelled on the support ship, the *Olwen*. The joke on the *Edinburgh* was that the Prince truly had a wife in every port—Fergie. She was on the quayside to meet him as the *Edinburgh* sailed into Sydney Harbour—and that was before they even started their tour of Australia. She waited for him in Hobart in Tasmania, Adelaide, and Fremantle. She would arrive at the dock at six o'clock in the morning to make sure that she was present and correct when his ship was no more than a dot on the horizon—determined to be the first person he saw when the boat came in.

On one of those occasions she had seen Andrew rather more recently than it appeared. Seasickness was troubling her en route to Adelaide, and, hearing of her plight, Andrew rushed to comfort her. In the middle of the navy's sea manoeuvres in the southern Indian Ocean he was given permission to fly in his Lynx helicopter to call on his wife. Her seasickness seemed to have vanished as she stood on the deck of the *Olwen*, scouring the sky through binoculars for his arrival. As soon as he landed, he walked toward her and said, 'How's your seasickness?' and then they went off to her cabin, where they remained for two hours.

They pulled a similar trick a year later when HMS *Edinburgh* arrived back at Rosyth in Scotland after some time at sea. The official welcome home was to take place a few days later at Leith, and come that day there was Fergie waiting on the quayside with baby Beatrice, standing with the other officers' wives as they waited for the ship to berth. The Duchess was one of the first on board for a reunion hug and kiss from her husband.

Actually it wasn't quite the reunion it appeared. Fergie had seen her husband only the night before—as well as the two nights before that. For three nights on the trot Andrew had travelled from Rosyth to where Fergie waited for him, presumably looking her prettiest, at the Queen's official Scottish home, the Palace of Holyroodhouse. And there they spent secret nights together.

There's a certain charm about such good, old-fashioned, lusty loving that provides a marvellous contrast to the virgin sacrifice that was the marriage of Diana and Charles. This is not to say that Diana was being sacrificed to him—rather, to the job.

There's no sense of lustiness about Diana. Somehow, even after two children and ten years of marriage, she is still innocent: pink, white, and untouched in spite of all her enjoyment of schoolgirl dirty jokes (a taste she shares with Fergie). A lot of the time she is bored. But it is not being Princess of Wales that seems to bore her. She does that job with great style and has carved herself a niche doing the caring things. She is warm and amazingly good at putting people at their ease and has a gift for communication with old people, young people, and handicapped people. She shows a genuine compassion. She even took the trouble to learn sign language so that she could communicate with the deaf and mute. Princess Anne does the same things equally well, but differently. Her style is more clinical. Anne is the brusque, reassuring matron. Diana the loving big sister or mum. The impression is that Diana loves her job and gets better at it every day. The rather dim young woman who never got an A-level at school has completely disappeared. She has grown into her job and educated herself while doing so. Those who work with her on her various charities are delighted by her grasp of their causes and what they are trying to do. She is the perfect example of the work making the woman.

She also does the quiet good deed or makes a thoughtful gesture out of what one could call, without exaggeration, the goodness of her heart. Just before Christmas 1987 thirty-one people were killed in the appalling fire at King's Cross underground station in London. Unexpectedly, and completely without ceremony, Princess Diana arrived at the memorial service. She arrived alone, dressed entirely in black, and sat in a separate seat in the front pew, close to the bereaved families. She joined with full voice in singing the hymns, and the relatives of the dead and the injured were touched that she had cared enough to attend the ceremony herself instead of sending a representative. Earlier in September the same year, when she heard that Kenny Murdoch, the young baker who provided the bread for Balmoral, had been killed in a car crash, she drove to his home and spent half an hour comforting his widow. Exactly a year later she took the trouble to call again.

Diana does and says the right thing instinctively and with sensitivity. Not because she is attempting to create a good image for herself, but because she is a genuinely kind and caring person.

There is nothing artificial about her love and concern for children, and her most spontaneous acts are reserved for them. On a trip to Washington in October 1990 she visited a home for eight small children, all stricken with AIDS. She was instantly down on her knees, helping them play with their toys. A three year old, known at the home as First Lady, particularly charmed her. First Lady, a little black girl, wore a bright pink jump suit and had a pink bow nestled in among her plaits. When Diana asked about her life expectancy, the matron of the home burst into tears.

Visibly moved, Diana gave the child a hug and a kiss. 'You're a lovely little girl and I'm going to tell my two sons about you,' she said.

When the Princess was ready to leave the toddler tugged at her skirts and asked: 'Please can I have a ride in your car?'

'Of course you can,' said Diana. She picked the child up and carried her out to the waiting British Embassy Rolls-Royce. While First Lady sat on Diana's lap and waved to the crowds, a massive police escort accompanied the Rolls 400 yards to another entrance to the home.

'That was very, very nice,' First Lady said solemnly as the Princess handed her back to a member of the staff.

But Diana's compassion is not only for children. While she was visiting her husband at the Queen's Medical Centre in Nottingham where he was receiving treatment for his broken arm, Diana heard that a young father in a nearby room had been in a coma and on a life-support machine for four weeks.

She had bumped into his mother in the hotel corridor, noticed how unhappy the woman looked, and asked what was the matter. Mrs. Woodward explained that her son, Dean, had suffered head injuries when his van crashed with a lorry.

On four separate occasions Diana sat by the young man's bed and talked to him even though there was no response. She sent his mother a huge bouquet of flowers and took William and Harry to meet the family. She also asked to be kept informed of the young man's progress.

After her fourth visit, Dean Woodward regained consciousness.

The Woodwards are convinced that the Princess's interest in their son went a long way towards helping him to recover.

She did not visit Mrs. Murdoch or sit with Dean Woodward because she was looking for good publicity. The stories came out only by chance. But she does like the limelight and can handle it, as the Royal family began to realize not long after the marriage. In the early days she behaved quite impossibly at Royal meals when the whole clan gathered. She toyed with her food and appeared to be sulking. The truth probably was that she was paralyzed with nerves or numb with boredom, but the Queen, who would hardly see her own family as either nerve-racking or boring, was appalled.

'I don't know how she'll cope with a State banquet if she can't even cope with a family dinner,' she said privately to Prince Charles when he and Diana were on honeymoon at Balmoral.

To everyone's surprise Diana adored State banquets and shone at them like the star she is. State banquets were a lot less scary than the Royal family en masse. Heads of State hold no fears for her. When she and Charles made a State visit to Portugal she embarrassed the portly President, Mario Soares, by playfully twanging his suspenders. She was wearing an off-the-shoulder dress at the time and asked the scarlet-faced President flirtily, 'If I get cold, will you warm me up?'

Charles was not amused.

It was not until after the wedding that the Prince of Wales fell in love with his young bride. They really began to know each other on the honeymoon. Lazily cruising the Mediterranean, they went to bed early and rose late. For the first time in his life Prince Charles was not called in the morning, and their small staff let them strictly alone after supper was served. Diana spent a lot of time roaming the ship and chatting to the young sailors, but up on the veranda deck, enjoying the Queen's private quarters and eating cold food discreetly left on trays for them to help themselves, they might well have been alone on a wide, wide sea. They even took a naughty picture or two of each other, which though they have fallen into press hands, no newspaper has yet been bold enough to publish.

Diana was undoubtedly a woman in love. And Charles's attitude toward her changed. As she grew in confidence and beauty and flirted outrageously with him, even in public, Charles began to act like a man in love. But things started to go wrong after the children were born. Diana began to find that her husband was a touch staid and middle-aged and that she was missing all the fun the average twenty-year-old regards as her due. She realized she had married the archetypal bachelor, a man deeply set in his ways and used to doing exactly what he pleased in his private life. Even Stephen Barry, who after twelve years in Royal service had retained deep regard for his master, had to admit that the Prince could be astonishingly selfish. Basically, he had never had any reason not to be selfish and didn't realize there was another way to behave.

'After all,' said Barry, 'he had never had to consider anyone but himself, though in fact, he could be extremely considerate because by nature he is a thoughtful man.'

Not thoughtful enough to restrict his hunting, his polo, his opera, his elderly esoteric friends and some of the more glamorous feminine ones once he was married. He did accompany his wife to the odd pop concert, looking miserable and overdressed in a formal suit. The experiment was abandoned, and Diana began to punish her husband with sheer, unpredictable naughtiness—flirting with other men and behaving publicly in a way she must have known would alarm her in-laws. She quite deliberately created minor scandals. She did not behave at all well.

Sadly, it seems that her discontent was to do with being Charles's wife and finding herself part of a family who is rigidly traditional. The Queen's family is hidebound by rules, doing everything at exactly the same time so unchangingly that you could set Big Ben by them. They also expect new additions to the family to enter wholeheartedly into their habits. For Diana, who at the beginning was trying hard to keep on doing things *her* way, it must have been like plodding through treacle. The Royal family engulfs people. Everyone must dance to the family's tune and do things their way. Take, for example, a Royal wedding. A Royal wedding has precious little to do with the bride or groom or their parents. Anyone marrying into the family hardly has any say in what goes on. The system takes over.

Both Lady Diana Spencer and Sarah Ferguson had perfectly good homes of their own from which they could have left in the normal way on their wedding day, but both were required to leave from a Royal home—Clarence House. It was there, in the middle of London, away from their own families, that they spent their last nights as single women. Of course, there are all sorts of practical reasons, such as the necessity of being near a church that is big enough to house the number of guests invited. Even so, both women were disappointed that when it came to 'their side' of the church, space was limited for their own families and friends in comparison to the numbers of people who were there for diplomatic reasons. The Foreign Office lobbies for space for important overseas guests, and then there are the magic four hundred or so regulars on the Queen's visiting list who must be taken care of. These four hundred people could be pretty sure that they would be on the guest list, even if there was no room for Diana and Fergie's friends and relatives.

But then every cloud has a silver lining, even if only from the viewpoint of the father of the bride. The Queen picks up the bill for the entire occasion! A blessed relief for Major Ferguson no doubt, but the Earl of Spencer could well have afforded to pay for his own daughter's wedding. He spent more than £100,000 on his son's, and traditionally he wasn't even responsible for that one.

Royal nuptials are a bit back to front by normal standards. The church is crammed to bursting with people, many of whom are complete strangers to the bride and groom, while the reception is small. This takes place behind closed doors at Buckingham Palace, and hardly more than forty people sit down to the wedding breakfast —mostly close family. Close Royal family. Close friends are not included, and often there isn't even enough room for the parents of some of the bridesmaids and pages. They eat in the household dining room, along with the Equerries and ladies-in-waiting.

So that acquaintances don't feel slighted when there simply isn't room in the abbey or cathedral, the Queen gives a prewedding dance two nights before the big day. But Fergie and Diana were allowed only about a hundred invitations for theirs. Both must have secretly felt that it wasn't so much their wedding as a State occasion, Diana probably resenting it more since her family's circumstances are so much grander than Sarah Ferguson's.

Resentments fester. And it was toward the end of 1987 when it began to look as if there was some foundation to all the gossip about the marriage of the Prince and Princess of Wales heading for the rocks. There was Diana, fighting to retain her own individuality in the face of the family togetherness and coping with the problems of an age gap and lack of common interests between her and her husband. After seven years of togetherness it appeared that they were barely speaking to each other. They were not seen publicly in each other's company for thirty-five long days. Prince Charles was brooding (or perhaps sulking) up in Scotland, while his wife and the mother of his children appeared to have reverted to her Sloane Ranger lifestyle. She was whooping it up on the town with a gang of faintly raffish friends introduced by her best-friend-this-term, the irrepressible Fergie.

For a while it did seem as if the Waleses had agreed to differ and were going their own ways. The compulsory heir and a spare had been provided, and once that has been achieved, living separate lives is not an uncommon way to run a marriage in Royal circles. Diana was becoming more of a clotheshorse, more fascinated by meeting famous pop people of her own age, and less and less interested in the stately routine of the Royal way of life. She had found her own set of friends, forged her own career, and appeared to be making her own life. The years between the end of 1986 and the spring of 1988 were a bad time in their marriage.

When they married, referring to the thirteen-year age gap between them, Charles joked that she would keep him young. Unfortunately, he was already older than his years and set in his ways, and she wasn't able to do much about that. When the troubles that led to rumours of divorce began in 1987 she was twenty-six. She had met him when she was nineteen and married him at twenty, and as we all know, ad nauseam, she was a virgin. Not having sown her oats, she proceeded to sow some. Presumably she was angry with Charles, perhaps for nothing more than being older and stuffier than she. Certainly they were both unhappy. He let his work go to pot. His favourite charity, the Prince's Trust, drifted rudderless for weeks while he hid himself in Scotland. He spent a lot of time talking to his grandmother at her Balmoral home, Birkhall.

Diana was behaving in what can only be described as a frenzied manner. It seemed as if she was deliberately doing everything that she knew would annoy and alarm the Royal family. She took to wearing leather trousers and short leather miniskirts, no doubt egged on by Fergie, who likes the same kind of gear. It probably didn't help that she had discovered she was a desirable woman who could make men go weak at the knees and that she knew how to flirt.

She flirted with several men, all introduced by Fergie. The one who attracted the most attention was Philip Dunne, a city banker and very much a ladies' man. His sister, Millie, is one of Diana's closest friends, and Diana spent a weekend at their family mansion, Gatley Park at Leominister, while his parents were skiing in France. It also happened to be at a time when Charles was out of the country. Dunne escorted her to Ascot, and she spent a lot of time dancing with him in a rather abandoned fashion at various society parties. At the Marquis of Worcester's wedding, she ran her fingers through Dunne's hair and kissed him on the cheek for all to see. One could hardly blame her, since Prince Charles, who was actually *with* her on this occasion, spent most of the evening talking to another guest, Anna Wallace, the girlfriend Diana succeeded and the one who had walked out on Charles—a striking blonde from Charles's past and the very one who gave Diana the most reason to be wary of his ex-girlfriends. After spending two hours talking over old times with Anna, he eventually left around 2 a.m. Diana opted to stay on and retaliated by returning home to Highgrove well after dawn.

She continued to make her point about the women that Charles had been tipped to marry. In November 1987 she refused to go to the wedding of Amanda Knatchbull, Earl Mountbatten's granddaughter, the pleasant but rather plain girl that Uncle Dickie had tried so hard to persuade Prince Charles to marry. Charles went to the wedding along with the Queen, Prince Philip, and his brothers and cousins but without his wife. It was all rather embarrassing. As the unfortunate Amanda had not been that keen on marrying Charles herself, she must have felt that it was a bit unfair to hold her grandfather's machinations of long ago against her, particularly on her wedding day.

*

Matters came to a head the night Diana went off alone one evening to the home of her friend heiress Kate Menzies (of bookstall fame) for dinner. It couldn't have been more innocent. After dinner they played bridge, Kate Menzies's partner and a friend of Diana, Major David Waterhouse, making up the foursome. When the time came to leave, the Princess, casually dressed in red trousers tucked into boots and a satin bomber jacket, was in a giggly mood, and by the time she was in the mews below her giggles were becoming uncontrollable. Unfortunately for her, a photographer, Jason Fraser, had followed her and was hovering at the entrance to the mews. As she and Waterhouse were fooling—he was pretending to run her over while she stood in the headlights of his car—the photographer snapped away and promptly had his collar felt by Ken Wharf, her detective. Swearing and furious, the detective demanded the film.

Jason Fraser felt no obligation to comply and had no intention of doing so until the Princess, in tears, begged him to give it to her. She told him how few friends she had anymore, how difficult her life was, what little fun she had, and how much worse it would be if he published the pictures. Her genuine dismay left him little choice. He handed over the film, and she wrote down his address and telephone number on a small block of white cards that she took from her handbag. She promised that the film would be developed the next day and any other pictures, apart from those of her, would be given back to him, as indeed they were.

It was a fairly dramatic plea for what would have been no more than a picture of Diana prancing about in the headlights of a car. But perhaps neither she nor the detective were certain of exactly what Jason had photographed. Fortunately for her and unfortunately for him, he had missed the best shot. The Princess's giggles were brought on because she had placed a condom over the exhaust pipe of Waterhouse's car. It had inflated when he switched on the car engine, and this she thought hysterically funny and a splendid jape. Diana has a bawdy sense of humour (she tells some truly frightful, quite unprintable jokes when with close friends), and she was indulging in a harmless, silly schoolgirl prank in Sloane Ranger style. But it was hardly a suitable pastime for the future Queen, and she knew it. Her anxieties must have been over what the pop newspapers would make of her having a condom about her person—or at least the availability of one! She needed that reel of film and humbled herself to get it.

Prince Charles, not surprisingly, did not approve of all these goings-on and didn't care who knew it. He took to spending time with his ex-girlfriends, and psychologists studying pictures taken of the Prince and Princess of Wales in their rare moments together declared that their body language told a tale of two people deep in conflict.

Diana was not aiming to please at that time. She was doing her own thing. And the most dangerous of all her friendships, say Royal watchers, was with David Waterhouse, a thirty-two-year-old Guards officer who is a nephew of the Duke of Marlborough. There was anxiety that her friendship with him was not simply a flirt and that she was really smitten. At first people had thought that he was a blind for Philip Dunne, but the conviction grew that Dunne was a blind for Waterhouse.

Waterhouse first appeared when he took her to the David Bowie concert in 1987. He was seen in her company often, though the press was concentrating on Philip Dunne. Dunne, whose father is the Lord Lieutenant of Hereford and Worcester and whose godmother is Princess Alexandra, is supposed to have been warned off. It is said that he was told to keep away from Diana, probably through the Royal network of the Queen's private secretary having a quiet word with the Queen's Lord Lieutenant of Hereford and Worcester. All during the speculation Dunne had still been involved with his ladylove of three years, Katya Grenfell, daughter of Lord St. Just. After being quietly told to stay out of Diana's life, he married someone quite different —Domenica Fraser, daughter of a former Rolls-Royce chairman. The wedding took place in February 1989. Romantics insist Dunne was on the rebound from Diana, but there she was at the wedding, her usual giggly self (seeing a great number of her friends in the congregation wearing her cast-off clothes set her off) and looking stunning in jade green. Prince Charles was absent; he was hunting in Wiltshire.

That was the end of speculation about Philip Dunne, but then the insiders had never quite believed the Dunne stories. Sensibly. Much was made of the fact that he escorted her at Ascot, but he had been a member of the Queen's house party on that occasion. Her Majesty would have been unlikely to have invited him if he were up to mischief with her daughter-in-law. The weekend she spent at Leominster was well chaperoned by a dozen other people, and his sister is her great friend. Neither of those occasions was of any real significance.

But Waterhouse was still about. His name still appears on the guest list of private parties when Diana is present. In March 1989 they were spotted when they slipped out to the cinema together after a quiet dinner at the home of friends. The film was *Rain Man*, and she was just about to kiss him good night outside the cinema when a press photographer appeared. Diana didn't handle the situation well. She bolted for her Jaguar while he leaped over barriers to get into his BMW. Not the behaviour of people with nothing to hide, but, to be fair, it was probably nothing more significant than panic.

Charles was home at Kensington Palace at the time, entertaining a group of European visitors. Since Diana speaks no foreign languages, for her an evening with Major Waterhouse and Dustin Hoffman was no doubt preferable. But Charles could not have relished the press coverage his wife was receiving. When she was seen letting her hair down in discos and dining with other men, even though other people were present, it could have demeaned the Crown, and the constant reporting of her activities must have humiliated the Prince. Perhaps he consoled himself by remembering that the popular press has always focused on the supposed extramarital activities of the Royal family. For many years Queen Victoria was referred to as 'Mrs. Brown'—a reference to her gillie, John Brown, with whom she was rumoured to have had a long affair after Prince Albert died. No doubt there was truth in it, judging by the way the bad-tempered Scotsman ordered her around. But to this day, no one has been able to prove it. Even so, the first thing that Victoria's son, Edward VII, did when he came to the throne was to chuck out the statue of John Brown that stood in the hallway of Balmoral. It now stands in the woods, overgrown with ivy and scaring the wits out of anyone who encounters it at dusk.

The question is, was there any truth in the rumours about Diana? Yes and no. Most of the time Diana's rendezvous with other men were as part of a crowd (which the press wasn't wasting column inches explaining). No one mentioned that she had known David

Waterhouse since she was a child and that he too was an old friend. No one pointed out that she was rarely alone with any of what her friends call her crushes. To a great extent she was doing no more than testing her pulling power a little late in the day and enjoying finding that it was pretty formidable. Naively, she was surprised and a little alarmed at the uproar her flirts caused. She went to great length to get a message to Royal reporter Harry Arnold, who works for Rupert Murdoch's *Sun*, the largest selling daily newspaper in Britain. She asked a close aide to tell Arnold, 'Just because I go out without my husband doesn't mean my marriage is on the rocks. The stories are nonsense.'

In the end, poor old Fergie got blamed for it all, and it is true she had some responsibility in the matter, as Prince Charles pointed out forcefully. The friendship with Fergie was cooled.

Today it seems that the attack of the verging-on-seven-year itch has subsided. The flirting has stopped, and the marriage seems to be back on course, even if it does not appear as deliriously happy as in the early days when Charles could not keep his hands off his wife. The burning question is, what caused the trouble? It is hardly fair to put the blame squarely on Fergie's broad shoulders. Diana is a big girl too. She did not have to go along with the giggling, the rowdy behaviour, the dinner parties, and the diet of crude jokes and bitchy Sloane gossip. As Royal advisers point out, she could and should have backed off much earlier, before so much damage was done.

So why did she join the nonstop party? Perhaps a clue lies in a small incident in 1984 when the Waleses were on a State visit to Italy. They were being ushered through a Venetian gallery when Charles's artistic eye was caught by one particular painting. He stopped, drank it in, stood back, and said to his wife, 'Wouldn't it be marvellous, darling, if we could come back and look at this on our own one day soon?'

Diana replied in a sad, small voice, 'But we never are alone, are we?'

Charles simply isn't with her most of the time, and when he is, they are always with the family. This does not seem strange to Charles. He is used to being with the family always, since it is only with family and a few close and trusted friends that Royals can let down their hair and relax. The company of family also helps keep one safe from the pressing curiosity of the outside world. It took Diana endless columns of newspaper gossip and some blazing rows with her husband to realize that the sort of friends that Fergie found for her were simply not safe. Not only did they push Diana's private life into the public spotlight with a series of incidents that worried the Royal firm, but they also gossiped too much to other friends, perhaps boasting about their Royal connections. They *had* to go.

Before those two frenzied years Diana was undoubtedly lonely. She was lonely in the days before the wedding, when she wandered through Buckingham Palace on her own, waiting for Charles to come home. She was lonely waiting for him at Highgrove during the courting days while he went out hunting. She was probably at her loneliest when with his cerebral friends, who frankly bored her to tears.

She took to setting her detectives in a panic by suddenly jumping into her car to speed off alone—sometimes through the Gloucester-shire lanes around Highgrove, sometimes very late at night through the London streets. She once frightened herself doing this in London when she found that her car was being chased by another car full of Arabs. She might have been grateful for the presence of a young paparazzo on his motor bike who was also following her had she not managed to shake off the other car.

The advent of Fergie and a whole set of introductions to lively rich young people with no thought except where the next bit of fun was coming from was irresistible.

That phase of her life is now over. She still tries to keep some independence, and she can still be difficult. She fights Palace routine and won't do as she is advised. She accepts invitations to weddings, christenings, and parties given by her friends and then informs her private secretary. This loyalty to her friends is commendable, but not for those who are attempting to run her engagement diary. Unplanned outings disrupt the Royal schedule. Sir John Riddell, who was her private secretary, was so bold as to complain to Prince Charles, who agreed that Diana was complicating life and these casual acceptances to casual invitations must stop. Diana did not agree. She made it clear she would see who she wanted when she wanted. Sir John threw up his hands and eventually resigned.

Even so, she has yielded to some pressure. The more raffish of her friends have been blacklisted by the Palace. A discreet series of telephone calls from Royal advisers informed them gently of this. With them out of her life, Diana is busy rebuilding her marriage. She now meets girlfriends for lunch, but the evenings are spent in more serious company.

The woman who admits to liking to iron while watching TV and who once found great satisfaction in keeping her own flat neat and tidy will never need to do for her husband any of the homey things a normal housewife does. The cookery course she once took in preparation for an ordinary marriage will never be needed except for cooking lunch and supper for her children on weekends, which she likes to do. But she is fast becoming the wife Charles needs and has always wanted. She is a sophisticated, self-assured young woman who believes in his causes and has taken on many of her own. They work together. He helps her with her speeches and is her greatest supporter. The woman who was too self-conscious to open her mouth in public has become an accomplished speaker.

Her second major speech was made at the relaunch of Dr. Barnado's, a children's home dating back to Victorian days that is striving to change its image. Diana is the charity's president, and in the most personal speech she had ever made she spoke of the importance of a loving home life in a society where divorce is common and unhappy children can become the victims of prostitution and drug addiction.

She said she understood that the pressures and demands on modern parents were enormous and stressed: 'I know family life is extremely important, and as a mother of two small boys I think we may have to find a securer way of helping our children—to nurture and prepare them to face life as stable and confident adults.'

Significantly, toward the end of 1988, when her own marital troubles seem to have calmed, she took on Relate, an organization dedicated to saving marriages, as one of her charities. She has made many visits to their centres where people with marital difficulties go to air their problems. She has learned how couples are taught to quarrel constructively and she has sat in on sex-therapy sessions, perhaps learning something about her own marriage at the same time. At the organization's golden jubilee lunch she said, 'Despite all the changes around us, the family remains the bedrock on which modern society is built.'

These were hardly the words of a woman contemplating ending her own marriage.

When Charles was in hospital at Nottingham for an operation on his broken arm, Diana made at least four separate visits to see him. Not the action of a wife with no love for her husband.

It is true that they appear to be apart more than they are together, but these days Princess Diana is perfectly capable of handling even a difficult public appearance alone. Therefore very few of their engagements are joint ones. It makes sense for the couple to operate separately. It doubles their work load and shines up the image of Royalty, giving no cause for the public to grumble that they are not worth the money we pay them.

Separate engagements add to the impression that they are not getting along and indeed it is true that they take separate holidays. It is also said they sleep in separate beds. Certainly from day one of the marriage they had separate bedrooms. There was a night at Highgrove not long after the honeymoon when they were cuddled up in her bed in her bedroom. They were disturbed by a noisy party being given by one of the staff and they moved from her bedroom and bed into the Prince's bedroom and bed where the noise was less obtrusive. The Prince can sleep through anything as long as the room is dark. Diana is a light sleeper. The next day she obtained some ear-plugs in case the staff gave any more parties.

The press's preoccupation with Royal sleeping and holiday arrangements shows a lamentable ignorance of the habits of the British upper classes. Aristocratic people have almost always had separate bedrooms, taken separate holidays and frequently spend more time with their own individual friends than with their spouses. Among the titled classes the women have always been free to do pretty much as they like.

The Waleses are merely following in the family footsteps. Prince Philip has always taken holidays away from the Queen, and when they were younger that, too, caused rumours that their marriage was on the rocks. He and the Queen have always had separate bedrooms — though, as every Buckingham Palace footman knows, they are not always both in use. Each morning a footman must take up the Duke of Edinburgh's calling tray (a tray holding tea and biscuits) from the kitchen. His only problem is that he has to know where the Duke is sleeping. Will he be at the Queen's end of the suite of bedrooms? Or is he sleeping in what is called the Duke's side? Royal bedrooms are usually divided by dressing rooms and bathrooms. If the Duke's personal footman informs the duty footman that the Duke is at the Queen's end, the tray is left outside her door. Bobo, the Queen's maid, or one of her assistants then takes it in. If Philip is in his own bed, at his own end, the tray is handed to his valet. This is the way the Royals arrange their private lives. Undoubtedly Charles and Diana have exactly the same arrangement regarding their morning cuppa.

Those who insist the marriage is over except in name only point out that there are no signs of Diana increasing her family. She does not need to increase her family immediately—any more than the Queen did. Diana has provided the heir and spare—just as the young Princess Elizabeth did in the early days of her marriage. Diana now has time to perfect her job and will no doubt begin her second family later, following the pattern set by her mother-in-law.

The magic of the early days may have gone, as it inevitably does for both Kings and commoners, but some kind of professional rapport has come to take its place. In time, if Diana continues to mature so impressively, and if Prince Charles becomes a touch less stuffy, perhaps the magic might just quietly come back.

*

Before Mrs. Tom Trowbridge—or Baroness Marie-Christine von Reibnitz as she had reverted to calling herself—met Prince Michael of Kent, he was a laid-back sort of fellow, rather good-looking and athletic but certainly the most low-profile member of the Royal family. So low profile, in fact, that some of the younger members of the family joked that they were not absolutely sure which one he was. It was an undemanding role on the Royal stage, which suited him very well. He was popular with everyone in much the way that his sister Princess Alexandra is popular, and he appeared to be quite happy with his comfortable soldier career. Though not rich, he managed quite nicely on income from investments. He was a private person who didn't have to do anything in public like planting trees, laying foundation stones, or unveiling brass plaques on walls. Prince Michael was ambling gently through life, usually with a good-looking woman on his arm.

Marriage was to change all that. Princess Michael of Kent, without doubt the most controversial of all Royal wives, had him out of the army in no time. It was not well-paid enough. With the help of Uncle Dickie, Lord Mountbatten, she persuaded Michael that they should cultivate a higher profile. She personally was good at planting trees, laying foundation stones, and unveiling plaques and yearned to be asked to do so. She yearned also for a country mansion fit for a Princess. Having turned down Highgrove (which Prince Charles eventually purchased) because it was too small, she found one —Nether Lypiatt Manor in Gloucestershire, a house that needed a great deal spent on it to bring it up to her exacting standards. She had, after all, once been an interior decorator. This meant that her husband had to cash in large amounts of his investments to pay for the manor and the refurbishments. He then found that in order to heat the place, or indeed eat in it, he had to locate companies willing to employ him as a director—basically for the use of his title on their notepaper.

His wife began giving parties for the right kind of people, those who were both socially acceptable and who might just be interested in hiring him, and before you could say 'pushy,' he had a nice little income from a nice little collection of prestigious companies. None of the fees he was paid was enormous, so Marie-Christine set about adding to the family income by writing books. Her first tome, about European Royal Princesses, caused the publishers some problems when an author or two accused her of plagiarism. The good news was that the resulting publicity did not appear to do the book the slightest bit of harm. The bad news is that she is having problems selling her second book about Royal Courtesans. More money came in when, on occasion, she asked for payment for personal appearances. Strictly speaking, Royals are not supposed to do this. Marie-Christine's argument for asking for the odd gratuity is a perfectly valid one. She points out that she and Michael have all the problems of being a Royal without any of the privileges.

That is true. Her husband is one of the Queen's favourite cousins, but he is too far down in the Royal pecking order to be required for official duties (only first sons of Royal Dukes are required, and Michael is a second son). He is not, therefore, entitled to income from the Civil List. Marie-Christine finds this extremely galling. She considers it most unjust that they are omitted from this annual governmental handout, passed on by the Queen to a selected number of Royals who are on the duty roster. The fact that the Michaels of Kent have constant money worries makes it all the more irritating.

The truth is the worries are of their own making. The Princess works on the theory that having become an HRH she might as well live and act like one; therefore, lack of funds does not prevent her from owning Nether Lypiatt, the obligatory (as far as she is con-cerned) Rolls-Royce, three horses, and a formal staff that includes four gardeners. They also have to run their grace-and-favour apartment in Kensington Palace.

In the early days of the marriage, Marie-Christine constantly undertook unnecessary and expensive appearances to keep herself in the public eye. She believed that if she worked hard enough for the Royal firm, eventually she and her husband would be put on the Civil List. She also believed that it was her duty as a member of the Royal family to do these things.

Actually, it was not her duty. She had no obligation to do anything at all and no reason why she should not live in a quiet and dignified manner that she and her husband could afford. The Queen had said officially that she did not require Michael to carry out Royal duties. And if she did not require Michael, she did not require his wife, Marie-Christine.

This was bad news for Princess Michael. Being out of the limelight was not at all her style. For a long time she continued to accept engagements at her own expense, but the shortage of money led her to foolishly say in public that she would go anywhere for a free dinner, a remark that has lingered to haunt her. Like Fergie, she accepts gifts of clothing and airline tickets, and she has involved herself in a series of publicity stunts. She opened the St. James Club on the island of Antigua in the Caribbean for its owner, millionaire Peter de Savary, and appeared at a promotion for the British yacht in the America's Cup challenge. In return for her gracious presence she wanted a present and, it is said, was given a valuable brooch.

'The trouble is she's always grabbing,' commented one of her ex-aides, John Barrett, who then went on to recall an occasion when she walked away from an electrical firm with several free TV sets— for the servants.

In fairness, she has calmed down a great deal, but still the Royal family finds itself in a quandary. They are all fond of the kind, quiet, unpushy Prince Michael—which is why he was given the Queen's permission to marry Marie-Christine von Reibnitz in the first place. But permission might not have been given if the Queen in a burst of clairvoyance had seen the kind of problems the lady would create. They find her embarrassing, which, unfortunately, she often is. Worse, they don't like her all that much. Prince Charles has been heard to refer to her as that 'bloody woman,' and when he was taking his girlfriend, Anna Wallace, around Windsor one Ascot week before he married, he told her behind his hand, 'Don't bother to curtsey to Princess Michael.' When Marie-Christine wanted to buy Nether Lypiatt Manor, a scant canter from the Gloucestershire home of the Prince and Princess of Wales, Charles tried to stop it. He made it clear that he did not want her living near him. Obviously, he could hardly forbid her to buy the house, and when he realized she was going to move in regardless of what he thought, he exploded angrily, 'She can do what the hell she likes.'

She was never invited to Highgrove. The Waleses are also neighbours at Kensington Palace, but they are not exactly in and out of each other's homes. She once saw fit to lecture one of Prince Charles's staff about his language and received a curt, handwritten lecture back from Prince Charles on minding her own business. And she was irritated to be woken up one morning by what she described as 'some sort of disturbance going on downstairs.' She rang the policeman at the gates to see what it was.

It was Princess Diana's birthday and a group of children had arrived at the Palace to sing 'Happy Birthday.' Marie-Christine complained, and an amazed Prince Charles said, 'You're not really going to make a fuss about a few little girls singing "Happy Birthday"?' Oh but she was.

Her problem is that she cannot accept that she and her husband are not really important in the Royal scene, and what the grander members of the family get, she wants—and goes to great lengths to get it. Sometimes the results of her persistence are hilarious. When Charles and Diana moved into Kensington Palace, the Department of the Environment (the Government department in charge of Royal palaces) put in the most superb roof terrace for the Waleses to enjoy.

It is large, a suntrap, and runs the full length of two apartments. There is a greenhouse in the centre, a barbecue, and a lot of garden furniture. It is also completely private and can be viewed only from a helicopter.

When she heard about it, in spite of the fact that a small garden goes with her grace-and-favour apartment, Princess Michael decided she wanted a roof terrace. She sent for the man in charge of maintenance at Kensington Palace and put in her request. It was turned down flat on the grounds of expense. But Marie-Christine was not to be defeated. In an inspired stroke of cunning she invited Michael Heseltine, the Secretary of the Environment at the time, to dinner and raised the subject with her captive audience over the pudding.

Michael Heseltine apparently wriggled, but with the lady's extremely good meal inside him (the Princess is a superb hostess) it was difficult to refuse. He agreed that she could have a balcony terrace.

It proved rather less spectacular than the Waleses'. It hangs on the side of the building and can be viewed by both Charles and Diana and their staff if they lean out of the bedroom windows. It is tiny, with room for just two chairs, and it has plastic grass.

Just occasionally the Michaels of Kent have been asked to act in an official capacity, and on each occasion their appearance has been a great success. Marie-Christine adores being the Princess Michael, and in this she is an asset to her husband. The first time Lord Mountbatten saw her in action he said with delight, 'She's a natural.' And she is. Her instinct in public situations is spot-on. She has the ability to make people warm to her. But she has in equal proportion a gift for getting it all wrong behind the scenes. One of their few official overseas appearances was in Belize. When the Royal family goes on such a trip it is given a reasonably good allowance by the Foreign Office (i.e. the taxpayer) to buy appropriate clothing. Anyone accompanying them also gets a dress allowance. On hearing this splendid news, Marie-Christine went on a shopping spree. She spent the allowance and a good deal more before the plane tickets had even arrived. Then she tried to talk the Foreign Office into covering the extra expenditure. The Foreign Office was impervious to any special pleading. Rules are rules. They declined.

Humiliatingly, in the end the Michaels' private secretary and the lady's maid gave up their allowance to help balance the ever-unbalanced books.

There is no doubt that Prince Michael is proud of his wife, whatever headaches she causes him. This maverick Princess, depending on her mood, is not always lovable, but she is more intellectual and more cosmopolitan, has more taste and style, and is a more interesting all-round person than anyone else in the Royal family. Whatever she undertakes she finishes; *failure* is not a word in her vocabulary. She enjoys beating the rest of her in-laws at their own games. Having found herself a member of a horsey family, she took up hunting. She also took up dressage at an age (thirty nine) where most women (including Princess Anne) say good-bye to it. She even learned to ride sidesaddle, something only the Queen ever does. It was not a tactful thing to do, but tact and diplomacy are not Marie-Christine's forte, though she can display both when she wants something. She is strong, and she is very beautiful. Unfortunately, she can also be arrogant and is definitely the most frightful snob. Friends from the past whom she now feels are beneath her are ruthlessly cut dead.

Some who know her well say that the problem with Princess Michael is that there is an area where she is not in control of herself. Her temper can flare frighteningly. She can switch from being perfectly charming to a virago. According to her staff, her husband is slightly alarmed by her when she lets off steam, but he can sometimes laugh her out of a tantrum. Like the rest of the family, he is a good mimic and can be very funny, but even he could not calm her in the early days on the occasions when, for some misdemeanour, she received reprimands from the Queen. Reprimands from the Queen come by way of Her Majesty's private secretary to the private secretary of the member of the family who has offended. It is then the job of the unhappy private secretary to pass on the Queen's displeasure as tactfully as possible. For Marie-Christine's private secretary this was never a welcome task. Unfriendly missives from the Palace made her rant and rave. Princess Michael was in trouble for various things in the early days, some big, some small. The trivial were not unnaturally the most annoying. Having been advised, reasonably enough, to wear black to a funeral, one of the gentler rockets launched at her—more of a damp squib really—came when the Queen sent a note after the sad occasion, saying tetchily, 'When I say black I mean black. Not a black handbag with gold clasps.'

Marie-Christine is convinced she is disliked because she is divorced, foreign, and Roman Catholic. These are, of course, not the true reasons. It is unfair, but basically she is unpopular with her in-laws because she is cleverer, more glamorous, and much, much grander in her behaviour than they are. Worse, she is too smart. Smart the Royals do not admire. In fact, they positively distrust it.

There is some demon in the Princess that makes her contrary, which could explain why she and Princess Anne don't get on too badly. Having found herself married to a Prince and living in Britain—probably the most xenophobic country in the world—she is determined to be perceived as foreign. She now has a faintly Continental accent. This is puzzling since, from the age of five, she was brought up in Australia. Now Australia, though different, is not exactly what the British would call foreign. All her school days were spent in Sydney; she had her first working experiences there, and when she left for Europe after her unhappy love affair, she sounded, as one would expect, like an Australian. Since then she has worked at moulding herself into what she wants to be and, completely ignoring environmental influences, says, 'I'm as foreign as could be and being foreign means thinking differently, having different values, getting excited about different things. English people, for example, tend to retain a diffident manner even when they are really not shy or unconfident—foreigners don't. I am central European through and through.'

The Royal family could be forgiven for feeling that she uses her so-called foreignness as an excuse for behaving in a way that is unacceptable to them. 'She's much too grand for us,' they say rather smugly.

In the early days of the marriage it was just one darn thing after another for Princess Michael. Her charming, but not very forceful, husband would not have been human if he had not begun to wonder if the whole thing hadn't been a dreadful mistake. In April 1985, just when his wife had managed to get her profile megahigh, the news broke that her German father had been a member of the Nazi party and of Hitler's SS. In truth, the story was blown out of all proportion. Marie-Christine's papa was not a wicked, jack-booted bringer of terror, but quite a decent old buffer attempting to save his and his family's skin—as many did in wartime. But for a while, some among the British public were beginning to believe that he was (or rather had been, since he was dead) Attila the Hun, Adolf Hitler, and Genghis Khan in one murderous package.

The furore gave the Princess the opportunity to make an extremely effective television appearance defending herself. She did it against all advice and succeeded in winning the nation's sympathy by simply insisting she didn't know a thing about her father's part in the war. Which was absolutely true. On the day the news broke she was overheard giving her mother an extremely bad time on a long-distance telephone call to Australia for having left her in ignorance of her father's past.

'We still love you, Princess Michael,' proclaimed the headlines, but however blameless Marie-Christine was, the news did her little good with her in-laws. Her father's past gave the media the opportunity to regurgitate the wartime exploits of Prince Philip's German relations. But the Royal family could hardly complain. Even if Princess Michael had not known that her father had been a minor member of the SS, the Queen most certainly did. Marie-Christine's background would have been thoroughly investigated as a matter of routine before the marriage, as are the backgrounds of anyone entering the family. It was, therefore, impossible that the Palace did not know about Baron von Reibnitz's membership in the SS. The truth most likely was that they did know but had sensibly decided to ignore it.

Marie-Christine could give herself full marks for handling herself brilliantly throughout that crisis. She was not so successful a few months later when there was a brand-new drama. For her efforts this time she should have been given about a three on a scale of ten. But her problem was that she did not know what she was up against.

The whole episode was bizarre. It appeared highly likely that Marie-Christine was up to mischief. Someone within the Palace, or certainly close to Palace circles, decided that this time she was going too far and something had to be done to bring her into line.

Though she did not know it, the world started to collapse around her elegant blond head on a Tuesday morning in May 1985. A journalist, Stuart Kuttner, who was then an assistant editor of the *News of the World*, was meeting one of his many contacts at lunchtime. They had a drink and a snack and then, since it was a fine, sunny day, decided to take a stroll.

As they neared the River Thames, the contact said casually, 'Have any of your people noticed how often Princess Michael of Kent visits America?'

Stuart Kuttner said, 'I'm not sure that they have. Why? Should they?'

There was a brief silence, then the contact added, 'It might just be worth examining the record of her visits. Particularly this year. She seems to be going quite often. And they are private visits.'

Kuttner asked, 'Is she playing away from home?'

Silence, but a nod.

'I'll need a name,' said Kuttner tentatively.

'True.' A pause. 'Try Hunt.'

'Do you mean Hunt as in Texas?'

'Exactly.'

Back at the office, Stuart Kuttner found that Texas had an astonishing number of wealthy Hunts but none who would seem obviously to fit the bill. He asked his Deep Throat for guidance and was told, 'The answer to your question is Ward.'

'As in hospital?' Kuttner asked.

As in hospital it was.

At that moment, ignorant of her doom, Princess Michael of Kent was preparing to fly back to Heathrow Airport after a week-long trip to California. She had been staying at the Santa Monica ranch of her wealthy friend Princess Esra of Hyderabad. Princess Esra was not there. Mr Ward Hunt was.

Ward Hunt was forty-four years old and a cousin of the megarich oil tycoon Bunker Hunt. Though a rather minor figure in the Hunt dynasty, he was in property and worth several million. A cuddly looking chap, not unlike Robert Redford, he had been divorced from his wife, Laura, in 1984, and she had custody of their three children. He lived alone in an expensive apartment in Dallas. In an unusual judgment for the United States, his and his wife's divorce papers were sealed so that no one could discover what the financial arrangements of the parting were, but everyone knew it had cost him.

He and Princess Michael had first met in 1983 at a fund-raising dinner for the United States Friends of the English National Opera group in Texas. Since the divorce, he and Princess Michael had managed to see each other quite often. He even came to Britain in 1984, chaperoned by his mother, and they were both guests at Kensington Palace. On one occasion Marie-Christine and Prince Michael visited Dallas on business. Michael flew off to New York, leaving his wife to catch a later plane. She missed it. The hired chauffeur, instead of taking her to the airport as he had expected to, drove her and her luggage to Ward Hunt's apartment.

Princess Michael was taking enormous chances with her marriage. There is little that the Royal family's advisers miss, and they were aware that something was going on. But when, completely recklessly, she asked Hunt to come to Britain and spend a week with her in London, those in the know were horrified. Princess Michael rarely takes advice, and she did not do so then. She continued making arrangements to bring Hunt to her own doorstep. Stuart Kuttner's contact rang him to say there was an important development. Hunt was arriving in London on Monday, June 24. Journalistic digging revealed that a Mr. Hunt had been booked into the Carlton Tower, a luxury hotel in Cadogan Square. Furthermore, with a lamentable lack of discretion under the circumstances, he had been booked into the hotel by the office of Princess Michael of Kent.

For the next few weeks neither Princess Michael nor her friend, Hunt, made a move that was not observed by those stalking them. Then Stuart Kuttner received another message, which said, 'Change of plan. Hunt is still coming, but the Princess has arranged a private flat for him . . . It belongs to the brother of Princess Esra of Hyderabad.' Further research indicated that Hunt would arrive on his flight from Dallas, but before reaching central London, the Princess accompanied by Princess Esra would be at the apartment waiting there for him. *News of the World* reporters discovered that Princess Michael proposed to spend a day or two with Hunt there, and then arrangements had been made for them to spend the rest of the week at Rosie Northampton's country home at Moreton-in-Marsh.

And that proved to be exactly the sequence of events. Unaware of planted photographers, the Princess arrived at the Eaton Square flat of Princess Esra's brother, carrying groceries and wearing a rather unbecoming red wig. Later Ward Hunt arrived and was let in, and there they stayed. Princess Michael had to pop in and out for engagements—including one with her husband at a Masonic cocktail party, followed by a dinner given for the American ambassador. It was at the dinner that the Princess suddenly said she must leave. She was heading for the Gloucestershire house of her great friend, Rosie Northampton, and it was a long way to drive.

All true. What she understandably didn't mention was that Ward Hunt was waiting for her back at the Eaton Square flat. They were going to drive to the country together.

Curiously, it was at this moment, just as the *News of the World* was about to share all this fascinating information with its readers, that someone—Deep Throat?—let it be known to Princess Michael that she was caught and that the story of her liaison with the cuddly Texan would be headlines in the morning.

In a panic she sent a bewildered Ward Hunt straight back to the States, a journey that began with a helicopter arriving in Rosie Northampton's grounds and taking him to Manchester Airport and on to the New York plane. Once he was safely gone, Marie-Christine announced she was suffering from exhaustion, which she probably was. She went straight into hospital, where she stayed for a few days until the fuss died down. She emerged to be photographed beside her husband at the Wimbledon tennis championships.

In spite of all this, the marriage survived, which would suggest that Princess Michael has qualities as a wife that are more important to Prince Michael than the occasional lapse. For there had, in fact, been another lapse when she appeared to be overly friendly with Senator John Warner of Elizabeth Taylor fame.

Both incidents pose questions. Happily married people do not play away from home. Was Princess Michael unhappy? Was she finding the strictures of being Royal plus her unpopularity with her in-laws too much to bear? Was her good-looking, easygoing husband a touch dull?

Perhaps she was only asserting herself as Princess Diana did for a while. But Princess Diana was only playing at being a bad girl. Marie-Christine's actions were much more dangerous and serious. The chances she took with Ward Hunt indicate that her feelings for him must have been real. If they were not, for an intelligent woman her behaviour was foolhardy in the extreme.

Some say she had toyed with the idea of going off with Hunt, who was not as rich as his relatives (particularly after the astronomically expensive divorce). But Marie-Christine had worked hard to become an honest-to-God Princess and in a country where the title had real meaning and prestige. Thinking it over in the cold, black glare of some very juicy newspaper headlines, she must have decided that being a hard-up Princess in Great Britain offered more status than being a wealthy society hostess in Dallas. Ward Hunt, who was in love with her, is said to have believed that she would leave Prince Michael for him. He was doomed to disappointment. Despite his rapid dismissal, he kept his dignity and his mouth shut.

What were the motives of the Royal Deep Throat? Who gave him or her permission to inform on this Royal wife? It is unlikely that anyone that close to Royalty would have been able to embark on such a course on his or her own initiative, and it seems incredible that the Palace would deliberately use the dreaded press in such a way to make its point. Some in Royal circles say that only the Queen, or someone very close to her, could have given permission for a newspaper—and the one with the largest circulation in the Western world—to be given a minute-by-minute account of Princess Michael's extramarital activities. That stretches credulity as much as the story itself. But the story was copper-bottom true.

If the passing on of the information that trapped her and ended the affair was meant also to end the marriage, the ploy failed, though perhaps the 'source' had in mind a warning shot. The couple is still together, and the Princess has become a great deal more circumspect in her behaviour. She occasionally makes the odd mysterious trip to the States under different names, but these days when she has crossed the Atlantic she no longer heads for Dallas. Whatever happened between her and Ward Hunt is finished and done, and only time will tell how badly their relationship damaged the Michaels' marriage.

Once again Princess Michael survived brilliantly and has lived to fight another day—which, with her temperament, she may well have to do. After a bruised Ward Hunt had gone from her life, she really made only one intriguing comment on the whole sorry scandal.

'I do not,' she stated grandly, 'own a red wig.'

Perhaps she borrowed one.

*

There was one marriage in the Royal family that was an unqualified success, but sadly, like that of Queen Victoria, it did not last long. The Queen Mother, whose union with her Bertie, the Duke of York, became a pattern of what married life in a perfect world could be, has now been a widow for many years longer than she was a wife. Those who know her say that she still misses the King and that not a day goes by when she does not think of him.

Her consolation must be that she and her husband were truly happy together and that they gave their daughter, the future Queen, a secure, loving, and normal childhood—something that few Monarchs have been fortunate enough to have had. The Queen Mother can also look back on a marriage that, after much hesitation and hard thought, was of her own choice. If she had had doubts, once the deed was done Elizabeth set about making the marriage an enduring one. And her remarkable personality, charm, and dedication to duty made the union a fortunate one both for her family and the nation.

If Britain had had a different King and Queen in the days of war, the outcome could have been different. And without Elizabeth at his side, the King would never have become the symbol of strength and goodness that he was.

From the time that her in-laws, King George V and Queen Mary, first met Elizabeth in the early twenties, they liked her, as did virtually everyone who knew her. After the April wedding in 1923, George V wrote to his son: 'You are indeed a lucky man to have such a charming & delightful wife as Elizabeth' and 'The better I know and the more I see of your dear little wife, the more charming I think she is & everyone falls in love with her.'

Elizabeth was a wife before she was a Duchess and still very much a wife when she became a Queen. She was always at her husband's side. They were a team, a partnership, and where he went she went. She rarely undertook engagements alone as Royal women do today. He needed her with him. History will record that it was she more than any other who changed the Royal family. Her son-in-law, Prince Philip, succeeded in modernizing the palace and castles and made them cheaper and more profitable to run, but it was Elizabeth who much more importantly gave the Monarchy a human face—and did it without the slightest loss of dignity. And her daughter has admirably carried on the example her mother set.

Elizabeth was a wife any man would envy, totally loyal to her husband. But it was in smaller, more gentle ways that she kept her family unit so content. Instead of creating palaces she created homes. Their London home, No. 145 Piccadilly (which no longer exists), was tall, narrow, comfortable, and unpretentious. The house was neither large nor grand. It was a home, something her husband had never enjoyed. She and Bertie slept on the ground floor, but in the curious Royal and British upper-class manner, both had their own bedroom. Hers, which had a big, double bed, was furnished in the misty blues she still prefers today. Her kidney-shaped dressing table was always immaculately neat. Her rooms always were and still are flower filled. Bertie's bedroom had more of an air of a naval cabin about it. But the heart of the house was the nursery suite on the top floor—big, comfortable, sunny rooms that opened out on to a large hall under a rounded glass dome. It was here that the present Queen kept her first stable—thirty wooden horses on wheels, each about a foot tall and standing in a circle. They were unsaddled and unbridled every night before the two Princesses went to bed.

When her children arrived, those who were to look after them were chosen with meticulous care. The governess, Marion Crawford, was young, and Queen Mary disapproved. 'Crawfie,' as the children called her, was aware of this and mentioned it to her employer. The Duchess laughed. 'There is an idea going round that someone older would have been a better choice,' she admitted, 'but the Duke and I don't think so. We want our children to have a happy childhood which they can always look back on.'

Crawfie won over Queen Mary, stayed, and recalled, 'The Duke and Duchess were so young and so much in love. They took great delight in each other and in their children. Looking back on it, it often seems to me as though while we were there, the season was always spring.'

The Duchess and her husband were never Royal with their family. They behaved like normal parents in that they saw a great deal of their children, played with them, and bathed them before bed when it was possible. The Princesses were not escorted by nanny down to the living room, dressed in their best for half an hour after tea for Mama and Papa's inspection before being whisked back to the nursery. They were involved in the family. They had their tea at five and after tea went downstairs to join their parents for at least an hour and a half.

They would play family card games until it was bath time, and then the Duke and his wife would go upstairs to join them. According to Crawfie, hilarious sounds of splashing would be heard coming from the bathroom, followed by pillow fights in the bedroom while Alah, the nanny, begged her employers not to get the children too excited. Another ritual was the use of the weighing machine in the bathroom, where the children's height and weight were regularly recorded. Then the Duchess would read her children bedtime stories, usually from the Bible. At Christmas the Duke and Duchess would creep upstairs and fill the children's stockings after they were asleep.

The children were not confined to the nursery—the whole house was their home. There was no question of being seen and not heard. They were allowed in the kitchen where, Mrs. MacDonald, known as Golly, reigned. With the Duchess's approval, Mrs. MacDonald made cakes for blind soldiers, which the children would help decorate with silver horseshoes and bells. The house rang with laughter, and toys could be taken anywhere. They called their mother 'Mummy,' not 'Mama'—most unusual for Royalty of the time—just as the present Queen's children call her 'Mummy.' The Queen Mother's influence lives on.

Most ordinary people can remember their own parents behaving in just the way the Duke and Duchess did with the future Queen and Princess Margaret. Bath time, stories, Christmas stockings, helping making cakes are the stuff of family life. But for Bertie, all such simple things were as magic for him as they were for his children.

He had had an appalling childhood, terrorized by his nannies and terrified of his fierce father and regal mother, who, though loving, had no idea how to communicate with her children. Along with his brothers and sisters, he saw little but the nursery as a child. All these new warm experiences were a source of amazement and deep happiness to him. He was thrilled to see his girls grow so confident and so free-spirited and socially able at so young an age. 'We used to be so shy,' he would say, wonderingly, remembering his own stunted childhood. He basked and expanded in the new life that his marriage had given him. His official biographer, John Wheeler-Bennett, said that marriage 'brought him much for which he had long craved in deprivation—love, understanding, sympathy, support. All these things were now his in generous abundance, and his whole conspectus of life changed accordingly.'

His childhood had created in him the temper that could send his courtiers scuttling for safety. No doubt it was brought about by the frustration of living with a bad stammer, which made speech making and simple communication almost impossible for him. It was a sad situation for a Royal prince to be so handicapped. His wife could calm his temper with a gentle word and a smile. And it was she who persuaded him to visit an Australian speech therapist, Lionel Logue, who had perfected a new method of curing a stammer. Elizabeth frequently went with him to the therapist. She learned the breathing exercises that were part of the treatment so that she could work with her husband at home. And when, after long and arduous training, he was able to speak in public with some degree of skill, she was always there at his side, smiling and serene, her strength and encouragement sustaining him. The perceptive author Frances Donaldson says, 'Onlookers have described how he would sometimes turn and look at her across a room and how when he did this, she left what she was doing and went to his side. He then seemed enabled to carry on.'

It was as if there was some telepathy between them by which she was able to transmit her own confidence to him. It was awesome to watch.

It was fortunate that Elizabeth persisted in her determination to cure her husband's stammer. On January 20, 1936, King George V—called 'Grandpa England' by the little Princesses—died. Uncle David, the Prince of Wales, acceded to the throne. The Duke and Duchess of York, happy in their Piccadilly home with their little family, must have rested easy that though the Duke was now heir presumptive, there was little chance of much change in their lives. David had been trained to be King, was charismatic of personality and loved by the people. Mrs. Wallis Simpson was a cloud on the horizon, but the Royal family was sure that he would now put her aside and concentrate on his duties to both the Crown and his people.

Unfortunately, he did neither. He had been a playboy Prince for too long to change. The man who had been a brilliant Prince of Wales was a bad King. He had to go.

He reigned for less than a year, was never crowned, abdicated, and married the American woman he loved. To Bertie and Elizabeth's horror they found they must be King and Queen. After the initial shock, they both rose to the role magnificently.

They were crowned together five months later, on the day—May 12, 1937—that the new King's elder brother was to have been crowned. George VI, untrained and in poor health, was more alone than any other King in history, but no King ever had a better consort. Queen Elizabeth involved herself deeply in the Coronation. She went to planning meetings, sent out the invitations, and went to rehearsals, but more importantly, she worked with Logue, the therapist, to school the King in the ordained responses that he must make in Westminster Abbey. On the momentous day she sailed through with smiling confidence. For her shy husband the ancient ceremony was an ordeal.

It was good-bye to the house in Piccadilly. From now on Elizabeth's family would be housed in the headquarters of Monarchy, the six-hundred-roomed Buckingham Palace. It took five minutes to get out into the garden, and none of the living rooms or bedrooms faced south. There was electricity, but some of the bedroom lights could be turned off only by a switch halfway down the hallway. Furthermore, the Queen was separated from her children by both a flight of stairs and what seemed like a mile of red carpet. 'People here need bicycles,' said Princess Elizabeth, who set up her beloved toy horses in a long row down the corridor outside her bedroom.

Much changed about their lives. The bath-time romps were an early casualty—there simply wasn't time anymore. But the Queen insisted that she spend part of every morning with her children. And the family couldn't wait to get out of the Palace every weekend to drive to Royal Lodge, their country home in Great Windsor Park. It became the haven where they could be a family again.

Today the Queen Mother lives in Clarence House, the grand house on the Mall where the current Queen started her married life with Prince Phillip. The Queen Mother owns Birkhall on the Balmoral Estate, but Royal Lodge in Great Windsor Park is still her favourite country home, since it is one that holds the most memories of her idyllic married life.

Royal Lodge was in a state of disrepair and needed complete redecoration when Elizabeth and Bertie took it over. In typical fashion, Elizabeth hesitated to do the work when it first became theirs. It was 1931 and Britain was in the grip of the Depression. Both she and her husband felt it was not seemly to spend so much when others had so little.

When restoration work began it took a year to complete. They planted the garden together on happy weekends when the pomp of Royal life was forgotten and they were simply a family again. Everyone—the King, the Queen, their children, and some staff, including the detective—put on old clothes. The King was a bit of a slave driver, cutting back dead wood, pulling up dead plants, and lighting huge bonfires. Everyone had to work as hard as he did. The Queen worried about her husband's fierce cutting implements, imploring the children not to touch them and warning them to look out for brambles. Gradually the wilderness became a garden, and today it is still exactly as the King and his Queen planned it.

When war came two years after the Coronation, Royal Lodge was abandoned for the duration, and the family was split. The children were evacuated to shelter behind the vast stone walls of Windsor Castle. To be with the people, the Queen and her husband stayed in London, where they had many narrow escapes. Buckingham Palace was hit nine times by bombs and rockets. Four were direct hits. On one occasion the King saved his wife from serious injury by pulling her to the floor as the windows of their sitting room exploded. A German bomber had flown out of low clouds and streaked straight up the Mall, just above the treetops. Once over the shock, they agreed with their policeman that it had been a magnificent piece of bombing. The King actually saw the bombs fall as he pushed his wife down and they lay together on the floor, debris falling around them.

As they got to their feet, they heard the sound of water coming into the room. The bombs had burst the mains and penetrated the palace's antiquated sewers. The result was a great deal of serious damage, a fearful smell, and days of rat hunting. The Queen said, 'I'm almost comforted that we've been hit. It makes me feel I can look the blitzed East Enders in the face. They are so brave.'

As was she. She never once showed real fear, except when the King went overseas to inspect his troops in North Africa. 'I have had an anxious few hours,' she wrote to Queen Mary, 'because at 8.15 I heard that the plane had been heard near Gibraltar and that it would soon be landing. Then after an hour & a half I heard there was thick fog at Gib & that they were going on to Africa. Then complete silence until a few minutes ago when a message came that they had landed in

Africa & taken off again. Of course I imagined every sort of horror and walked up & down my room staring at the telephone.'

They were a perfect King and Queen for a country at war. Along with their subjects, they were rationed and restricted. When Eleanor Roosevelt visited Buckingham Palace in 1942, she was astonished by the paucity of the food served, albeit on gold plates. When food became scarce they had one egg a week, as did their subjects. The Royal family asked for no privileges. They faced the blitz like everyone else, leaving their beds for an air-raid shelter. Not that bolting inelegantly was the Queen's style. While everyone else was running for the shelter she would be unhurriedly dressing and gathering up a favourite book to pass the time in case the raid proved to be of long duration.

It was a matter of pride to her and her husband to live as the people lived. Even those who had been pro-King Edward VIII found it impossible to visualize Mrs Simpson in the role that Queen Elizabeth handled so brilliantly.

Frequently the couple toured the bomb-damaged areas of the country. One day the Queen saw a woman crying in the blitzed ruins of her home. She stopped to comfort her and learned that the tears were because the woman's pet fox terrier was too frightened to come out of the rubble.

'I'm rather good with dogs,' said Her Majesty. She got down on her knees and coaxed the terrified dog to safety.

It was little wonder that Prime Minister Winston Churchill was to say, 'Many an aching heart found solace in her gracious smile.' Or that Germany's Hitler called her the most dangerous woman in Europe.

The end of the war released the British and their King and Queen to more normal life. For the Royal family, state routine and public appearances of a less harrowing kind were gradually resumed. Their eldest daughter wanted to marry, and like any other parents, they had their doubts and suggested waiting awhile. When they did give permission, the wedding gave the people something to celebrate in the dark postwar days, when food, warmth, housing, and money were still in short supply.

Six months after the wedding, the Queen celebrated her silver wedding anniversary, and there was a service of thanksgiving in the magnificence of St. Paul's Cathedral. At the time she remembered the hardships that the country had been through and spoke of the joy her much loved home and family gave her. But she referred too to others less fortunate. 'My heart goes out,' she said, 'to all who are living in uncongenial surroundings and who are longing for the time when they will have a home of their own.'

It was not long afterward that the King's health began to fail. Though his wife never faltered, inwardly she was distraught at the possibility of losing her husband. Naturally, he had the best possible medical care, but in 1951 he lost a lung. The operation was carried out in a Palace room converted to an operating theatre. The Queen never left his bedside for a week. She was nurse-in-chief, doing what she could to assist the medical team in charge of her husband and hiding her own fears behind a calm, confident manner.

He was fifty-three when he died, his Queen a widow at fifty-one. She had been at his side for almost thirty years, and she bore her loss with a fortitude that led Churchill to refer to her as 'that most valiant woman.' What was she going to do with her life? No longer Queen consort, no longer mistress of the Palace, she seemed to have no role. And when she purchased the ruin of the Castle of Mey in Scotland and set about restoring it, the rumour was that she was retiring from public life.

Those who know her well say that her painstaking restoration of the castle and continuation with her work saved her sanity at that time. Mey was not a bolt hole; it was another home to enjoy between periods of work. Three months after the King's death she was as busy as ever, living up to her own adage that work is the rent you pay for life.

And if ever a woman has paid her dues, it is the Queen Mother.

— 5 —

Love Lost

WITH UNSWERVING patience, the present Queen won the man she wanted. Her little sister, Margaret, was not so fortunate. Princess Margaret is undoubtedly the most passionate of all the Windsors, though her nephew, Andrew, runs a close second. Her wide, sexy mouth and her challenging eyes have been dead giveaways since she was a small, shapely young woman surrounded by suitors —all of whom one by one dropped out of the competition. No doubt they realized, each in turn, that Margaret possessed a character that could never be completely controlled. Sexy she might be, beautiful indeed, but she was also wilful, contrary, and an impossible mixture of tenderness and arrogance.

God had made her volatile, and her parents had done little to tidy up His handiwork, though governess Crawfie did struggle to have some effect on the capricious little girl. Margaret was spoiled by the King and Queen both as a child and as a young woman. And in fairness, it was almost impossible not to spoil her. As difficult and provoking as she was, her charm was such that all bad behaviour was almost immediately forgiven, even by those as stern as her grand-mother, Queen Mary, who described her as *espiègle*, or roguish. 'She is so outrageously amusing one can't help encouraging her,' the old Queen remarked. Her parents also encouraged her. If her father attempted to be angry with her, she would look at him teasingly and say, 'Smile, Papa, smile,' and his wide mouth and solemn face would spread into an uncontrollable grin.

She was eminently spoilable, the beauty of the family. A tiny little girl with unbelievably perfect skin (though not as fine as her sister's),

130

huge, come-hither blue eyes, and, once the baby fat faded from her small bones, an hourglass figure. It would have broken her father's heart had he known what grief and pain her love for Group Captain Peter Townsend would cost her. But then if the King had not been so close to the end of his life the affair would never have been allowed to blossom.

Margaret was also spoiled because her parents were aware that throughout her life she would have to play second fiddle to her older, more serious sister. They did their best to compensate. And while they were compensating, Elizabeth complained, 'Margaret always wants what I want.'

Unfortunately, Margaret, though she has always stoutly denied it, was jealous.

By the age of twenty-one she had a fair bit to be jealous about. Her sister was heir to the throne, happily married, and mother of an adorable baby boy. Margaret was deeply in love with her father's Equerry, Group Captain Townsend, a man who was sixteen years older than she, married and divorced, and the father of two boys. Her family hadn't noticed love growing between them, but she must have been well aware that when they did they would not easily give her their blessing.

She seriously believed she could get away with marriage to Townsend and managed to persuade him of it too. Why not? Her father doted on her. She had never been denied anything she wanted if it was possible to give it to her. Eileen Parker noticed how the King would gaze at his pretty daughter admiringly and compliment her openly. 'All she had to do,' she said, 'was give him a spontaneous hug of affection to bring a glow of pleasure to his face. And then she would tease him for exposing his feelings.'

'I know I shouldn't spoil her,' the King would say, 'but I can't help it.'

She was showered with gifts from her parents. Eileen Parker remembers an occasion when she was with Margaret, Michael Parker, and Prince Philip in the Buckingham Palace lift. They were going to a party at the Dorchester Hotel.

'Do you like my new necklace?' Princess Margaret asked, arching her throat to display a string of pearls the size of peas. 'Mummy gave them to me tonight. I honestly don't know what came over her.'

Says Eileen Parker, 'Prince Philip turned to Mike and myself with raised eyebrows.'

Philip never put up with the younger Princess's airs and graces. If she deliberately dillydallied outside a lift, keeping him waiting because the precedence was hers, Philip would give her a shove to settle the question.

He was never a member of Princess Margaret's fan club. He thought her shallow and spoiled, and his not being on her side was to have an adverse effect on her love life. It was Philip who was implacable in his opposition to her marrying Townsend. Her immediate family, programmed into always giving Margaret her own way, hesitated and tried to think of ways around the problem. In the end, it was Philip who got his own way. The marriage never took place.

Margaret, the passionate lover, never managed to fall in love with anyone suitable. Sadly, most of her love stories have to do with this book's chapter on divorce. The men in her life—and unlike her sister there have been quite a few—have always caused problems to both her and her family. Her life has a habit of taking wrong turns, probably because of her own perverse nature. As a young girl, her contemporaries say, she had every intention of marrying young, just as her sister had. She saw herself settling down with one of the aristocrats that, once she was grown-up, her father invited to Balmoral and Sandringham house parties. These gatherings were then, as they are today, occasions when the younger members of the Royal family find their only opportunity to get to know members of the opposite sex.

Obviously, she intended, in the Royal manner, to find a *suitable* husband. Sunny Blandford, the present Duke of Marlborough, would make a suitable husband, she confided to her family. Unfortunately he fell in love with someone else. Then by her twenty-first birthday she was head over heels in love with Townsend, but since it was a love she could not declare, she invited the handsome young Earl of Dalkeith and Billy Wallace, a rather vapid-looking young man who was heir to a seven-figure fortune, to join her at Balmoral to celebrate the occasion. The press was certain that an engagement to one of these two highly suitable young men would be announced. Billy Wallace, the son of a Scottish landowner, was socially ambitious and forever asking Princess Margaret to marry him. But the odds were on the immensely rich Johnny Dalkeith, who was to inherit vast estates in Scotland, along with not one but three stately homes.

It was a prospect that much excited Sir Alan Lascelles, the King's private secretary, because he was related to Johnny Dalkeith's mother. Princess Margaret would become one of the family, as it were. But Dalkeith also fell in love with someone else. This was no great disappointment to the Princess, but maybe it was for Alan Lascelles and would explain the role he played in scuttling the romance between Princess Margaret and the love of her life, Townsend.

Of course, the affair was doomed, even if Margaret couldn't see it. Her first meeting with Group Captain Peter Townsend, DSO, DFC, and Bar was at Buckingham Palace on February 16, 1944. He had been dispatched to see the King, who was looking for an Equerry from the services, one with a record of bravery. Townsend certainly qualified. He had been flying night and day throughout the Battle of Britain. He had once been shot down into the sea and miraculously rescued by a passing trawler, had cracked up, recovered, returned to flying, and this second time round found himself so possessed by fear of death that he was taken off active service and put in command of a flying training school. He described himself as nerve-racked and sleep-starved at this time. The job at the training school should have come as a merciful release, but he was bored. He grabbed the opportunity to serve the King.

The King immediately liked him, perhaps because Townsend too had a stammer. And the man was sensitive looking, handsome in a fine-boned way, haggard by experience. After the King had finished his interview and Townsend was leaving, the two Princesses were told that an RAF hero was in the Palace. They darted off to contrive to meet him in the Palace corridors and found him. They were then introduced to their father's new Equerry, who had just been appointed for a three-month tour of duty.

Margaret, who was nearly fourteen at the time, does not remember this meeting. Townsend does.

Townsend had a wife. He had made a hasty wartime marriage, one that both he and his wife, Rosemary, came to regret. The new job was to accentuate all the weaknesses of the marriage. Working for the Royal family is akin to being married to them. They show little consideration for the outside lives of those who serve them, which is almost certainly why so many homosexuals work at the Palace.

Homosexuals usually do not have families sitting at home and asking where they have been. Rosemary Townsend, who already had a small son, was rapidly disillusioned with this wonderful new job. By the time their second son was born, she was bored and embittered, complaining she never saw her husband. Later, according to the wife of another Royal courtier, she became irritated by the wide-eyed devotion shown to her husband by 'a girl barely out of long white knee-socks' and his preoccupation with her.

Indeed, Margaret admits to having had 'the most terrific crush' on the Byronic Group Captain, but since she was correctly described as a schoolgirl, it seemed harmless enough. Perhaps, much later, her family had become accustomed to the crush and did not spot when it became the real thing. They liked Townsend very much. He was treated as a personal friend, in the same way that Prince Philip would treat his private secretary, Mike Parker, and with similar disastrous results.

It was in 1947 on an official family visit to South Africa that the romance between Margaret and Townsend blossomed. It was the two Princesses' first official overseas tour; the King had planned it as a thank-you to General Smuts for his support throughout the war. An unhappy Princess Elizabeth was stoically doing her duty. Prince Philip had proposed and she had accepted before they left Britain for South Africa, but the King had refused to make the engagement public and told her she must wait. But Margaret, age sixteen, was having a wonderful time. The poetic, heroic, handsome Townsend was deputized to keep her amused and under control. She spent a great deal of time alone with him. There were long, romantic shipboard evenings. In South Africa they went riding alone. She spent most of the time in his company. For her the South African trip was marvellous.

There was no difficulty in carrying on the deepening friendship back in Britain. She was seventeen when her big sister married Prince Philip, and she was suddenly left without the steadying influence that Elizabeth had always provided. She appeared to be happy enough. She took to night-clubbing and had her own set. For the rich and aristocratic being one of the Princess Margaret set was the ultimate achievement. She was daring in her dress and smoked with a long cigarette holder (surprisingly, at Queen Mary's suggestion). She was beautiful, challenging, and as wilful as ever. And while she was flirting with a dozen swains, she was all the while in love with Peter Townsend.

What is so amazing is that no one seems to have noticed—except the King, but he realized too late. At first he had completely trusted Townsend, who was, after all, almost double Margaret's age. But eventually, the King, who adored his youngest daughter, would have felt that prescience a father experiences when another man comes into his daughter's life. Certainly if he had not been so ill at the time he became aware of the relationship, the Townsend affair would never have happened. But when Margaret was twenty-one and Townsend was buying her a sheepskin saddle for her birthday present (they rode alone whenever they found the opportunity), the King was fighting what he thought was pneumonitis. It was, in fact, lung cancer. And it was too late to prevent the affair.

Townsend obviously recognized that the King was the danger to their relationship. Once when he was sleeping on the moors at Balmoral he woke to find Margaret's 'beautiful face' close to his. 'Your father is watching,' he warned as she tenderly covered him with a coat. On another occasion at Balmoral when the family were picnicking, the King came downstairs to find two cars being loaded at the door.

'Why two cars?' he wanted to know.

'Peter and Margaret are having their own picnic,' he was told.

'Oh, no, they're not,' he said, and the second car was sent away.

The King died in February 1952, and by then he had done something that again made Margaret feel that she was forever number two. The King had noticed that his father, King George V, had not made allowances for the Crown going to a female—as it would when George VI himself died. The old King had made provision for his sons' children and the children of his sons' children to be born Princes and Princesses, but not the children of his sons' daughters.

Five days before Prince Charles was born, George VI authorized that the children of his daughter Elizabeth were to be born Princes and Princesses. It was a necessary move or Charles, the future King, would be titled, but not a Prince. The King did not include Margaret's future children in this decree. It was another small disappointment for the Princess but was forgotten when her father died. She was shattered by his death and turned more and more to Townsend for comfort. He and his wife had decided on divorce, and there was no question of his doing the decent thing and taking the blame. He was granted the divorce on the grounds of his wife's adultery, and he and Margaret began seriously to dream about the possibility of marriage.

Still no one noticed what was happening under their noses. The new Queen had problems of her own without worrying what her sister was up to. And the Queen Mother seems to have simply ignored the whole thing. Margaret, her timing appalling, told the Queen and her mother just a few weeks before the Coronation that she and Townsend were in love. The timing was bad but fairly typical Margaret behaviour in that it brought the attention back to her at a time when the impending Coronation had cast her out of the family limelight. At the same time, Townsend made his confession to Alan Lascelles, who had taken over the role of private secretary to the Queen. As Lascelles saw the chances of having the Princess as one of the family disappearing, his reaction was that Townsend must be 'mad or bad.'

Elizabeth was kinder. Townsend said how impressed he was 'by the Queen's movingly simple and sympathetic acceptance of the disturbing fact of her sister's love for me.' What he didn't say was that the Queen was also deeply shocked by the implications of their wishing to marry. Philip decided to treat the news as a joke. Townsend said stiffly, 'Prince Philip, as was his way, may have tended to look for the funny side to this poignant situation. I did not blame him. A laugh now and then did not come amiss.' The truth was that both Townsend and Margaret were hurt by Philip's flippant reaction to what was, to them, a matter of the heart. But then there was little rapport between the poetic Townsend and the abrasive Prince. Philip's lack of sympathy may have been because he suspected Townsend of having advised the King against him when he had first wanted to marry the young Princess Elizabeth.

Philip may have joked to Townsend's face, but he was saying privately to the Queen that Townsend should be sent on his way. So was Alan Lascelles. And the Prime Minister, Winston Churchill, when told of the situation, advised exactly the same thing. There are rules even for Queens. If Elizabeth had wanted to give her sister her blessing, she could not do so. She was obliged to consult Churchill under the rules of the Royal Marriages Act of 1772. Churchill said that such a marriage would be a disastrous start to the new reign. He suggested that Margaret wait until she was twenty-five, when she would be freer to make her own decision. In the meantime, nothing must be said; Margaret and Townsend's relationship must not become public. Townsend offered to go away, but the Queen would not hear of it. She at least could rule that he would stay in Clarence House and be treated, as he had been for years, as nearly a member of the family. Not only did the Queen not relish the idea of breaking her sister's heart, but she liked and respected Peter Townsend.

The headstrong Margaret could only chafe at the restrictions that her lofty position put upon her. Any other woman in the land was free to marry whom she chose. Because of who she was, Princess Margaret was bound by rules that could not be broken. Without the Queen and the Government's permission, no clergyman in the land, or indeed registrar, would be legally able to marry her.

Elizabeth did not give that permission. She could not. But at least she had given Margaret breathing space. Her decision to let things go on as they were no doubt had an element of hope that perhaps the problem would solve itself. And this time indulging Margaret was to have disastrous consequences.

It was at the Coronation that Princess Margaret, perhaps deliberately, made the gesture that told the world she was in love with a divorced, older man. The newly crowned and anointed Queen had driven off in her carriage and the rest of the family was sheltering in the Abbey porch from the driving rain when Margaret pulled a little thread from her Peter's RAF uniform and then ran her hand affectionately along the row of medals on his chest. It was a loving, intimate gesture, and it was spotted by the press. The British newspapers still held back, but the foreign ones felt no constraint. As had happened before when the Duke of Windsor was wooing his unsuitable bride, the British public was kept in ignorance, until one newspaper pulled the old journalistic trick of printing the foreign stories and then knocking them down: 'The story is of course utterly untrue. It is quite unthinkable that a royal princess, third in line of succession to the throne, should even contemplate a marriage with a man who had been through the Divorce Courts.' Speculation was instantly rife, and the brand-new Queen had a scandal on her hands.

If Margaret's gesture had been one of defiance—for surely with all her experience with Royal watchers she must have known it was a dangerous thing to do—it backfired. Perhaps she had thought by exposing the situation, public sympathy would be with her and something would have to be done. After spending nine years and four months of his life serving the Crown, Peter Townsend was exiled.

Again, at this new time of crisis, a trip to Africa—this time Southern Rhodesia as it then was—was planned for Margaret and her mother. Townsend, who had become the Comptroller of the Queen Mother's household, had planned the whole thing and intended going with them. Suddenly he was told that he would be accompanying Elizabeth and Philip to Northern Ireland instead. Princess Margaret, perhaps now appreciating what her sister had felt on that previous trip to Africa, sailed away without him. She was in Umtali when she was told that Townsend had been posted to Brussels as Air Attaché. He had chosen Brussels out of the three postings offered him because it was the nearest to Britain, the woman he loved, and his two sons. Margaret cried. She spent a day crying. Her engagements were cancelled. Migraine was the excuse.

The next day the Princess, managing to smile, continued in her Royal tour.

There followed two long and painful years of waiting, though the couple was permitted to meet after a year, but then only briefly and in secret. The public was not to know. There were no restrictions on letters and phone calls, but the Royal family must have hoped that the affair would not survive two years of separation. Perhaps it might not have if everyone, including Alan Lascelles, had not given Margaret the wrong idea that when she was twenty-five she would be able to marry. It was a stale crumb of comfort. She believed all she had to do was give the Privy Council twelve months' notice of her intention to marry once she was twenty-five, and if Parliament raised no objection, she and Townsend would be free to marry after a year.

She saw him once briefly in those two years when he flew home incognito to meet her at Clarence House, and then it was back to letters and the telephone. Time passed slowly for Margaret, and then he was in Britain again—seven weeks after her twenty-fifth birthday. He had four weeks' leave from his Brussels job. Margaret, who had been in Scotland with her mother, travelled to London on the night train, and the couple met, alone at last, in the privacy of Clarence House. Two years had changed nothing. Even after the long separation, Margaret knew she still wanted to marry him.

The following few days must have been a nightmare for both of them. The press harassment that Peter Townsend suffered was probably the worst that anyone has ever endured, and he had to endure it without any official backup. There was an army of journalists on his heels, and it was a battle every time he set foot outside the Marquess of Abergavenny's flat in Lowndes Square, where he was staying. Women reporters clung to the open door of his car as he tried to drive off or flung themselves across the bonnet. Amazingly, he stayed calm and courteous. But the pressure became too great to bear. The couple fled to the Berkshire country home of Margaret's cousin, Jean Lycett Wills, the daughter of the Queen Mother's sister, Lady Elphinstone. There they found some peace, though the press still clustered outside the gates.

In London the problem that the Queen had hoped would go away was back in her lap. Margaret and Peter Townsend wanted permission to marry from the Privy Council. She was advised by her new private secretary, Michael Adeane, as she had been advised by Alan Lascelles, that the marriage was simply not a possibility. The Church agreed and the new Prime Minister, Anthony Eden, a divorced and remarried man himself, also was negative. Prince Philip was still insisting that the marriage would diminish the dignity of the Crown. Predictably, *The Times* thundered 'no' while the popular papers said 'why not?' and asked if the public really wanted her to marry one of the chinless wonders who had made up her set. *The Times* had authority. The tabloids did not. The only course left open to Margaret was to defy the Queen and Government, marry abroad, and retire into private life—without, of course, her allowance from the Civil List. And it was this that caused the couple to pause.

Margaret made one last attempt. She went to London to dine with her sister and her brother-in-law at Buckingham Palace, and there she pleaded her case. Philip conducted the proceedings, and it was he who finally, almost brutally, made Margaret see that she could not be Mrs. Townsend and part of the Royal family as well. He was adamant there could be no marriage, until finally Margaret broke down in tears.

She telephoned her lover the next day and cried bitterly as she told him that the situation looked hopeless—unless they left Britain and lived on Peter's salary, which for Princess Margaret would be tantamount to living on love. And more, it would rob her of her status. According to columnist Nigel Dempster, it was Townsend who wisely decided that this would be impossible. Margaret was ready to give up all, but, being older and wiser, he could see that such a dramatic change for the worse in her personal circumstances would have a disastrous effect on the marriage. He felt they had no choice but to accept the inevitable, and it was he who sat down to write the Princess's poignant speech of renunciation, which she delivered to the nation on October 31, 1955.

'I would like it to be known that I have decided not to marry Group Captain Peter Townsend. . . . Mindful of the Church's teaching that Christian marriage is indissoluble, and conscious of my duty to the Commonwealth, I have resolved to put these considerations before any others. . . . I am deeply grateful for the concern of all those who have constantly prayed for my happiness.'

The news could have been broken earlier, but the Queen agreed to delay it. A sad Peter and Margaret were allowed one last weekend together in the country.

And so, Margaret relinquished the love of her life for duty, and now, thirty-four years later, it all seems so unnecessary, a tragedy that need never have been.

Today there are few who would not agree that giving up the man she loved was beyond the call of duty. And yet had she gone into private life, many would have complained if she had continued to be paid her Civil List allowance. And had she remained as part of the Royal firm, continuing to launch ships and plant trees, the Church, and many God-fearing people, would have been deeply offended.

In the end, she and Townsend did what was the right thing at the time, probably for themselves as much as anyone else. And if blame is to be apportioned, the guilt is his. A man in his thirties, trusted by his master, should have known better than to involve himself with a young, impressionable girl, who, unfortunately for them both, happened to be a Princess of the realm. He should have understood that the situation was an impossible one.

As for Princess Margaret, her tears were soon dried. Perhaps the two-year separation had taken some of the urgency out of her feelings. Perhaps she was disappointed that Peter Townsend made the decision that the marriage was impractical. It might have been a sensible conclusion to reach that they could not live on his money, but it was hardly a romantic one.

Princess Margaret doggedly got on with her life. There was nothing else she could do. And back on the scene came Billy Wallace, who still wanted her.

She continued to say no to him, but things had changed since her affair with Townsend began. All the suitors who had made up her 'Margaret set' were spoken for. Billy Wallace was the only one left, and he renewed the pressure on her to marry him. Eventually she listened. Townsend was in the past. In a rather dated fashion, he was going round the world to forget. Margaret had been left at home to do the same thing, and, aged twenty-seven, she felt she was on the shelf. She was not in love with Billy, but he was 'suitable.' He had money, he understood and even aspired to her life-style, and she and he had been friends for a long time. She said yes, but no official announcement was to be made until the Queen's approval was received. It seemed Margaret had settled on someone suitable at last.

Unfortunately, before the announcement, silly Billy went on holiday to the Bahamas. There he indulged in a last fling with a willing lady. When he came home he took his time about calling the Princess. Indeed, eventually, knowing he was back in England, she was forced to telephone him. When they met, he was staggeringly unwise enough to tell the Princess how he had been passing his time in the Bahamas. It does not seem possible that he had the sauce to be both amazed and disgruntled when she reacted by throwing him out of her life in a fury.

He continued to protest his dismay at her reaction long after, but could he really have been stupid enough to think she would accept the news with a happy smile and continue planning the wedding? Or was the confession his own way of getting out of what, with time to think about it in the sunshine of the Bahamas, he may have decided could only be a difficult marriage? He died of cancer in 1977, so we shall never know, but it is difficult to believe that a man of thirty, as he was then, could be so naive as to believe that a woman of the Princess's temperament would accept such a blatant insult.

It was in 1956 when the last of the Margaret set, her kind, good, and rich friend Colin Tennant, married. And it was at his wedding that she briefly met a young Eton- and Cambridge-educated photographer called Tony Armstrong-Jones. Later, she was to meet him more formally at a small dinner party given by Lady Elizabeth Cavendish. She was instantly attracted to him that night. He was not wearing the regulation suit, but a casual jacket and boots. He was only a few inches taller than she, and he walked with a pronounced limp. When Princess Margaret fancies someone, it shows. The young Armstrong-Jones was not one to miss an opportunity, and here was a chance that he was not going to let pass. Princess Margaret was giving out 'I'm available' signals, and Tony was quick to pick them up. It took only a little while before he was showing her his Pimlico Road studio, office, and living quarters. They were just round the corner from the palace, but definitely on the wrong side of the tracks. The studio had a spiral staircase that went down to the basement living area, which he had decorated with a curious mixture of fine antiques and junk. The Princess was enthralled—sufficiently enthralled to share this new man in her life with his current girlfriend, an exotic Oriental model called Jacqui Chan. Being with Tony made her feel daring, she said, and though Tony once again was 'not suitable' in the eyes of the Queen and Prince Philip, life began to look better.

Again, much of the drama of Princess Margaret's marriage to Armstrong-Jones has more to do with divorce than love. But at the beginning, they certainly were in love. As with Andrew and Fergie, theirs was an obviously strong physical relationship. Even in public they could not keep their hands off each other. It could be embarrassing for others. And, curiously, even when the marriage was at its end, the physical aspect was still very much alive. Without that, it would have undoubtedly ended much earlier. Perhaps if Princess Margaret had not been Royal, the relationship would have been no more than a torrid affair that would have burned itself out quickly.

One of the most difficult problems for Royals is conducting a courtship. They have so little privacy as the rest of us know it that ordinary courtship for them is almost impossible. Prince Charles used to moan about the difficulty, but Princess Margaret told him rather sharply that with all the houses the Royal family owns she couldn't understand his problem. Even so, an HRH in love gets to know his or her partner after marriage, rather than before. Royals are never alone. There is always a detective or two hovering close by, and in their homes, servants are within call—servants who notice what is going on. But Princess Margaret, bolder and less discreet than her sister, did manage to begin a furtive affair with Armstrong-Jones.

At first she stayed the occasional night in the Pimlico flat, but there was always the chance that Jacqui might unexpectedly appear. Jacqui had a key, and it took Armstrong-Jones some while to get around to saying good-bye to the model who, not unnaturally, wasn't going to exit from his life of her own accord. He found a flat to which Jacqui did not have the key. It was in Rotherhithe—a dockland area of London that is fashionable today but was not then. It was territory that must have been as unfamiliar to Princess Margaret as Swaziland. All through 1957 she visited Tony there, not always returning to her bed at Clarence House. This caused the Queen considerable concern. She wanted no more gossip about her sister. The Townsend affair had already caused enough angst. But this time the Queen Mother was on her younger daughter's side in the matter. She felt Tony and Margaret (Tone and Pet, as they called each other) were a well-suited match. Both were a touch bohemian, both interested in theatre and the arts. Armstrong-Jones's name began to appear regularly on the lists of dinners and functions at Clarence House, the Queen Mother's London home that she shared with Margaret. The indulgence of Princess Margaret by her mother had not stopped.

At Clarence House Margaret and Tony Armstrong-Jones were never alone. In Rotherhithe they were. It was a flat without servants. When Margaret and her new love shared intimate meals, she found herself helping to lay the table and, after they had eaten and shared a bottle of wine, helping with the washing-up. It was a perfectly normal situation for the rest of the human race, but heady stuff for a Princess. Different and exciting. Of course it would be unrealistic to suppose that the passionate Margaret and Tony only held hands until she went home the next morning after these candle-lit suppers in the flat where the Thames flowed below. Their love affair that had begun in Pimlico continued in Rotherhithe, and the scruffy area itself was protective colouring. Who would expect to find Princess Margaret there? When alone in Tony's bedroom they must always have been aware of the detective waiting outside in the Royal car. Perhaps that gave it all an added excitement and piquancy, but miraculously they were able to carry on the affair in secret. The normally alert media suspected nothing. It was all far too unlikely. It was not until May 1959 that they were spotted together in public, and even then the press did not manage to put two and two together. There was one very good reason: many people quite mistakenly believed that Armstrong-Jones had no interest in women.

But the Queen and Prince Philip's anxieties about the friendship grew. Prince Philip couldn't see why Margaret couldn't marry one of his many highly suitable German relations. Princess Margaret had no intention of doing anything of the kind. She had inherited her mother's dislike of the German relations. That autumn there was a family row, with Margaret telling her sister and her brother-in-law that this time she would do what she liked. She emphasized her point by not appearing at the family dinner arranged to celebrate the Queen's tenth wedding anniversary. On November 20, while the Queen sat down with all her closest relatives, Princess Margaret was conspicuously absent. She went to the Coliseum to see a musical show and afterward dined, somewhat ostentatiously, at the Savoy Grill.

And who can blame her for boycotting a celebration of her sister's marriage when she had been denied marriage to Peter Townsend and was once again being told that the new man in her life was unsuitable?

To someone as contrary as Princess Margaret, the opposition would have made her more determined. But there was another factor involved. At the beginning of 1960 she received a letter from her ex-lover, Peter Townsend. He was marrying a twenty-year-old Belgian woman, young enough to be his daughter, just as the Princess had been.

'That evening,' said Princess Margaret, 'I decided to marry Tony. It was not a coincidence.'

On February 26, 1960, the Princess and Armstrong-Jones announced their engagement. The Queen had met this unlikely suitor and, possibly to her own surprise, taken to him, though she did not approve of the wedding. Nor indeed did Armstrong-Jones's friends and family. All implored him to reconsider, but he was determined. Added to this was the sexual chemistry between them, and Margaret, just twenty-nine, was at her most stunning. The birthday pictures that he took of her, in profile, show a regal, but softly beautiful, young woman. The world might forecast disaster, but the couple was convinced that true happiness was theirs.

There were problems. The unfortunate rumours regarding Tony's sexual predilections were revived when he asked Jeremy Fry, of chocolate firm fame, to be his best man. The Establishment had kittens when it was discovered that in 1952 Fry had had a homosexual conviction. Fry retired from the job, pleading a convenient attack of jaundice. Maybe Tony was being mischievous, but his second sugges-tion was the politician Jeremy Thorpe, who much later was to become the leader of the Liberal Party. Unfortunately, the special branch of the police pointed out that Thorpe too had homosexual tendencies. Eventually someone comfortably heterosexual was found to fill the role, but it was hardly surprising that the Queen's face was set in lines of stern Victorian disapproval all through the wedding ceremony in May 1960. She did not even crack a smile when the Princess dropped her a formal curtsey when leaving Westminster Abbey. Perhaps Her Majesty had a pretty shrewd idea that this marriage of two people who were far too alike was not going to work, as indeed it did not. However, the Queen did give her sister's new husband an Earldom. And even today, long after the marriage ended, the Queen and the Earl of Snowdon, as he became, are still friends.

Margaret's marriage had not been going well since 1966, when Tony had gone to India on a photographic assignment for the *Sunday Times* and the Princess was left bored and lonely. One of her closest friends was Anthony Barton. Barton was married with two children about the same age as Margaret's, and he and his wife spent family holidays with the Snowdons. While Margaret was alone, Barton travelled from his home in Bordeaux, where he runs a wine business, to inquire after the health of his goddaughter, Sarah Armstrong-Jones and to ask for news of Tony, whose father had recently died.

Perhaps not surprisingly—Barton is a very attractive man—Margaret found herself attacked by a plague of hormones and believed herself in love with him. For the space of just a few days they became involved. The romance was all over in practically five minutes and would not have mattered or caused any damage if Margaret hadn't done the unforgivable. She rang Barton's wife to say how sorry she was it had happened. She also told her husband.

Amazingly, both marriages survived the episode. Not only did she and Tony seem closer than ever afterward—for a while—but even the family friendship between the Bartons and the Snowdons went on. Margaret may have done the unforgivable, but Royals are forgiven where lesser mortals are not.

Tony was still often away, and Margaret was bored. She had never been one to undertake any more Royal duties than necessary, and she had little to do. For a while she saw a lot of an old friend, Dominic Elliot, and she developed a heavy crush on another of Snowdon's friends, Derek Hart, who worked in television. For a while the Earl of Lichfield was in the frame, but she dismissed him to her friends and relatives as no one to worry about. 'He's a kissing cousin,' she said.

More complicated was the flirtation that began with Robin Douglas-Home, the nephew of a former British Prime Minister, Alec Douglas-Home. He had been in her life since the days of the Margaret set, when the lucky nightclubs, lush, plush, and pink, had Princess Margaret and her group of lords and landed gentry as habitués. The young Princess, slender and beautiful with her large Egyptian eyes ringed in black, held court, a tapering cigarette holder between her fingers, her shoulders rounded, shining, and bare above strapless sequined gowns. And the man at the nightclub piano, playing his signature tune, 'I'm in the Mood for Love,' was more often than not Robin Douglas-Home.

He had an impeccable background, educated at Eton and then commissioned in the socially correct Seaforth Highlanders. He came from an old and honourable aristocratic family. That he had no money was not important. He and Margaret were friends, and she constantly asked for him to be invited to house parties and would send her own car to pick him up and drive to the country with him. In their friends' homes, she would sing to his piano playing, and those who knew them then are still convinced that he could have married Princess Margaret long before Anthony Armstrong-Jones came on the scene. Unfortunately, at the time Douglas-Home was in love with another Princess, the blond and curvy Princess Margaretha of Sweden. They wanted to marry, but King Gustav of Sweden had different ideas. He made sure the marriage never took place.

In 1967 Lord Snowdon was sent on a long assignment to the Orient, again for the Sunday Times, and the lonely Princess Margaret turned to her old friends—and most particularly Douglas-Home. This time round, Robin fell deeply in love with the Princess and told his friends of his hopes that one day they might be together. He said that she felt the same way. The press had seized on the friendship since the couple was seen together so frequently in public and Tony's Far East trip gave the relationship a new credibility. Snowdon, kept informed by newspaper reports of his wife's behaviour, did not approve but kept a poker face in public. The besotted Robin was pressing Margaret to make decisions. She went to the Bahamas and thought about it. She realized the situation was getting out of hand, and when she returned to Britain, she wrote to Robin Douglas-Home and gently dismissed him from her life.

After he received the letter he said bitterly to a friend, 'She put the Crown before her heart. I really didn't think she would do it. I thought we would be together.'

Robin Douglas-Home was a man of great charm but not noted for his stability. He eventually committed suicide, leaving an embarrassing legacy of tender letters, written in affectionate terms, from Princess Margaret, which had found their way to auction in New York. The letters were printed in full in the States and round most of the world. But British copyright laws prevented their publication in Britain.

For Margaret there were other comforters, including the comedy actor Peter Sellers, who was much more fun than the melancholy Robin, and eventually she and Tony made an agreement to go their own ways—as long as everything was done to keep up appearances. Princess Anne and Mark Phillips were to make the same arrangement some years later. It wasn't a situation that made the Princess particularly happy, but she had little choice since at this stage divorce was unthinkable.

Even so, her actions had given her husband the greatest possible excuse to play around himself, and he took it. He was constantly seen with attractive women, and then in late 1969 he began a yearlong affair with Lady Jacqueline Rufus-Isaacs, a stunningly attractive young woman of twenty-two. When it became public knowledge, the affair ended. Snowdon had told Jackie that he could 'get rid of Princess Margaret anytime [he] wanted.' When it came to the crunch he couldn't bring himself to raise the matter with the Queen, even though his marriage to Margaret was falling apart at the seams.

Margaret had a host of defensive reasons for the looming failure. She was angry that Tony had bought a country house she disliked; they quarrelled about the children's upbringing. She felt he didn't love her anymore, and she was embarrassed and angered by his public appearances with so many different young women—women younger than she. No one had ever explained to her that what is sauce for the goose is sauce for the gander, and she refused to accept that it was she who had opened the floodgates with her five-minute fling with Barton. So used to having her own way, she believed she could get away with anything but was discovering time and time again that she could not.

Still the marriage limped on, the Snowdons superglued together by protocol, the tender age of their children, and Margaret's determination not to embarrass her sister with a divorce.

The meeting with Roddy Llewellyn in September 1973 eventually changed all that, though she could not have imagined the future when with her two children she was invited to join her friends Colin and Anne Tennant for the last week of their summer holiday in Scotland. She had originally turned down the invitation but suddenly telephoned to ask if she could change her mind. The Tennants were in a quandary. Lord Snowdon was not of the party, they were a man short, and it was unthinkable that the numbers should be unbalanced, particularly with the Princess as a guest. But who to ask at such short notice so late in the summer season? Colin Tennant rang Mrs. Violet Wyndham, one of London's better-known hostesses, who also happens to be his great-aunt by marriage. It was she who suggested Roddy Llewellyn.

It took awhile to track down Roddy. He was not and probably never will be a man with a tidy lifestyle. He agreed to join the party, even though he had never met either the Tennants or Princess Margaret. Leaving Cornwall, where he had been staying, he got himself on the shuttle to Edinburgh, armed with his instructions to be at the Cafe Royal, just off Princes Street, by 1:00 P.M. His fare was to be paid by Tennant, since Roddy was somewhat impecunious.

The lunch was a great success. In spite of his being so much younger than the Princess (he was nearly twenty-six, and she was forty-three), he and she hit it off at once. In retrospect, Margaret was ripe for what the media call a 'toy boy.' She knew her husband was in love with his production assistant, and though she herself had hardly behaved well through the marriage she was humiliated and hurt. In many ways her flings and crushes were understandable. Her husband's treatment of her was cavalier in the extreme. Friends say that Tony was deliberately provocative with his wife—even more provocative than she was capable of being herself. He certainly made her very unhappy. He was often hostile, rarely spoke to her, and left her alone most of the time while he continued with his work. His marriage to a Royal Princess had helped him in his career, but the Royal Princess now felt herself to be extraneous to his life.

She needed an adoring swain, one she could control. And here was this attractive man who, though taller, looked not unlike the young Tony. Unlike her husband, Roddy shared her passion for music. That first evening at Glen House, Colin Tennant's Scottish home, she and Roddy played and sang at the piano. They had talked all through lunch. Princess Margaret was giving out signals again, and not only was Roddy picking them up, he was throwing out a few of his own.

There is no doubt that they did fall in love. They were in contact immediately after they reached London, and Roddy rushed to tell his brother, Dai Llewellyn, that he was in love with the Queen's sister and that his feelings were reciprocated. Not surprisingly, Dai was amazed.

So was everyone else in her set. Her family was not pleased but resigned. There was no attempt to persuade her to stop the friendship, although the Queen Mother was the only one of the Royal family to receive Roddy, inviting him for weekends at Royal Lodge. The Queen steadfastly refused to meet her sister's new lover. This was understandable, because of all Princess Margaret's unsuitable suitors, he took the prize. Roddy was the son of Colonel Harry Llewellyn, star of the show jumping ring and a friend of Prince Philip, but he was not so robustly masculine as his father. He had already tried to commit suicide twice, was quiet and a little shy, had no money or career, and was generally drifting through life. Before Margaret, he had been sharing a flat with a self-confessed gay.

It was a romance verging on the bizarre. According to friends, not too much in the way of bed was involved. It was more a companionship. As one said, 'They went beddie-byes once or twice. That was not hugely successful, but there was a lovely bond between them.' Roddy is said to have confessed that he found the physical side of their relationship difficult to cope with.

Six months after their meeting, Margaret took Roddy to her home Les Jolies Eaux on the island of Mustique. They travelled separately. It was her treat. It was always her treat. The romance finally finished seven years later when he fell in love with and married Tania Soskin, a girl three months his junior. Once Margaret had weathered the shock, she said generously, 'I am really happy for him.' But she did add ruefully, 'Anyway, I couldn't have afforded him much longer.'

Much had happened before the day when Margaret gave a small luncheon party to celebrate her ex-lover's engagement. Roddy had been obliged to remember that his love was also a Princess and must be treated accordingly. He made lists of her likes and dislikes, enemies and friends, and puzzled out which situations to avoid. Princess Margaret's friends and lovers have to learn to cope with her mood swings, from being one of the gang to sudden reversion to being the Queen's sister. All of this caused him acute anxiety, and after a year of it, in 1974, he just freaked and fled the country. He took the first plane available and landed up in Guernsey in the Channel Islands, having phoned Princess Margaret to say he was going away and didn't know when he would be back. He next took off for Turkey and spent three weeks there exploring the country by bus. He had every intention of going to India, but he never got there. Most likely his money ran out. And then he slipped back into England.

In the meantime, what with living with Tony's silences and insensitivity and Roddy's disappearance, Princess Margaret was quietly close to a nervous breakdown. She took enough pills to make her sleep through a day and a night and afterward said it did her a power of good, even if the aftereffects made her miss a few engagements. A month or so later, Roddy did much the same thing with the help of Valium (the Princess used Mogadon). The aftereffects for him were more serious. He landed up in hospital for three weeks, spending some of the time in a ward for disturbed people. One might say the affair was not going well.

Tony was having a much better time. In 1973 he had taken on a production assistant to help him with his television documentary work. She was Lucy Lindsay-Hogg, a tall, good-looking, understated brunette divorcée, totally different in temperament, style, and looks from Princess Margaret. Working together, often abroad, Snowdon and Lucy were strongly attracted to each other. While Roddy was having his nervous breakdown, Snowdon was working in Australia and was away for eleven weeks. He and Lucy began an affair. This time it was serious, and Princess Margaret knew it. Where she had been reasonably tolerant of Tony's other women friends, she called Lucy Lindsay-Hogg 'that thing.'

Back in London, Snowdon spent much of his time at Lucy's flat in Kensington Square. Princess Margaret was not amused. 'There he was, living in my house,' she said bitterly, 'thinking he could have a lovely affair. I asked him for a separation, but he laughed in my face. I would only know he was back at night when I heard him banging about the bathroom—it was all hours.'

Margaret was not seeing Roddy, though they were in touch by telephone while he recovered his health. He became involved in an upper-class commune in the countryside near Bristol. Eventually his health recovered sufficiently for him to see the Princess again. She visited him a couple of times at the commune, declared it all great fun, and invited Roddy back to Mustique the following February.

He accepted. And it was then that disaster struck.

The *News of the World*, a sensational British Sunday newspaper, had sent a journalist from its New York bureau, posing as a school-teacher, for a holiday along with his wife on Mustique. His assignment was to get an incriminating picture of Princess Margaret with Roddy Llewellyn. It took a while, but the journalist eventually managed it when the Princess took a small group for a drink at the one and only beach bar on Mustique. When the photograph was printed, it showed just Roddy and Margaret, the rest of the group having been carefully cut out of the picture. The couple had been made to appear as if they were alone.

Though Roddy and Margaret had been together for two-and-a-half years, and therefore were frequently alone, they had never been photographed before. When the picture appeared on the front page of *News of the World*, it gave Snowdon just the lever he had been looking for—the chance for a divorce.

— 6 —
Royal Divorce

*L*OOKING BACK over the years to the romance that shattered Princess Margaret's life, it seems extraordinary that such an event could have happened in 1953. Today, only thirty-odd years later, it seems impossible that any couple could be kept apart by Monarchy and Government. The Townsend-Margaret drama was more a scenario for the turbulent Middle Ages or days of the Tudors. The rules have been modified since she loved and lost, but, depressingly for Margaret, the changes came too late for her. She was a victim of her time.

In 1953, when Princess Margaret's affair with Group Captain Peter Townsend became known, divorce was simply not socially acceptable in aristocratic circles. It is difficult today to remember just how different things were, how narrow the thinking was. No one who was divorced was invited to Buckingham Palace or any of the Queen's homes, not even to the Royal yacht. Guilty parties in divorce cases were not permitted in the Royal enclosure at Royal Ascot. To be divorced was social death. When Townsend himself divorced in December 1952, it was essential that he be the innocent party. The divorce itself could have cost him his job and certainly would have if the King had been alive. However attached to Townsend the King might have been, his totally Royal upbringing would not have countenanced a divorced man among his courtiers. It was fortunate for Townsend that the decision as to whether or not he should stay rested with the Queen and the Queen Mother. For them, perhaps with a little urging from Margaret, his being the innocent party was sufficient excuse to keep him at the Palace.

Interestingly, when Michael Parker, Prince Philip's private secretary, was told by his wife that she wanted a divorce, he instantly said, 'You'll have to be the guilty party because of my job.' Since her husband was having an affair, Eileen Parker was furious and certainly not prepared to take the blame publicly for the marriage breakup. She also feared that if she agreed she might lose the custody of her children. She petitioned for divorce from her husband, citing his adultery, and though both the Queen and Prince Philip urged him to stay, Parker resigned. He did the honourable thing for the day, but it is likely that there was a more complicated reason. Prince Philip had been aware of Parker's liaison from attending parties where Parker and his mistress, Marion, were together. It is possible that Parker feared Philip's condonation of his adultery might come out in the divorce court, to the detriment of his Royal employer. In Britain in the 1950s divorce still came with a stigma.

Margaret was prepared to live with that stigma, but her chances of marriage to Townsend were sunk in the end by the Privy Council — that powerful body to which belongs the true ruling class of Britain. Their thinking on the matter had not changed in two years. The Queen's sister could not remain third in line to the throne, receive a Civil List income of £15,000 a year (as it was then), and be the wife of a divorced man. It would not do. Even those who felt pity for her agreed.

There were those in the Cabinet, notably the Marquess of Salisbury, who felt so strongly that they threatened to resign should Margaret be permitted to marry a divorced man. Salisbury was a close friend of the Queen Mother, and his opposition strengthened her own feelings that the marriage was wrong. The Queen Mother had done nothing to calm her daughter's growing relationship with Townsend in the early days. Now, faced with Margaret's defiance and determination to go ahead, it was too late. The Queen Mother was aware that her husband would never have approved, but she was still unwilling to interfere in her daughter's life. It was not her style. All she could hope for was that Margaret would make the decision to end the affair of her own accord.

Divorce in Royal circles was simply not accepted. King Edward VIII had been prevented from putting Mrs. Wallis Simpson beside him on the throne not because she was an American, and not because she was no aristocrat, but because she had been divorced—twice. Much later it was the unfortunate Margaret who was to be in the position of not being permitted to marry a divorced man and then having to live through the misery of a desperately unhappy marriage because she did not wish to embarrass her sister by asking for permission to shed him. Margaret, like her sister, does not believe in divorce, but the hostile and vindictive treatment that she was receiving from Lord Snowdon was making her ill. The divorce came about only because Snowdon wanted to marry someone else. When the Mustique picture of Roddy Llewellyn and the Princess together appeared on the front page of a sensational London newspaper, Snowdon declared himself humiliated and said that his position was intolerable. On these grounds he asked the Queen for permission to divorce. Before the Queen agreed she talked with her sister and her mother. Even Margaret, who had tried to keep the marriage together for the sake of the children (Lady Sarah Armstrong-Jones was only fourteen at the time), accepted that the time had come to part. The Queen reluctantly gave her permission—holding up, incidentally, the announcement of Prince Michael's engagement. The Establishment thought it wise to ration out the shocks.

Tony was given his freedom. The Queen might not have considered saying yes if the Royal family had not become fond of him over the years. Perhaps she and her mother, who still see him regularly, felt that he too had had his crosses to bear. The Queen, summing up the situation, also took into account that the divorce would free Margaret, who had now been married for eighteen mostly unhappy years. The family had to bow to the inevitable.

The news broke on May 11, 1978, when Kensington Palace announced in a brief statement, 'Her Royal Highness the Princess Margaret, Countess of Snowdon, and the Earl of Snowdon after two years' separation have now agreed that their marriage should be formally ended.'

They were fortunate that the divorce laws had been changed so that blame was no longer apportioned. Sufficient grounds for divorce were the irreversible breakdown of marriage. As Margaret and Tony had been living apart for two years, those grounds legally applied. Even so, being Royal did not protect the Princess from the case's having to be heard in court, though since it was undefended it was heard under a 'special procedure' petition, which meant that neither she nor her husband had to appear. Margaret had been ill when the divorce was announced and was 'convalescing in the country' when it was granted.

The divorce was like anyone else's in the land, sad and unglamorous. The legal proceedings were handled by Her Majesty's solicitor, Farrer and Company, and listed in court: 'Farrer and Co, WC2 SP3628b HRH The Princess Margaret Rose, Countess of Snowdon v Armstrong-Jones ACR Earl of Snowdon (5684/74).' The petition was heard at the London law courts on May 24, 1978, along with twenty-eight other 'quickie' divorces, including those of a barmaid, a chamber-maid, and a woman who was living with her boyfriend. A seventy-one-year-old judge who had been happily married for forty-five years granted the decree on the grounds of two years' separation by consent. The divorce itself cost the small sum of £16. The judge then sat in private to discuss the custody and financial arrangements for the couple's children. Princess Margaret was given custody but had to make a six-figure settlement with her husband. She no doubt felt it was worth it for her freedom.

But the real end did not come until later, when on December 17 of the same year Lord Snowdon married his production assistant, Lucy Lindsay-Hogg. The couple had a daughter, Lady Frances Armstrong-Jones, on July 17, seven months after the wedding. Both events, the wedding and the birth, came as a considerable shock to Princess Margaret. Her ex-husband had not had the courtesy to give her warning of either. For once public sympathy was on her side. Curiously, the divorce brought considerably less public outcry than her love for a divorced man when she was a young, impressionable girl. Times had changed. But still Princess Margaret was the first person so high in the line of succession to involve the Royal family in divorce since Henry VIII legally shed Anne of Cleves.

In the years between her ardent love for Townsend and her bitter divorce from Snowdon, much had changed. In October 1955, at the height of the Townsend crisis, when the world was agog asking 'Will she, won't she?', *The Times* thundered that the Princess should not forget she was the sister of the Queen 'in whom her people see their better selves reflected.' The newspaper pontificated that if she married Townsend she would be 'entering a union which vast numbers of her sister's people . . . cannot in conscience regard as a marriage. . . . The Queen's sister married to a divorced man (even though the innocent party) would be irrevocably disqualified from playing her part in the essential royal function.'

When the news of the impending divorce was announced in 1978, *The Times* took rather a different line. The thunder had died to a rumble.

'The Queen and her family reflect as well as represent the community. . . . They are exposed to the pressures of modern life like the rest of us. All that may reasonably be asked . . . is that in their private lives they should act within the broad limits of customary conduct among the people of this country. Divorce now comes within these limits.'

Perhaps her marriage to photographer Antony Armstrong-Jones had never been a very good idea. But Margaret, walking up the aisle of Westminster Abbey on a sunny May day in 1960, her dark hair held high in a Princess's tiara and in her gleaming gown, was perhaps the most beautiful and radiant of all Royal brides of this generation.

*

There are those who say that the Margaret-Townsend affair did at least encourage the Church to take a more liberal view of divorce. But there is little sign of it. The Church of England does not accept divorce, and orthodox Church of England vicars generally will not remarry divorced people. As a rule, the most that can be hoped for is a blessing in church. Nor, unlike the Roman Catholic Church, does the Church of England have its own procedure for religious annulments. Therefore, since the Queen is the Defender of the Faith—that faith being the Church of England—the idea of divorce in the Royal family sends shudders through the Establishment even today. Divorce may be commonplace for commoners, but not for Kings and Queens.

Royal marriages have their ups and downs like everyone else's, and frequently the downs become glaringly apparent, which causes constant press speculation. At the end of August 1989 the obvious crack in the marriage of Princess Anne finally became a yawning chasm. A twenty-six-word statement—'Her Royal Highness the Princess Royal and Captain Mark Phillips have decided to separate on terms agreed between them. There are no plans for divorce proceedings'—issued by

Buckingham Palace on September 1 ended years of speculation about the state of this extraordinary marriage. The Palace picked its moment for this revelation brilliantly. The Queen was at Balmoral with her family and 'unreachable,' Princess Anne was working in South America, and it was just two days before the papers and television would be full of reports pertinent to the fiftieth anniversary of the start of the Second World War. The timing, however, did not stop the popular newspapers from devoting many pages to the story for the next two days.

It had been stretching credulity for years to ask the Queen's subjects to believe that this was a marriage that worked perfectly well by its own rules. If one took the trouble to add up the days per year the couple were apart from each other, in some years the sum came to roughly ten months. A truly happily married couple would not wish to be separated so much, however demanding their careers. Ten months is a long time, with plenty of opportunities for two young, attractive people to get into mischief. Princess Anne is apt to say, 'One's horse does not know one is Royal.' Neither do one's hormones! Nature has a habit of making its presence felt. It was hardly surprising that every now and then throughout the marriage their names were linked with other people's.

Yet the marriage had looked so good on paper, with the Queen Mother insisting that they could have been picked by computer as the perfect couple. She is usually right about such things. This time, sadly, she was not.

Much of the trouble with the marriage was caused because from the beginning Mark refused a title and held out against joining the family firm. Anne is very much a member. Ask her to name her favourite holiday and her face lights up. 'Oh, Balmoral, with the family,' she says. But Mark couldn't be bothered with Balmoral or Sandringham and involved himself as little as possible in Royal family matters. Anne did not mind his refusing a title—that was done entirely with her approval—but she did want him to be one of the family.

Friends say that he was never comfortable with his in-laws. He must have been aware that Prince Philip did not particularly care for him. Philip thought he was dull and boring. Mark is a shy man and none too articulate, and by Prince Philip's abrasive judgment maybe he is dull. Worse, he married a woman who is a great deal more quick-witted and forceful than he could ever manage to be. His wife left him with egg on his face in countless situations. She even managed to make a fool of him at their joint television appearance that took place after the engagement was announced. He was hardly allowed a word in edgeways, which made the nation, as well as his future father-in-law, decide he must be a touch thick. But nevertheless, his and his wife's common interest in riding held them together for a long time. In fact, they appeared to be inseparable. They were photographed together at dozens of equestrian meetings, and when they were not riding together they were working together on their Gloucestershire estate. But they began to drift apart, and friends say that his preoccupation with money had something to do with it. Anne dislikes his obsessive interest in his bank balance, not appreciating that she has always had plenty of cash and that people who start without any are often obsessively interested in the stuff. They had one good skiing holiday together not long before they split. Then he went and spoiled it all by moaning about how much it cost because he had picked up the bills.

In the beginning he resented the fact that he could not compete financially with his wife and that Gatcombe was hers, bought for her by the Queen for £300,000 and put in her name alone. If Anne is anything like her Aunt Margaret, who was forever complaining that Lord Snowdon was making her miserable *and* in her house, she was probably making the same point every time she and Mark quarrelled. Eventually he stopped joining Anne's family at the traditional Balmoral and Sandringham holidays. He pleaded pressure of work on the farm, and she and the children went without him.

And then a telltale policeman, Peter Cross, who had been her bodyguard, came on the scene with tales of the tender feelings that he and Princess Anne had once shared, and nothing was ever the same again.

It was nine years after their wedding day when the Phillipses' marriage began to change. Speculation about the couple was at its worst when the titillating tale of the pouting Princess and the passionate policeman was all over the front pages of Britain's newspapers not long after Zara's birth. The story almost got away. It was two years after the policeman had been sent back to uniformed duties in 1980 that the torrid tale surfaced. 'Anne and the Sacked Copper' read a big, black headline on the front page of the *Sun* on July 6, 1982.

Harry Arnold, the paper's Royal correspondent, wrote, 'A royal detective has been sacked over allegations that he was 'over familiar' towards Princess Anne. The detective, a sergeant, was summoned before Commander Michael Trestrail [who was later fired himself] who is the Queen's bodyguard and the head of the Royal Protection Squad.

'He was told that his conduct did not come up to the standards expected of police officers who guard the Royal family.'

The unnamed sergeant had quit the police, but Harry Arnold pointed out that Captain Phillips had been angry over the officer's behaviour, while Princess Anne defended him.

'His departure left a rift between the Royal couple which has never been healed,' said Arnold.

Three years later, in 1985, Cross sold the inside story of this unlikely friendship to the *News of the World*, Britain's largest-selling Sunday newspaper, also owned by Rupert Murdoch. With some justification Cross was instantly dubbed 'rat of the century.' If he and the Princess had been as close as he made out, telling all was a pretty cruel thing to do. Like all traitors, he had his reasons of course. When the story appeared he justified himself by saying, 'I was a victim of the Establishment. I want to get even with those who ganged up so unfairly after our friendship [his and Anne's] was betrayed. Telling my story will help me do that.'

Telling his story also lined his pockets, and in retrospect one can see all too clearly that the end of the affair (if an affair it was) spelled the beginning of the end for Mark and Anne's marriage. Mark gritted his teeth and put a brave face on it, but the screaming headlines must have been hard to take.

Unfortunately for the Royal family, Peter Cross's revelations made for riveting reading. And, as is so often the case, the first part in what was to prove the story of the year came from a woman scorned.

Peter Cross—blond and balding, with bright blue eyes and a lot of charm—was something of a womanizer. His time at Gatcombe had wrecked his own marriage, and when he left the police force he joined an insurance agency as a salesman. There, one of the employees, Gillian Nicholls, became his mistress. His wife threw him out, and he left her and his two children and moved into Gillian's home. She confidently expected him to marry her. He didn't. He ditched her and married another woman a few weekends later. He didn't feel it was necessary to mention the nuptials to Gillian. When Ms. Nicholls found out why he had gone missing, she retaliated by telling the press the story of her ex-lover's mysterious phone calls at the insurance office, all from a woman who called herself Mrs. Wallis but who was really Princess Anne.

Cross had made no secret of having been in the Royal Protection Squad, and his fellow staff members recognized Anne's voice when the calls came through. Eventually, Cross admitted who the persistent Mrs. Wallis really was.

Before Cross left his wife, Linda, she too was answering phone calls at least once a week from a mysterious woman who never gave a name but asked if she could speak to Peter. Linda did not have to inquire who was calling. Princess Anne's clipped, upper-class tones were unmistakable. The family got used to the kids shouting up the stairs, 'Dad, it's Princess Anne on the phone for you.'

The friendship between Cross and the Princess began on the backstairs at Gatcombe Park, where they used to sit telling each other their troubles, he one step up from her, her head dangerously close to his knee. And it was on the backstairs that Cross began to feel what he described as tender feelings close to love. It was also where he first kissed her but, fearing that they might become 'something that the butler saw,' they moved into the library where he kissed her again.

He says they began spending as much time together as they could, allowing for the week-on, week-off rotation he worked. Cross went so far as to claim a night in Buckingham Palace. But Mark Phillips, who is not as dense as he's painted, had obviously noticed what was going on. On one occasion, Mark drove his wife home after a dinner, leaving Cross to follow in the Princess's car. Anne asked him to slow down—he was driving at such a speed that the policeman was having difficulty keeping up.

According to Cross, Mark is said to have asked curtly, 'What are you worried about? The car or the man driving it?'

Not long afterward, Cross was on the carpet in front of his superiors and sent back to uniformed duty as station sergeant at Croydon Police Station. He resigned from the force shortly afterward.

Cross was removed from Gatcombe probably at the insistence of

Mark Phillips. Cross left the Princess's service in September 1980, protesting that the familiarity hadn't been one-sided. There wasn't so much as a squeak of denial from the Palace to give Mark Phillips some comfort. The only excuse forthcoming was a rather feeble one, under the circumstances. Sergeant Cross was said to have 'mistaken the Princess's friendship.' Mark was more positive. He said Cross's allegations were 'a load of rubbish . . . in the realms of fantasy.'

Princess Anne had been abroad at the time the sergeant was removed from Gatcombe, and she had no idea that he had been dismissed until she returned home. Cross claimed that she wrote to him, saying that when she came back to find him gone she went to her room and cried. He could not produce the letter. Hand on heart, he said that out of loyalty to Anne he had destroyed it.

The friendship apparently went on for two more years. Anne first sent a Christmas present—shortbreads for Cross's children and a signed photograph of Anne for him—through a policeman on the Royal Protection Squad. He took back Cross's note of thanks. A few weeks later, the police officer reluctantly set up what the police call 'a meet' with Cross at Victoria Station. He came straight to the point.

'The lady wants to see you,' he said.

Cross hesitated at first but eventually agreed to go to Gatcombe at an arranged time. He waited in the library, and she came in, then about five months pregnant with Zara. The Princess asked why he had gone. She had been told that he had asked to be moved because of domestic trouble, and, said Cross, she was angry when he told her the truth. Their friendship started up again, and they began to meet regularly, using a secret code. She would telephone and ask him if he would like a 'day in the country.' That meant she was free and presumably that her husband was away. They met at the home of another policeman who gave Cross the keys to his house. They also met at an unused cottage on the Gatcombe estate. And when Zara was born on May 15, 1981, he claimed that he was the second person to whom she told the news.

It is very much a story of ordinary folk rather than Royalty. One does not expect Royalty to go on like that. But was it all realms of fantasy, as Mark Phillips insisted? Probably not. It would have been a happier situation for all concerned if Peter Cross had been making it all up, but the evidence strongly suggests that there was truth in it.

Sergeant Cross did name the high-ranking policeman who acted first as go-between when Anne made contact again. The officer has never denied what Cross said had happened. Many people confirmed the phone calls from Mrs. Wallis, and none had any doubt that the voice was that of Princess Anne. Pictures of her with the Sergeant, who of necessity as her police protector was always at her side, show the body language of two people who are comfortable together and standing just a little bit too close to each other.

No doubt Cross, now married to a dental nurse, was a philanderer. He certainly knew how to attract women, and the Princess in her ivory tower would not have felt the warning vibes a more streetwise woman would have. She had never been so close to a man of his experience and background before. She had no yardstick to measure him by, and living with a husband who fell asleep most nights in front of the television, she was vulnerable. The persistent phone calls, the enormous chance she took in involving another policeman, and perhaps even writing the letter that Cross said he destroyed are all the actions of a woman in love. And in fairness, even Cross's jilted mistress said he believed himself in love with Anne and was devastated when his Royal duties ceased. But, sadly, not devastated enough to keep his and the Princess's secrets safe when a chequebook was waved in his direction.

It all ended when he told Anne he was involved with another woman. Whenever he tried to ring her again, she was never there.

After the policeman went from her life, Anne's marriage followed a path similar to that of many other marriages. She and her husband stayed together by staying apart. She flew to the less salubrious corners of the globe in her career as a caring Princess deeply involved with the Save the Children Fund, and he was busy with his many business activities, which constantly took him abroad or to other parts of Britain.

Neither ever seemed to stop for breath, as if they were both grasping the work ethic as a lifeline. He began giving riding exhibitions, mostly abroad. He worked sixteen hours a day. Once he opened his three-million-pound riding centre at the luxurious Gleneagles Hotel in Scotland, he was making sufficient money to be completely independent financially from the Royal family, and, more particularly, his wife.

He was boosting his farmer's income by lecturing at equestrian weekends around the world. He was also sponsored by Land Rover. And he has his own rooms at the Gleneagles Hotel, where he spent (and still spends) much of his time. Anne had been there only once, and that was to give the place a boost by declaring it open. There was an inside joke that said the nearest they got together was when they passed in airplanes going in opposite directions.

In 1988 Mark was away from Britain for four months at one stretch, which raised questions of whether the marriage was in trouble. From April 1988 to April 1989 Mark and Anne spent only forty days together with their children. But the telephone bills were high. They phoned each other often. There was an occasion when Mark was away abroad and Anne was trying to reach him. It was late, and he was not in his room. Anne asked the manager to find him. Her husband was indulging in a little gambling with some colleagues when the manager came into the room. 'Mr Phillips,' he said, 'your wife wants to know why you aren't in your room.'

Was she jealous? Was she wondering what he was up to? Her reaction was that of any wife, and Mark Phillips's reaction was that of any sensible husband. He went smartly up to his room to call her back.

She herself tells a pertinent story of meeting a member of the Newcastle Townswomen's Guild. The Princess asked the woman what had made her join the guild and was told, 'I had two young children and never got out of the house. Now I'm out with the guild four nights a week, and my husband doesn't like it!'

'They're all a bit like that,' replied the Princess, perhaps thinking of her husband's disappearances and, possibly, his discontent with hers.

Yet when the first cracks began to appear, when Anne was working in Britain and Mark was in residence in Gatcombe, she did make the effort to touch base each night, however late it might be. For reasons of appearance? To see the children? Or to be with her husband? Who knows.

A lot changed about the relationship after they married in 1973. He was the easygoing one who married a great horsewoman who was also a surly princess, disliked by the public. Today her role has changed. She is a star. Since her daughter Zara's birth in 1981, she has devoted her life to her charity work, and she believes deeply in the worth of what she is doing. And so does the nation. She was the first Royal to clock up five hundred engagements in a year. Since then it has grown to more than six hundred—and that takes up a lot of time.

Early on in the marriage she attempted to juggle the two roles. She said, 'You've got to put being a wife and mother first when the occasion demands. Whether I'm getting the balance right or not I'm not sure. It's too early to say. I've been a Princess all my life, but I've become a wife and mother comparatively recently.'

Just as her mother enjoyed being a navy wife, Anne's happiest days were when her husband was still in the army and she was an army wife at Sandhurst, the military academy. Mark had been sent there after the marriage as an instructor and was promoted to the rank of Captain. He and Anne moved into married quarters, which were rather grander than the average officer would have been given. They were to live in Oak Grove House, a five-bedroom residence that had been the home of Sandhurst's director of studies. It was a house that would normally have been leased only to a Colonel, but the circumstances were a little unusual. The only snag was that the new Captain had to pay the rent of £400 a year, which he felt excessive as his pay was well under £3,000.

It is understandable why the Princess looked back at those days with some nostalgia. She has always longed to be ordinary, and the time she spent at Oak Grove House is the nearest she is likely to get to being that. She asked that she be treated as the wife of a serving officer and that protocol should at least be partially forgotten. It took awhile for Mark's fellow officers and their wives to get over their shyness, but eventually Anne did become one of the crowd. Their friends of those days recall that her favourite place to sit was the floor and that she was perfectly content round the kitchen table with a Coca-Cola in her hand. But if she was invited to dinner, she had to be given a list of the other guests before she accepted, and the obligatory 'ma'am' remained as the order of the day. Protocol didn't entirely disappear.

It was a two-year posting to Sandhurst, and after it Captain Phillips had intended to return to his regiment in Northern Ireland as a Company Commander. He then discovered that it was out of the question for a member of the Royal family to serve in that particular sector of conflict. But unless he saw such service he would never achieve promotion. It was this that made him determined to leave the army and seek a new career, just as the Duke of Kent, another career soldier, had been forced to do for the exact same reason.

He became a farmer, a choice that could not have pleased Anne more. She likes country life. She says, 'To a great extent I've been brought up in it. If I'd been asked before I was married I would have said, "Farming is the way I would like to live more than any other." Now that we are farming I find it fun to be involved with it more closely.'

She was and still is very involved. There are chickens in the driveway—truly free range. 'My chickens have a liberal regime, and I do not look closely to see what they are eating,' she says, 'but their eggs are excellent.' Her house looks lived in rather than *Homes and Gardens* perfect. There are wellie boots and riding boots in the hall and riding macs and ordinary macs ready to grab. Her girl grooms wander in and out, while in other Royal homes the outside staff never goes inside. At Gatcombe there is no formality. Even the food served is simple. It's a family trait never to throw food away. 'Economy was bred in me,' said the Princess. And the family eats a lot of shepherd's pies made from leftovers. Unlike her brother Charles, Anne is no vegetarian. When British beef began to get a bad name in the summer of 1990, she stoutly defended the product and said that nothing would stop her eating it. Her family enjoys roasts and casseroles. Fancy cooking is out.

She has staff, of course, but they all wear casual clothes—usually trainers and jeans. A butler who came to fill in when her own was on holiday presented himself in the usual black-trousered rig. Anne looked at him doubtfully and said, 'Haven't you anything less formal? Our butler usually wears jeans.'

Perhaps the marriage might have worked better had Mark not been so determined to be independent of the family. He never came near to letting their tentacles close around him. From the beginning he made it clear that he did not wish to be Royal. He refused an honour from the Queen and has stuck to his rather quaint title of Captain (a rank so low in the military hierarchy that retired professional soldiers usually forget it). Mark's 'no' to a title was at the time much to Princess Anne's relief. She argued that since her husband would not be taking up any Royal duties, a title was unnecessary, and furthermore, she was anxious that any children she had should not be

Royal. The result is that Peter and Zara Phillips are the first grand-children of a reigning Monarch not to have a title of some kind. This bothers the Queen, and since Princess Anne has accepted the rank of Princess Royal—but only because she now feels she has earned it—the Queen may in time do something about the children's rank.

Once Anne was made the Princess Royal, she could no longer be known as Mrs. Mark Phillips. Until the spring of 1988, her correct form of address was Her Royal Highness, the Princess Anne, Mrs. Mark Phillips. There was a time when Anne thought the Mrs. was a bit of fun. Her mother did not agree and fifteen years after the marriage gave instructions that in the future her daughter must be known only as Her Royal Highness, the Princess Royal. It was fortuitous when you come to think about it.

So Anne is now the second lady in the land, one beneath the Queen and ranking above the Princess of Wales, whose rank comes only from marriage and is not in her own right. In the 350 years since the title was created by Charles I, there have been only six women who could call themselves Princess Royal. Queen Victoria gave her eldest daughter, Princess Vicky, the title when she was only eight weeks old, but usually it is an honour given to the eldest daughter once she has gained the affection of the nation. There are no financial rewards or any extra inheritance, nor does the title alter the line of succession. Becoming Princess Royal is a mark of the Monarch's and the nation's respect. Asked how she felt about receiving the title, Anne answered with her usual abruptness: 'Honoured.'

But the fact that she accepted this prestigious title does make it all the more odd that her children are plain Mister and Miss when Charles and Diana's and Fergie's offspring are princelings. The betting in Royal circles is that when the children are a little older the Queen will confer honorary titles on them by simply giving a title to their father, even though his marriage to Anne is at an end.

As in any broken marriage there were, naturally, happy times. Their home life was always so low-key that it warranted little attention. Therefore, what is not often remarked upon is that on the rare occasions when they were together, they were very much together, even if only as companions and working partners. At Gatcombe Park their lifestyle was that of gentleman farmer (which he is) and his wife. Though, unlike the average farmer's wife, Anne did not cook—except for scrambled eggs—or clean house, she did help on the land. Their togetherness came when they both wore old jeans to muck out the stables or get in the harvest. And the kids, Peter and Zara, were expected to help too. The whole family was hammering in posts and erecting fences when Mark persuaded Anne to open Gatcombe Park for a day for a horse trial. Anne was not keen about letting the public into her home, but she did it for him. That was in 1983, and Gatcombe has been open for that one day a year ever since. In September 1988, on Mark's fortieth birthday and only a year before they split, Anne arranged a huge surprise party for him with seventy guests, some from abroad, dining and dancing until dawn, followed by a shoot the next morning. She organized the whole thing herself and it was the surprise that she had wanted it to be. This was hardly the action of someone who hated her partner.

In fact, there never has been that bitterness and acrimony between them that so soured Princess Margaret's marriage. They could have gone on the way they were, living separate lives, but that is not Anne's style. She is too honest to live a lie, and she will not compromise over anything. For her a clean break was the only possibility.

When they were at home together they entertained friends, but again in a casual manner. So casual that on one embarrassing occasion Anne had asked Lady Leonora Lichfield, the divorced wife of Lord Lichfield, to dinner. Unaware of this, Mark asked Lord Lichfield. It was a rather uncomfortable evening, and it ended as uncomfortably as it had begun. Mark Phillips had invested in a new coffeepot—the type where the coffee is put into hot water and then pressed to the bottom of the jug with a plunger. He attacked the plunger with such gusto that everyone at the table was showered with coffee grounds. It does warm the heart to know that Royalty have their social disasters like the rest of us!

It is little mishaps like showering lords and ladies with coffee that gained Mark Phillips the nickname Fog, which infuriates him as it used to infuriate his wife. The nickname is unfair. It seems reasonable to suppose that the bright, intelligent Anne would not have chosen a thick husband. She called him Chief, or The Captain, and whatever their relationship was, she respected him, because, said a friend, 'he works jolly hard.' Nor can he possibly be that thick since he is successful at everything he touches. He has never trotted at Princess Anne's heels, he has always worked hard and made his own money, and he has become amazingly successful. It is estimated that he earns at least a quarter of a million pounds a year. It is just as well he created his own fortune in light of what has happened, though with his faintly distasteful payoff from the Queen, said to be around a million pounds, he came out of the marriage a wealthy man. In spite of his liking for money he is generous with it. The Christmas presents that Mark Phillips bought for the Royal family were not only more imaginatively chosen than anything they buy for themselves, they were also more expensive. Princess Anne once let it be known to Prince Charles that she would like a doormat for Christmas. And she got one. Mark would have been more likely to have bought her a beautiful piece of jewellery. And the money he spent, he made himself. Anne respects him for all this.

The press was certain that the marriage was over, which infuriated Anne. Yet she could hardly blame the media for the constant speculation about a breakup, even though the press is always eager to find some rift in a Royal marriage, as Charles and Diana know. But you cannot blame the newspapers for asking questions in the type of situation where Anne turns up for Princess Beatrice's christening, but Mark says he is sorry he cannot be there because of 'equestrian business.'

Nevertheless, all was reasonably calm until April 1989, when the nation became agog at the possibility that Anne had a lover. A mystery man handed the Royal correspondent of the *Sun* newspaper four letters written to Princess Anne over a period of eighteen months. They had been taken from the briefcase she kept either with her or at her private suite at Buckingham Palace. The letters, of course, were legally the copyright of the writer, as well as being stolen property. On these grounds the editor of the *Sun* promptly returned them to the Princess—having agreed not to divulge their contents. The newspaper then ran checks to discover whether or not the letters were genuine and, having found that they were, decided the story of their existence was too good to miss. Anne's private life became front-page news. Again.

Naturally, the media had an urgent question. Who was the romantic correspondent? He was said to be tall, dark and dashingly handsome and close to members of the Royal household, including the Queen. Word had it that one Sunday newspaper knew the name of the man. In an amazingly inept move, Buckingham Palace was panicked into shooting itself in the foot. When a reporter rang to check out one name, the Palace told him that no, he had got the wrong man. The reporter was astonished when a press officer then went on to read the details of a statement that the Palace was about to issue.

It said, 'The stolen letters were addressed to the Princess Royal by Commander Timothy Laurence, the Queen's Equerry.

'We have nothing to say about the contents of personal letters sent to Her Royal Highness by a friend, which were stolen and which are the subject of a police investigation.'

An Equerry is the male equivalent of a lady-in-waiting, and the job, always given to someone from the services, lasts for three years. Commander Laurence took over as Equerry in 1986 from Major Hugh Lindsay, who was later killed in the avalanche that narrowly missed Prince Charles at Klosters. Laurence had served on the Royal yacht, where the Queen first noticed him and liked his quiet confident manner. She also noted that he looked amazingly good in uniform — important for an Equerry, who is always on show a pace or two behind her. On ceremonial occasions a tall, good-looking man in a naval commander's dress uniform, complete with sword and medals, looks a good deal more impressive than a chap in a lounge suit. Equerries, therefore, are romantic figures, as Princess Margaret had found long before. And this particular Equerry was also a hero. At twenty-seven he had been mentioned in dispatches for gallantry in the fight against the IRA to stop the supply of terrorist arms to Britain.

Laurence was commanding his own vessel, HMS *Cygnet*, when the Queen sent for him to be her new Equerry. Hugh Lindsay had been Army. It was the Navy's turn for the job, and the Commander became part of the Royal household. His duties were mainly to look impressive, open doors for the Queen, wrap a blanket around her knees if she appeared a touch chilly, and keep tabs on all the information concerning the engagement they were attending. An odd position for a man trained for war, but one that leads to an honour from the Monarch, a higher rank on returning to service duties and a great deal of prestige.

He was only thirty-four, five years younger than the Princess, when the existence of the letters became public and his posting to Royal service had just a few months to go. In the time he had spent with the Queen he had become a Royal favourite, generating the same kind of affection that Peter Townsend once did. Like Townsend, he was very much part of the family, lunching with Princess Diana when her husband was away, escorting Princess Anne at Ascot when Mark Phillips did not appear, and joining the Queen's party for holidays.

The stealing of the letters caused a great deal of anger and embarrassment. Mark was beside himself, since neither Princess Anne nor the Palace had bothered to tell him of the theft or that a statement was to be made. It was thoughtless and rude but par for the course for Anne and, alas, for the Royal family. The couple had already agreed to separate before the existence of the letters was known. Lawyers were working on the details, and, as ever in this kind of situation, Mark's feelings did not rate high in the Royal family's priorities but took second place to finding out who the thief was. The finger of suspicion pointed at a member of the staff who had perhaps felt the sharp end of Anne's tongue once too often. The employee, who had already resigned, was working out notice when the theft of the letters was discovered. The accusation was vehemently denied, and since the Palace had already stated that there would never be a prosecution for fear of further embarrassment, that was really the end of that. The search, however, went on. The police fingerprinted one hundred members of the staff at Gatcombe and Buckingham Palace—as well as some on the staff of the *Sun* newspaper—but were unable to trace six sets of prints that were among many found on the letters. The case was finally dropped.

Royal watchers believed that Commander Laurence would have to resign. Not a bit of it. He did discreetly disappear for a day or two but was publicly seen back on duty by May 9. On that same day Anne permitted a photographer to take a picture of her riding with Mark and her two children. It was a show of solidarity, as if the Princess were saying, 'My marriage is fine.'

But the Equerry had not vanished from the picture. In August 1989, when the Royals were on their way to Balmoral for their summer holidays, Commander Tim Laurence was spotted again—back in favour and very much a member of the ten-day Scottish cruise on the Royal yacht *Britannia*. He was at the Queen's side when they visited the Queen Mother's Castle of Mey in the north of Scotland, and the following day he was laughing and joking with Fergie when she took a group of friends for a walk along the beach. The dark-haired officer rolled up his trousers and waded into the sea to help bring baby Beatrice ashore from the *Britannia*. Then the Commander joined the Queen, Prince Philip, Charles, Andrew, and Fergie for a barbecue at an old wartime bunker on the beach at Lossiemouth, Morayshire. The weather was appalling, but bad weather has never stopped a Royal picnic.

The press was beside itself with excitement, then an aide said primly, 'The Queen has always valued the Commander's services. She is very glad to have him with her on the cruise.' Indeed. But, as the newspapers said, it was significant how much time he was spending with the Royals, since they were supposed to be on a private holiday.

Once at Balmoral he picknicked with Anne on the moors and went out with the guns. Amazingly, on August 23 it was announced that the Queen had honoured him with the Royal Victorian Order—an honour that is the Sovereign's personal gift. It was given for his three years of service as her Equerry, and she pinned the medal on him on the last day of his Royal duties before he returned to normal naval service.

While it is standard for an Equerry to be given the RVO—they always are at the end of their Royal duties—the Royal family must have known that this presentation, so soon after it was known that he was the author of the letters, would cause raised eyebrows. The Queen's gesture made it clear that the Commander had been taken to the bosom of the family and that the young man had the Queen's complete approval, even if he had been writing letters to her married daughter.

And so Timothy Laurence was released for normal duties. In his place came another glamorous figure, this time from the Royal Air Force. It was time to say good-bye.

But was it? The question is, will Laurence see Anne again? He may still be invited to join the family occasionally, as the late Hugh Lindsay was, but opportunities will be limited since he will be commanding his own ship. The romance, if there ever was one, could fizzle out from lack of contact unless the Queen continues to encourage it by inviting the young man to join more family gatherings.

Not unnaturally Princess Anne does have men in her life, but her discretion is such that even a vigilant press is hard put to pin anything on her. The occasional photograph of her with a male companion has surfaced—one in particular, taken in Germany excited some interest. But the man proved impossible to identify. And it certainly was not Timothy Laurence.

However, while Captain Phillips boiled with rage over the letters, the wind was abruptly taken from his sails. At this most unfortunate moment, his name was linked with that of Pamella Bordes, an exotic Indian call girl with a gift for finding herself gentlemen friends in high places. When Mark's name cropped up in her shocking memoirs, the Palace agreed that it was true she had met him and that she had been to one of his equestrian weekends at Gleneagles, Scotland. She had also stayed in a cottage on the Gatcombe estate with one of Mark's friends while Princess Anne was away. The call girl said a lot more went on than that. But she would, wouldn't she? She was telling, and selling, her life story.

Whether or not she was telling the truth, Mark Phillips was, like his wife, finding himself in the position of having to explain something extremely embarrassing. Yet neither publicly showed any signs of anxiety. Anne went about her duties with a smile. Mark went on making money.

'Their marriage appears rather strange,' said Mark's father, Major Peter Phillips, in the middle of all the fuss. 'It's certainly not what I would want from marriage or other people would expect, but it is what they have chosen. But quite honestly the Queen and Prince Philip's life is different from the lives of normal individuals. If people are Royal they do not necessarily spend lots of time together. It is inevitable.'

Major Phillips, an elderly English gentleman, would have been telling the truth as he saw it. Indeed, when the news broke that the marriage was over, he was visibly distressed. He was fond of his daughter-in-law, and he and Anne got on well. He may also have felt that he had been misled into distorting the truth, since the lawyers were already hard at work on the financial settlement at just the time he had been attempting to pour oil on troubled waters.

Trying to redeem the situation, he said when the Palace issued the statement ending the marriage, 'They didn't make the decision to separate all that long ago. It wasn't at Mark's instigation—it was at

172

Princess Anne's. It is amicable, though. Her relationship with Commander Laurence played no small part in all this. They have both agonized over this decision and talked it over with the Queen. She is very upset, as you can imagine, but she helped make the arrangements for their future apart.'

Again, it was a brilliant move on the part of the Palace to let Major Phillips talk to the press. No doubt he was advised to do so. It was not an action that he would have taken on his own initiative. And the obvious distress of this recently widowed, charming gentleman helped create a wave of instant sympathy for the couple. His son was to live on Aston Farm, a property on the Gatcombe Estate for which he would pay the Queen a peppercorn rent, since the property belonged to her. The children were both to go off to boarding school, and Anne would be sole mistress of Gatcombe. Everything was neatly arranged, and no doubt in a couple of years' time—as happened in the case of the Snowdons—there will be a nice, quiet tidy divorce to wrap up the matter.

Why did the marriage go wrong? Was it that Mark could not cope with the stifling weight of the family? If that is the case, Diana will be sympathizing with him. She had the same problem. But the fault no doubt lies in themselves. As much as she strives to be ordinary, Anne is not. She is Royal through to the bone. She is a good, decent woman with courage and a sense of duty, but she is also a chip off the old block—her often rude and arrogant father. If she is in one of her moods, she doesn't give many civil answers. When asked the simple question 'How does it feel to be an aunt?' just after Prince William was born, she snapped, 'That's my business.' It was the *Washington Post* that branded her Princess Sourpuss, and she didn't make herself too popular when she told the American people that their national emblem of the bald eagle was a bad choice. It is impossible to blend being ordinary along with arrogance. The two don't mix, and arrogance, like cream (or scum), always comes to the top. At the beginning Mark was strong enough to quell her tempers. He stopped bothering long ago. He became bored with her prickliness.

In the end he irritated her. She has always been impatient with him, but then she is not difficult to annoy. For him the discovery of love letters written to her by the Queen's Equerry was the last straw. He'd had enough public humiliation. The time had come to say good-bye. And there wasn't a soul in the land who did not wish him well. Public sympathy was massively on his side.

But the Monarchy now must live with the fact that both the Queen's sister and daughter have broken marriages. The old school of thinking in Britain believes that Anne certainly, as the Monarch's daughter, should have stuck it out, which her husband was willing to do. But the Queen who can be so firm with others can deny her sister and daughter nothing. They were both allowed to part from their husbands, even though the Queen personally abhors divorce. She has since she was a young girl. One morning her governess found her depressed over newspaper reports of the divorce of an acquaintance of hers of whose children she was very fond.

'Why do people do it?' she asked. 'How can they break up a home when there are children to consider?' Now the Queen certainly cannot afford to have any more marriages come unstuck while she is still on the throne, and she cannot enjoy hearing the periodic talk of breakup surrounding Charles and Diana. If this gossip proved to be true and Charles and Diana parted, it would indeed be a severe blow to the Monarchy.

Certainly there was something seriously wrong two years ago, which led the press to speculate fulsomely whether or not divorce was in the cards.

Well, it made for some great headlines, but divorce was never a real possibility for a variety of reasons—the strongest being that it would be totally contrary to Prince Charles's temperament. He has been programmed from birth to appreciate that for him, marriage is forever. Diana, of course, was the joker in the pack. Since she came from a broken home herself, with a mother who was known as 'a bolter', no one was sure which way Diana would jump if the marriage became any more strained. But people had forgotten that Diana knew all too well the pain of a divorce for the children and that as a girl she had sworn that for her marriage would also be forever. Those who knew her well were certain she was unlikely to put her own children through the same misery she had suffered when her mother ran off with another man.

Had the unthinkable happened, Diana would have been the loser. Divorce would affect her husband considerably less than it would her. Even if Diana had bolted, Charles would not lose his inheritance—

though once King, and bearing in mind the Church's attitude toward divorce, he would have had a problem in retaining credibility as the Defender of the Faith and the Head of the Church of England. However, regardless of the views of the clergy, Charles, like his ancestor, the twice-divorced Henry VIII, could divorce in the normal way. It would cause no alteration to his status as heir to the throne. Once King he would not even need special permission from Parliament. All he would need would be a good lawyer. Henry VIII disposed of one of his divorce problems by beheading the lady. Happily for Diana, Charles would not have the same option.

But the complications would be considerable. Should Charles remarry, what would be the position of the children of his second wife, or 'the second bed' as genealogists call it? There is no precedent in either British law or tradition to cover it. A Diana bent on divorce might be putting her own children's inheritance in jeopardy.

Indeed, the one to suffer most would be Diana if she ever decided to break free. Since she dreads the day when she takes over the role, never becoming Queen would be unlikely to trouble her too much. She would be forced to relinquish the title of Princess of Wales but would remain a Princess. Once an HRH, always an HRH. It is a style of address that cannot be taken away (a fact that must have cheered Princess Michael of Kent on the occasions when her marriage has appeared rocky). It was also the practical reason, as opposed to the emotional reason, why the American Duchess of Windsor was never made an HRH after the King abdicated and married her. Quite apart from the new Queen Elizabeth's virulent dislike of the twice-divorced woman who caused her brother-in-law to abdicate from the British throne, the Establishment of the day did not feel that this could possibly be a secure marriage. The speculation was that when the ex-King realized 'what sort of woman she was' the marriage would soon be over. Had she been made an HRH she could have continued to divorce and remarry while retaining her title and thereby bring the Crown ridicule and contempt. As it happened, the Establishment was wrong. The marriage survived.

So though Diana would remain a Princess, she would lose something much more important to her than any title if she ever divorced Charles. Unquestionably, she would forfeit the custody of her children. Wills and Harry would be quietly removed from her. It would be unthinkable that she, as a divorced woman, should have care and control of the second and third in line to the throne. And since her children are the most important thing in her life—'coming home to the children is the best part of the day'—in no circumstances would she do anything to lose them.

Perhaps less important, but still significant, is that her financial circumstances would change very much for the worse. Any ordinary woman divorcing in Britain could expect to receive between a third and a half of the family estate. There would be no possibility whatsoever of this in Diana's case, even if she employed the legendary American lawyer Marvin Mitchelson to fight her divorce battle. Mr. Mitchelson would be hampered by not knowing exactly what the family estate consists of, since all Royal financial facts are a closely guarded secret. The best Diana could hope for would be a generous allowance (not a lump sum, since this would mean she was no longer dependent on the family). And a condition of the divorce and continuation of the allowance would be that she live abroad, as far away from England as possible, so as to cause no one any embarrassment.

The truth is that there is little chance that Diana would ever seriously want to break with her husband. As the Princess of Wales, she is fêted, loved and recognized as a worldwide superstar. It is fair to say that, with the possible exception of Marilyn Monroe, she is this century's biggest female attraction. Her face has launched a billion magazine covers, and every word printed about her commands a vast audience. Shy Di has become the most famous woman in the world. She also has all the money she could possibly need. But more important than the fame and the material possessions is that she has proved herself an extremely able Princess of Wales. She has matured into a likeable and deservedly loved young woman, doing serious and significant work. The girl who wasn't much good at school has brilliantly managed to turn being a Princess into a satisfying career for herself.

Why on earth would she want to lose all that? We can safely assume therefore that, though the marriage may not be entirely made in heaven, divorce is unthinkable.

In spite of the Royal attitude toward divorce, this unpleasant issue seems to have plagued the Queen throughout the last two decades, both directly and indirectly. Most of the latest crop of young Royals seem to be married into divorced families. Princess Margaret set the ball rolling when she married Antony Armstrong-Jones, whose father divorced twice and married three times; his mother married twice.

What with the divorced parents of Diana, Fergie and the Duchess of Gloucester, the Royal family has become quite blasé about who sits next to whom at Royal weddings. Parents are put at the front, and wife or husband number two (or three) simply gets shunted to the back of the congregation. But at least they get asked.

Which is more than the Earl of Harewood was to Princess Anne's wedding or the Duke of Windsor's funeral. Neither he nor his second wife received an invitation to either. Not being an HRH, strictly speaking the Earl is not Royal, but he is the Queen's cousin and he has a place of succession to the throne. At the time of his divorce from the first Countess in 1967, he was eighteenth in line. His mother was King George VI's sister, Mary, the Princess Royal who married Henry Viscount Lascelles, the sixth Earl of Harewood.

In the late forties Harewood, who is a classical music buff, fell in love with Marion Stein, the pianist daughter of Erwin Stein, a World War II Jewish refugee. Stein was one of the most respected musicologists in the world, and when he fled to Britain, he and his wife, Sophie, and Marion were given shelter at the flat of Britain's greatest living composer, Benjamin Britten. Marion Stein was an extraordinarily beautiful girl, and when Harewood met her he was instantly attracted. Also in love with her was the late Ronald Duncan, a talented poet and author who wrote most of the librettos for Britten's operas and tone poems.

Marion showed little interest in Duncan and, indeed, not a great deal in Harewood. Duncan was convinced that her young heart was set on Britten. The poet, a short, powerful man with a large head and a great shock of dark hair, observed her longingly but felt he had no chance because she was deeply in love with the composer. This was an unfortunate state of affairs since Britten was totally disinterested in women. And besides, his lifelong partner, the opera singer Peter Pears, was very much on the scene, and he could be very jealous.

Marion Stein was young for her age, but one must remember that in the forties homosexuality was not a conversational subject. Most well-brought up young people knew nothing about it. According to Duncan, Marion had absolutely no idea that Britten and Pears were lovers and had been for many years.

Harewood began courting her. Duncan says she was reluctant, but the Earl was persistent. He took her to meet Queen Mary, who approved and declared her a charming girl. All Harewood had to do was to persuade Marion to marry him and then get the King's permission to marry a German-Jewish refugee. Perhaps for Marion the idea of becoming a Countess was irresistible. Perhaps she learned of Britten's real sexual predilections, perhaps she learned to love George Harewood, but Marion Stein eventually accepted his proposal, and the King, urged by Queen Mary, gave his permission for the marriage. They married in 1949 in the presence of the entire Royal family. As they left after the ceremony, Winston Churchill is reputed to have said audibly, 'It's a pity old Harewood's gone down the Steinway.'

The marriage lasted until 1965, when, three children later, the couple began to live apart. According to friends the ex-Miss Stein had become insufferably grand in her behaviour—so much so that the Queen said of the Countess, 'Marion is the only woman I know who can make me feel like the cook!'

Living apart was acceptable in Royal circles, but the situation became uncomfortable when in 1959 Harewood met Patricia Tuckwell, an Australian fashion model. They found themselves sitting next to each other on a plane, and they chatted. They had a lot in common. Patricia's brother, Barry Tuckwell, the French horn virtuoso, was well known to Harewood. She was an extremely good-looking brunette, known as Bambi because of her dark doe eyes. She had been divorced by her photographer husband, Athol Schmith, ten years previously on the grounds of desertion. Her husband had raised their sixteen-year-old son.

She and Harewood continued to meet after the plane journey was over, and when he eventually applied for a divorce it was revealed that she was the mother of his two-and-a-half-year-old son.

The Queen, who most certainly did not approve of all this, was not keen to grant the divorce, but Harold Wilson, her Prime Minister at the time, persuaded her that it was the best thing to do. George Harewood was granted a decree nisi from his Countess—who eventually went on to marry Jeremy Thorpe, the liberal MP the Establishment turned down as Antony Armstrong-Jones's best man. Harewood immediately married Bambi Tuckwell with the Queen's permission, but the price he had to pay was being struck from the Queen's visiting list. Not a wedding invitation, even a funeral invitation, reached the new Countess and her husband.

It took ten years before he was back in favour, and he and his wife went to her first Royal occasion, the Silver Jubilee celebrations, in 1977. Was the change of heart due to the Queen's general good will during the celebration of twenty-five years of her reign, or was it that divorce had become so much a part of modern life that the Queen decided there was no point in leaving the Harewoods out in the cold any longer?

The decision was taken just in time. Only a year later Princess Margaret's name was read aloud in the divorce courts. Furthermore, it would have been truly hypocritical to continue Harewood's banishment once Prince Michael of Kent asked for permission to marry the divorced Mrs. Tom Trowbridge and was told that he could.

Yet divorce is not new in Royal circles. Prince Albert, the husband of Queen Victoria, was a victim of Royal divorce even in those long-ago days. His much-loved mother, the Duchess of Saxe-Coburg-Gotha, a lively and beautiful woman, left him when he was five years old. She created a scandal at the German court by her 'closeness', to put it delicately, with one of the Court chamberlains. Eventually there was a separation from Albert's father, who, it must be said, was something of a lady's man himself. The separation was followed by divorce. Cut from the Royal circle and banished to Paris, Albert's mother died, a sad and lonely woman, in 1831.

One of Albert and Victoria's daughters, Louise, was involved in a situation where a marriage would have been better ended but could not be, since Louise was a Royal princess.

Louise was the only one of Queen Victoria's children to completely escape the matriarchal ties of her mother and the Royal cage. Like the present Lady Helen Windsor, the Duke of Kent's daughter, she became an art student at the National Art Training School, now the Royal College of Art, which Prince Albert founded.

Queen Victoria bound her children, particularly her daughters, to her with ties of filial affection and duty. Louise, the only one permitted a life before marriage, even tried to get permission to live in a studio, like any ordinary art student. In this she failed. Queen Victoria considered the suggestion going far too far. Louise remained under the

179

Royal roof, and yet the girl was a talented sculptor and painter. Her statue of her mother, overlooking the Broad Walk in London's Kensington Gardens, still stands as confirmation.

When she was twenty-two Louise fell in love with Lord Lorne, the eldest son of the Duke of Argyll and an MP. In 1871 she married him, and Parliament, reluctantly, voted her a dowry of £30,000—a fortune in those days. Victoria, who had lost most of her daughters to foreign princes, was delighted that Louise was marrying into British aristocracy and would be settling in England. This was not to be. At first Louise lived in Scotland, and then Lord Lorne was made Governor General of Canada. It was there that the marriage went adrift. Louise left her husband in Canada and returned to Europe. She spent some time travelling around the Continent, visiting various relatives, and then made her home in England. From this time onwards the couple lived apart most of the time.

Nothing much had changed by 1937. King George V was dead, his widow, Queen Mary, lived on, and their eldest son, Edward, Prince of Wales, was proclaimed King. Proclaimed, but never crowned. A little matter of a twice-divorced woman got in the way. Wallis Simpson completely upset the course of English history. The King fell deeply in love with her, and their affair began while the lady was still married to her second husband, Ernest Simpson. Whether Mrs. Simpson fell in love with Prince Edward or whether the glittering prospect of becoming consort to the King of England beckoned, we shall never know, though Lady Monckton, the widow of Walter Monckton, the barrister who represented Windsor at the time of the abdication, was convinced that Wallis never loved him.

Lady Monckton, who had been a close friend of Edward VIII's before he gave up the throne, believed that the Duchess merely wanted to be Queen.

'She was too American to realize that could never have been possible,' she told journalist Caroline Blackwood, who in 1989 had the initiative to interview the few remaining ancient ladies who once were friends of King Edward VIII. Lady Monckton added, 'The Windsors may have been the romance of the century, but they certainly never had the love story of the century.'

Edward, like his uncle, Prince Eddy (who so conveniently died of pneumonia), was also a man of great charm but little substance and lacking in judgment. Pneumonia saved the British monarchy from one Prince Edward. This time Mrs. Simpson was to do the job.

Romantics say that the King gave up his throne for love. More likely the truth is that Edward VIII never could bring himself to believe that he would not get his own way. He saw himself on the throne with the needle-thin and needle-sharp Wallis at his side as his morganatic bride. It was not to be. He married Wallis, who became a Duchess but never an HRH, and neither of them was ever to live in England again. Royalty closed ranks and cut him from their privileged circle. He was never forgiven.

— 7 —

Royal Mother Love

'B ABIES,' as Princess Anne used to say, 'are an occupational hazard of being a wife.'

They are certainly an occupational hazard of being a Royal wife. The dynasty must go on, and for a woman who marries into the family, and certainly one born into it, not to have at least two children (the heir and a spare) is unthinkable. The night that Queen Elizabeth I heard that her rival, Mary Queen of Scots, had given birth to the son who became James I of England, the virgin Queen was so depressed that 'all merriment was laid aside.' One of her courtiers, Sir James Melville, recorded, 'The Queen sat down with her hand upon her haffett [cheek] and bursting out to some of her ladies how that the Queen of Scotland was lighter of a fair son, and that she was but of barren stock.'

And, of course, for the Scottish queen to have produced a son was an even bigger blow. When Queen Victoria's second child proved to be a much-longed-for heir, those around the bed let out a cry of joy. 'Oh, Madam, it is a fine boy.'

The exhausted Queen looked up from her pillows and said reprovingly, 'A fine prince.'

Victoria possessed the Hanoverian robust appetite for sex and did more than her duty to the dynasty with a brood of nine (there wasn't much in the way of birth control in those days!). But she disliked having babies. According to her, childbirth was 'a great inconvenience to us and particularly to the country, independent of the hardship and inconvenience to myself.' Victoria was completely unsentimental about both her own children and her grandchildren. 'I

182

fear the seventh granddaughter and the fourteenth grandchild becomes a very uninteresting thing,' she said sourly, 'for it seems to me to go on like the rabbits in Windsor Park.'

The present Queen's grandmother, Queen Mary, also loathed the whole business of childbearing, so much so that she said, 'Having babies is highly distasteful to me, though once they are there they are very nice,' sentiments that might be echoed by Princess Diana. For all she loves her children it appears she feels the same way. She grumbled that she 'never felt well from day one' throughout her pregnancies and that 'nobody told me it was going to be like this.' Queen Victoria complained that 'men never think, at least seldom think, what a hard task it is for us women to go through.' Diana is often heard to say that if men had the babies there would be only one in each family. But, whatever her feelings about pregnancy, like Queen Mary, Diana concedes, 'It's all worth it in the end.'

Royal mothers never bring up their own children. They are too busy being Royal. Motherhood is both essential and incidental to their role, and once they have done their duty and secured the line, they have no choice but to work if they are members of the Royal firm. Royal women are by no means similar in their attitude to motherhood. Having to work suited Princess Anne. She once said, rather defensively, 'I still think there are a lot of people who consider that women who go straight out to work immediately after having children verge on the irresponsible. In a perfect world they may be right, considering the long-term development of the child, but it doesn't necessarily help to do something to which you are temperamentally unsuited.'

Anne seemed to be implying that she was not suited for motherhood. She certainly disliked being pregnant, mainly because it stopped her riding. The Queen, while her daughter was pregnant with her first grandchild, had joked, 'We might well expect it to have four feet.' Others, less kind, had suggested that Anne might bring forth a centaur. Happily, Peter Phillips proved to be a perfectly normal, healthy, six-pound baby when he was born on November 15, 1977. The Princess was given an epidural, and Mark Phillips stayed by her side. After it was all over she said, 'Three-day eventing at Burghley is a doddle compared to this.' It just so happened that on the day of Peter's birth the Queen was giving an investiture at Buckingham Palace. She arrived ten minutes late, apologized, and, wreathed in smiles, said to the eight hundred people present: 'I have just had a message from the hospital. My daughter has given birth to a son and I am now a grandmother.'

A great cheer went up.

Anne has always put her work before both husband and children. There are those in the family who put their husbands before the children—as the Queen did and the Duchess of York does. Others, including Princess Margaret, put the children first. For all her personal problems and temperamental behaviour, Princess Margaret was a very good mother indeed. Even though she had a wonderful nanny, if David or Sarah cried in the night it was Margaret who climbed out of bed to comfort them. She breast-fed both babies and changed nappies between official engagements. Now the children are grown up, she has become an indulgent mother but has gracefully let her children go from her life. Quite a sacrifice. Margaret is often lonely, but she does not cling to Sarah or David; therefore they frequently take the trouble to call in to see her. They come because they want to and not because they feel obliged.

Lord Linley and Lady Sarah are favourites of the Queen. She is particularly close to Sarah; the Queen sees her as a second daughter and very much took the girl under her wing in the bad days of Margaret's marriage. The family is proud of the two children's achievements. They are charming and well-liked young people who are doing something positive with their lives, a freedom that would have been denied them had they been Royal. Margaret says firmly, 'My children are not Royal. They just happen to have the Queen for an aunt.'

Princess Michael longed to have children and says that they are the most important thing in her life. She contends her first husband didn't want babies, so she didn't waste a lot of time once she became a wife for the second time. Her first baby, Lord Frederick Windsor, was born in April 1979, just nine months and five days after her marriage to Prince Michael. His little sister, Lady Gabriella, joined the family in, again, April, two years later. This was by design. Marie-Christine discovered that April was the ideal time to have a baby. 'You can have the pram outside and the fresh air on that child for the whole spring, the whole summer, and the whole autumn,' she explained. 'That was why my second child was also born in April. I was as careful about it as

Sealed with a kiss: the Prince and Princess of Wales after their
St. Paul's Cathedral wedding in July, 1981

Happier days: Anne and Mark celebrating their
fifteenth wedding anniversary

Princess Anne with Detective Peter Cross. They became
too close and he was sacked as her bodyguard

Fergie's old flame, Paddy McNally, a wealthy
businessman involved in motor racing, seen with her
at a Silverstone Grand Prix

Princess Anne at Ascot in June 1987. On her left [black top hat]
is Commander Timothy Laurence

The Queen and Prince Philip relaxing at home
with one of their many dogs

Sandringham House. The most intimate and homely of the Queen's
residences, bequeathed to her by her father

Balmoral Castle. Like Sandringham, it belongs to the Queen

Prince and Princess Michael of Kent share a quiet,
close moment in the countryside in September 1984

Holiday snap: Princes William and Harry with the Princess of Wales
in Majorca in 1987

Charles and Diana out for an afternoon bicycle ride with William
and Harry in January 1989

The Queen Mother celebrating her eighty-ninth birthday in
1989 with the Queen and other members of the Royal family

Sarah, Duchess of York, with baby Beatrice in Scotland, April 1989

I could be so that both my children could have this benefit.'

Frederick and Ella are the best behaved of the new brood of young Royals because their mother would not have it any other way. She will not tolerate naughty children. She says and means, 'Mother's word is law.' Any misdemeanour brings punishment. Princess Michael punishes by deprivation. If Ella is naughty, her favourite toy is firmly put back in the toy cupboard. If Frederick, who is mad about football, is disobedient, he is not allowed to watch the football match on television or, alternatively, the plug comes out on his computer games. Princess Michael's theory is that all children have something that they are mad about, and that is the thing they must be deprived of when they behave badly. She does not believe in shouting or slapping, except when the children are rude. 'Rudeness,' she has said, 'gets a slap. There are only three things you can give your children after loving them as all children should be loved and that is discipline, good manners, and a good education.'

She also believes that there are aspects of bringing up baby—like nappy changing and making bottles—that are best left to a trained nanny. When they were little her offspring were wont to drive her mad if she was left alone with them for too long. Her former private secretary, John Barratt, recalled that she found it difficult to cope if the children didn't behave impeccably. 'She told me they got on her nerves,' said Barratt. 'She was always in a mess when there wasn't a nanny around and was often near to tears. I used to go and sit with the kids for a couple of hours to give her a break. She loves the idea of having children, but it has got to be in the context of someone helping to take care of them.'

Perhaps in self-defence, Princess Michael has a gift for training staff to her methods, and she turned one young girl into a first-class nanny. Unfortunately for her, the girl was promptly poached by Marie-Christine's neighbours, the Prince and Princess of Wales. As Charles and Diana had already pinched her butler, the Princess has every right to be a bit cross. But she kept on smiling and professed herself flattered that they should want her staff.

In time she found herself a new nanny, but nannies go on holidays. When hers went off for her annual break in the summer of 1988, the Princess went about solving the problem of staff shortages in a rather unusual way. A member of her office approached a British army woman, Captain Cheryl Atcheson, and asked if she would look after Frederick and Gabriella while their regular nanny was away. Captain Atcheson was serving with the Army Eduation Corps at the time. An ex-teacher, she had taught Lord Frederick at his Berkshire school before joining the army. She said she would see what she could do about this strange request and, astonishingly, obtained permission from her commanding officer to take over the nursery at Nether Lypiatt Manor on a temporary basis while still on army pay. When questions arose about this novel arrangement, Princess Michael, perhaps in a state of panic at all being revealed, referred inquiries on the subject to the Ministry of Defence, which was hard pressed to know exactly what to say. It is possible the Princess thought borrowing a nanny from the army a perfectly reasonable thing to do since both Prince Philip and Prince Charles have army batmen (paid for by the army) on their staffs. She would argue, therefore, why shouldn't she have an army nanny? The Duchess of Kent, Controller Commandant of the Women's Royal Army Corps, was said to be furious.

Some of Princess Michael's staff problems come about because she is not easy to work for. John Barratt remembers a relief nanny who was well liked by the children, but Princess Michael did not approve of the girl. She said to Barratt, 'You really have to talk to the nursery. I went in this morning and the nanny didn't curtsey to me.'

Barratt could not believe his ears. 'You must be joking!' he said. 'No I am not,' said Princess Michael. 'I wish you to instruct all the staff on the protocol.'

It is this *folie de grandeur* that causes her staff problems.

As in many a home where the mother has a career, a good nanny is very much a crown jewel in Royal circles. Since space and money are usually no object and there is considerable glory in working for an HRH, the Royal family doesn't normally have much trouble in finding nannies. Their children never question the system, accepting it as the norm. Prince Charles at age five once asked a small boy if the woman he was standing with was his nanny. She was the lad's mother, which quite surprised the little Prince.

Charles's great-granny, Queen Mary, relied entirely on nannies. Motherhood was simply not her forte; even her own babies held little appeal. When her eldest son was just a few months old she cheerfully went off on holiday to St. Moritz, dumping him in the care of a friend.

Sadly, she seemed incapable of showing her children any affection at all. On the rare occasions when she did see her children, they were hastily handed back to the nanny if they cried. Nor was she particularly good at picking nannies. The first one she hired was neurotic. Neither Mary nor her husband, King George V, had noticed that the woman was unfit for the job. She so doted on the eldest boy, the future Duke of Windsor, that she would pinch him to make him cry when in his parents' presence. His mother would then hastily have him taken back to the nursery, where she couldn't hear the screams. The nanny was so disinterested in the second son, who was to become King George VI, that she ruined his digestion by not feeding him properly. The children's parents were unaware of what was happening until the nanny had a nervous breakdown and was, happily, removed from all their lives.

As is often the case, Queen Mary proved to be a much better grandmother than mother. Princess Alexandra was once complimented on her perfect carriage. She smiled and said, 'You forget Queen Mary was my grandmother.' The present Queen and her sister were a little afraid of the old Queen when they were young, but Mary had their interests at heart. It was she who insisted that Elizabeth's education be broadened, particularly once her father became King. Queen Mary's intervention was necessary. All Queen Elizabeth wanted for her children was that they should be happy. Their governess, Crawfie, once said despairingly, 'She was not over-concerned with the higher education of her two daughters.' Elizabeth's recipe for bringing up her daughters was 'to spend as long as possible in the open air, to enjoy the full pleasures of the country, to be able to dance and draw and appreciate music, to acquire good manners and perfect deportment and to cultivate all the distinctly feminine graces.'

All very well for a life as a society belle, but her daughter was heir to the throne. The future Queen needed a great deal more in the way of education than social graces, and it was Queen Mary who made sure that Elizabeth learned languages, the constitutional history of her country, and how Britain and the Empire were run.

Queen Mary might not have cared for motherhood, but being a grandmother was quite a different matter. She adored being a grandma and, indeed, a great-grandma. She had mellowed, of course (not that she ever was as fierce as she looked). For some unknown reason, when

Princess Anne was little she would never curtsey to 'Gran-gran' as she called the dowager Queen; she just stood around shuffling her feet. Mary, usually a stickler for protocol, let her great-granddaughter get away with it.

The idea of grandchildren pleased Mary. When she heard that her daughter-in-law, Princess Alice of Gloucester, was pregnant for the first time, she wrote, saying, 'I was so thrilled and delighted at your good news this morning that I nearly fell off my dressing-table stool in my excitement!' Later she wrote in typical Royal, stingy fashion, 'Fortnum and Mason are so expensive that I think you had better go elsewhere for the cradle.' She concerned herself about anything to do with her grandchildren. When she heard that William of Gloucester was walking early, she wrote to Princess Alice, saying, 'So William is walking already. Much too soon. Don't let him get bandy.' Since bowleggedness runs in the Royal family, her note was less surprising than it sounds. King George VI had a miserable childhood with painful braces on his legs to straighten them, and as a little boy Prince Charles had to wear special shoes. Queen Mary worried a great deal about all her grandchildren and was forever putting her oar in about what should or shouldn't be done (a mother-in-law habit that wasn't always appreciated), and yet even as mother of the heir she had been quite indifferent to her own brood of six when they were young.

Indifference to children is not the way of the present Princess of Wales. If only she had the time Diana would be quite content to get rid of nanny forever and bring up the children herself. In her passionate feelings toward her children she is a reincarnation of 'Mother-dear,' Queen Alexandra's children's name for their mother. Alexandra's idea of bliss was to be able to 'run to the nursery, put on her flannel apron, wash her children and see them asleep in their little beds.' Her children, like Diana's, were unruly and noisy, but fun-loving and affectionate. They ran wild, encouraged by a mother who could never bring herself to permit them to be disciplined. Nor was she concerned about their education, since as a girl she had had so little herself, and lack of it had hardly held her back—any more than the same lack has held back Princess Diana. Queen Victoria was certainly not amused by Alexandra's offspring. 'They are such ill-bred, ill-trained children,' she said sniffily, 'that I cannot fancy them at all.'

One can appreciate her point. Alexandra's brood once managed to get a pony up into their mother's living room at Sandringham. All Alexandra said was that she was once as bad herself. And she did do the most extraordinary things for a Princess of Victorian times. Every year she gave a wonderful Christmas party for her children and their friends. One year the entertainment was decidedly different. She conjured up a small tribe of honest-to-God pygmies, who danced about the drawing room—naked. The present Dowager Duchess of Gloucester, Princess Alice, was a guest and, like the other children present, was fascinated. For weeks afterward, she and her sister Sybil were in trouble for dancing around without any clothes on when they were meant to be in bed. She has never forgotten that extraordinary afternoon of nearly eighty years ago.

All this made life very difficult for Alexandra's children's nannies—a familiar situation today in the Wales' nursery, where William and Harry's first nanny, Barbara Barnes, reputedly left because she was not permitted enough authority. Diana was determined that she was going to have a modern nanny for her children. This came as a disappointment to Prince Charles, who would have preferred, in the old-fashioned way, to have his nanny, Mabel Anderson, bring up William. He liked the idea of the continuity. Mabel Anderson had gone to work for Princess Anne when her first child was born, but unfortunately the arrangement hadn't worked out. All her life Mabel had been used to the roomy Buckingham Palace nursery, where she reigned supreme with two nursery footmen and nursery maids to do the menial work. Anne expected her to cope alone *and* cook Master Peter's meals. Mabel wasn't having that; she left and went to take over the nursery at a grander household where, as she put it, things were done properly.

There is no doubt she would have returned to Royal service if Prince Charles, with whom she was extremely close, had asked her. But in this case Diana wasn't having it. She wanted a young, first-name nanny and no uniforms. A pity, perhaps. William might have been better behaved if he had been left in the care of an old-fashioned nanny. As it is, he gets away with murder, and like his great-great-great-granny, Alexandra, Diana cannot bring herself to correct him. The lad has a temper that shows when he doesn't get his own way, and he is quite likely to burst into tears when corrected (not surprising, since it appears he so rarely is). It's fortunate that Harry is a much more amenable child and very like his father was as a little boy. Mabel Anderson used to say that no nursery could hold two Prince Andrews. Certainly no nursery could hold two Prince Williams. But Royal nurseries always seem to hold one holy terror. Once it was Princess Margaret, then it was Princess Anne, followed by Prince Andrew, and now young Prince William is filling the role with enthusiasm.

Wills may take after Auntie Anne, but his own mother was also quite capable of being a difficult child. She also liked her own way. She hated going for walks (today they are a favourite pastime) and would vanish if one seemed imminent. She saw quite a few nannies off until one named Janet Thompson tamed her. Diana hated eating the crusts off her bread, and Nanny Thompson, who looked after the Spencer children at Park House near Sandringham, said, 'I used to insist that Diana eat her crusts. I thought she was obeying me until one day I found at her place at the nursery table a little hidden shelf with a long line of crusts along it.' Nanny made sure that trick was never played again.

It was just the sort of thing that William does and just the sort of thing that makes Diana laugh instead of being cross, perhaps because she remembers how she was so very similar.

Diana can, however, control the children when she feels like doing so. In fact, she's rather good at it. Having once briefly worked in a nursery school, she knows how to distract a naughty child without causing temper tantrums. At one television photo session young William was beginning, rather aggressively, to run his toy car all over the photographer, interfering with his work. Diana did not tell him to stop or take the car from him. Instead, she turned the lad's attention to the photographer's pocket and suggested he park his car in there. To the photographer's relief, William took up the suggestion.

Given the choice, Diana is most unlikely to put her husband before her children. They come first in her life, though she is painfully coming to terms with the fact that it is her job that must be paramount. The well-publicized drama when she insisted on taking baby William on the tour of Australia showed early on which way her interests lie, though in truth it wasn't that much of a drama. The Queen, whose policy is to interfere as little as possible and let her family members learn by their mistakes, agreed to William's going and then waited to see what would happen. Diana, who firmly believes that separating mother and baby is deeply upsetting for them both, soon realized that it is, of course, totally impractical to tote a small child around when such high-pressure work is going on. She has quietly and reluctantly let go of the idea of never being separated from her offspring. The Australian experiment has not been repeated. Harry and Wills stay home with Nanny.

Poor Fergie, who received a roasting from both press and public for leaving Beatrice at home when she visited Australia, was in fact being extremely sensible. The child was, after all, in the capable hands of Nanny Alison Wardle. But after the official duties were completed Fergie decided to spend some time in the outback with her sister, Jane Makim and Fergie's real mistake was to stay away for so long once it was no longer officially necessary. Amid all the fuss and bother, Alex Makim, Jane's husband, said defensively, 'Jane and Sarah want to get away on their own and talk about babies. Of course she [Fergie] will miss the baby, but two more weeks won't make much difference. Sarah has not seen Jane for a very long time and they are enjoying being two sisters again.'

In retrospect, one can see that Fergie's disappearance was not quite as frivolous as it looked. It wasn't so much babies the two sisters wanted to talk about as the fact that Jane's marriage was tottering badly. She needed a sister's shoulder to cry on. It did, in fact, eventually come unstuck. Alex Makim blamed Fergie's elevation to Royalty for the break-up.

There was a time when it was taken for granted that Royal mothers left their children behind when they went off to do their duty. In 1927, when the present Queen was only eight months old, her parents went off on an overseas tour of both Australia and New Zealand. In those days such journeys had to be taken by sea, and the royal couple was to be away for six months. Her mother was deeply dismayed by the parting and wrote to Queen Mary, her mother-in-law, saying how the baby was so sweet while playing with the buttons on Bertie's uniform that leaving quite broke her up. When she returned home again she was sad to find she had missed the arrival of baby Elizabeth's first four teeth, just as the Duchess of York missed baby Beatrice's first steps.

The Queen in her turn had to leave Prince Charles when he was small, and it must have broken her heart when, after a long overseas trip, the solemn little figure waiting to greet her on her return at

Victoria Station did not recognize her and had to have his mother pointed out to him. And then he rather formally held out his hand to shake hers, rather than giving her a spontaneous hug and kiss.

Charles, well looked after by Nanny and Granny, was unlikely to have missed his mother, though the sentimental public preferred to think that he did. There was a rare picture taken of Charles crying at London Airport as he waved good-bye to his parents, who were flying off to Nigeria. The picture wrung a million mothers' hearts. Their sympathy was misplaced. Charles was having a temper tantrum because he 'wanted a ride in the airplane' and was upset that Mummy and Papa had said no. Princess Anne has no hard feelings about being left when her mother went off to work. 'I don't ever remember feeling deprived because nobody told me I was deprived,' she said. 'I accepted my parents' absences. When they came back they made a lot of time for us and spent holidays with us.'

Times change. When she was Princess of Wales the poor deaf and rather dim Queen Alexandra was in deep trouble with Victoria for taking her tiny children abroad with her. The Queen was furious when she learned that without her permission the baby heir to the throne had been taken off to Denmark to visit his maternal grandparents. Stuck as she was with an unfaithful husband, Alexandra made children her consolation. She was heartbroken when Georgie, her second son, married Princess May of Teck. She sighed, 'It is sad to think we shall never be able to be together and travel in the same way—yet there is a bond of love between us, that of mother and child, which nothing can diminish.' And having lost her Georgie to another woman, she clung, limpetlike, to her unmarried daughters, Victoria and Maud, and they in turn clung to her. So overprotective was she that the girls became known as Their Royal Shynesses. And so that Victoria could continue to be her mother's companion, the unfortunate girl was never permitted to marry. Alexandra's husband, the philandering Prince of Wales, said with some relief as he gallivanted through the Belle Époque, 'Her whole life is wrapped up in her daughters.'

Like Alexandra, leaving her children still tugs at the present Princess of Wales's emotions, even if it is only for a day. At a visit to a playschool when Prince Harry was just three, Diana confided in one of the helpers, Alita Connell, that she was worried about her youngest son and that she hadn't had much sleep because he kept climbing into her bed. Harry had some kind of bug and was not very well.

'As he looked up from his bed this morning.' she told Miss Connell, 'he said: "Don't leave me, Mummy, please don't leave me."'

She was sad and guilty about not staying at home and seemed to be feeling the strain of having to turn up at engagements when one of her children was feeling poorly. Miss Connell suggested she could always let his daddy look after him. The idea lightened the mood. The Princess burst out laughing. 'That would sort him out!' she said.

Though Diana has come to terms with much of the Royal family's unchanging routine and ways of doing things, when it comes to her children she has firmly brought the circumstances of their birth and upbringing into the twentieth century. When Prince Charles was born at Buckingham Palace, his father was playing squash with Michael Parker down in the bowels of the Palace. When Prince William and Harry were born, Prince Charles was at his wife's side in hospital, well away from the palace, in Paddington, West London. Though he didn't exactly enjoy the experience on either occasion, he said it was a very grown-up thing to do.

St. Mary's Hospital is where the Queen's gynaecologist, Sir George Pinker, delivers babies, both commoners' and Royals'. The Duchess of Gloucester was the first of the family to have her children in the Lindo Wing of St. Mary's. Then Princess Anne followed her example. There was a rumour at the time that Anne has the Rh negative factor and could have had a blue baby. More likely her blood group is perfectly normal and the story was invented to account for the break with tradition in the Queen's daughter going into a hospital. Anne herself explained it in her usual laconic fashion by saying, 'You go where the equipment is.'

When Princess Diana became pregnant, the old guard thought that the heir to the throne should be born at the Palace. Heirs to the throne had always been born in the Palace. It was traditional and expected. Sir George did not agree. A palace chamber converted into a lying-in room bore no comparison to his splendidly equipped hospital (equipment that had proved invaluable when the Duchess of Gloucester ran into complications with her first baby). King George VI had ended the seventeenth-century custom of having a Government witness or witnesses be present at a Royal birth. When the Queen and Princess Margaret were born the Home Secretary was elected witness, but Prince Charles was the first heir to the throne since the reign of James II to be born without some unfortunate man (or men) having to hover uncomfortably within the vicinity of the lying-in chamber. That particular custom had come about when gossip circulated that James II's wife, Mary of Modena, had not produced an heir at all. The baby in her bed was said to be a pretender—smuggled in in a warming pan. From then onward officials attended the births of Royal babies to make sure no jiggery-pokery went on. As recently as Georgian times, Royal births took place before a roomful of witnesses, including the Archbishop of Canterbury, the Prime Minister, and the Chancellor. And it must have been very embarrassing for all involved, particularly the mother.

As far as Diana was concerned, with this custom abolished there was no real reason for the birth to take place under a Royal roof. Besides, the young Diana was more inclined to take the advice of her distinguished gynaecological surgeon than listen to the old guard at the palace. Once again she got her own way. Both William and Harry were born in the Lindo Wing.

The room she occupied is, according to a subsequent occupant, pretty ordinary. No luxury at all. It has windows of one-way glass so that no one can see in; a basic hospital bed; utilitarian furniture, including a blue plastic armchair; and a functional tiled bathroom. When William and Harry were born, neither were put in with other babies in the ward—not out of snobbery, but simply for safety. The hospital's biggest worry was that there might be a kidnapping. St. Mary's is now accustomed to Royal mothers, and the ward has been made secure by those who guard the Royal family.

When Harry arrived in September 1984, his big brother was his first visitor. When Diana was informed that her first-born was on the way up to see her, she got out of bed and hid behind the door of her room. As soon as she heard William trotting down the corridor, she put her head out and called his name. He was in her arms in a second, shouting, 'Mummy! Mummy!' After being introduced to his new baby brother, he instantly made himself at home in the ward where he himself had been born, running up and down the corridor and pushing his head round the door of the nurses' room. 'May I have a biscuit?' he asked them and returned triumphantly with one to show his mother.

With both babies Diana was quickly in and out of the hospital. The spartan room does not encourage lingering. It is also a far cry from the grandeur of medieval Royal lying-in chambers where the Queen was made to disappear from public view toward the end of her pregnancy. Those chambers of long ago must have been mighty stuffy, since all the walls, ceilings, and windows were hung with draperies. Bedcovers and wall hangings were made of heavy fabric to stifle sound in case the Queen sufficiently lost her dignity to yell when the baby began to arrive. Only one window could be uncovered (not opened, mind you) in case the Queen felt like some daylight. The mother-to-be's food was served on special dishes and brought to her in bed. An altar where mass could be said was set up in the room, and there the hot, bored, and pregnant lady was left, with her ladies-in-waiting and a priest for company, until the little Prince or Princess arrived.

There was no question of her feeding her own baby. Mother and baby bonding had not been thought of. Queen Anne Boleyn wanted to breast-feed the infant Elizabeth I, but her husband, Henry VIII, put his foot down. He said it was not seemly. Royal mothers stayed in bed recovering their health for at least a month while the babies were immediately handed to a wet nurse, who gave them their nourishment until they were two or three years old. There was no other choice since neither cow's nor goat's milk was drunk at this time.

There were some Royal mothers who bucked the system. Catherine of Aragon insisted on breast-feeding her baby, as did Queen Philippa, wife of Edward III. But for generations it was not considered at all right and proper for Royal mothers to breast-feed. The present Queen ended this outdated piece of Royal etiquette when she breast-fed her children, and Princess Anne and the Princess of Wales followed her example. The Duchess of York breast-fed her first baby for three weeks and then settled for the modern equivalent of a wet nurse—the baby bottle.

Fergie was the first of the modern mothers to have her babies outside today's Royal system. Usually the Royal women all use the Queen's gynaecologist, who has now safely delivered nine Royal babies. The Duchess of York decided to stay with Anthony Kenney, who had been her gynaecologist before she married. He is the consultant at the privately run Portland Hospital, and after a lot of shilly-shallying, which gave the security people a headache, she chose to have her first baby in this expensive hospital, which is owned by an American company. The rooms, costing £300 a night, are luxurious, and the food is top-restaurant standard; perhaps this was why the Duchess did not come home with quite the speed of her sister-in-law. She stayed at Portland for four days after Beatrice's birth.

Like so many Royal mothers, Fergie did not enjoy her first pregnancy much. The baby was unplanned and therefore a bit of a surprise to all concerned. It is said that the second one was unplanned too. But having got over the shock, Fergie on both occasions declared herself ecstatic. On the day it was announced that she was expecting Beatrice she said, 'It would be fun to have quite a few, wouldn't it.' She obviously meant it. A month afer Beatrice's first birthday in September 1989 it was announced she was pregnant again. The first time round she had miserable problems with morning sickness, and water retention made her so heavy that she was completely exhausted most of the time. 'I feel like a horse,' she groaned in her usual self-deprecating manner. The poor lass looked like one too.

Beatrice was induced and born by epidural. The little Princess was born fifth in line to the throne, and Fergie got her wish. She had wanted a girl, knowing that it would be the first Princess born to this generation of Royal mothers. It would also be the first Princess born within the House of Windsor since the Princess Royal, Princess Anne, thirty-nine years previously.

The Duchess managed to remain in much better shape throughout her second pregnancy but the birth was not as straightforward. Princess Eugenie turned feet first, into the breech position, at the last moment and had to be delivered by caesarean section. She weighed 7 lb 1 oz and turned out to be a remarkably pretty baby. A delighted Andrew arrived at Portland Hospital bearing an enormous bouquet in the shape of a stork. Well chosen for the Duchess who adores cuddly toys, huge teddy bears and stuffed animals.

The Duchess of York is likely to be firm with her children. 'She has strong views on good manners,' said a friend. She will undoubtedly bring up both her offspring in the old-fashioned way, and that will find favour with her in-laws.

There was no fussing about buying a new pram or masses of new clothes for Beatrice. The Duchess used a friend's old pram and was quite happy to have secondhand clothes from her little half-brother and half-sisters. Her stepmother Susan Ferguson, dug out all Fergie's own baby clothes—some with a most beautiful kind of smocking that is not easy to find these days. The Duchess feels 'it's nice having old things,' and they'll be in use again for baby number two. This is the Royal family's way. Prams are kept in store for the next baby, and clothing is handed down. The same cot comes out time and time again. It is the family's old ethic of never wasting anything or spending money unnecessarily. The Queen must have quietly had a fit over the pure-silk rompers that Diana bought for her boys when they were young and the masses of clothes she cannot resist buying for them—clothes that are outgrown in weeks. Diana doesn't mind. She passes them on to those of her girlfriends who are also young mothers.

The Duchess of York is unlikely to be so indulgent. She likes children and is good with them, but she doesn't have Diana's obsessive feelings about babies and prefers children when they are old enough for games and conversation. She was furious, however, when in Canberra on the ill-fated Australian trip a spectator asked if Beatrice suffered from colic and then added snidely, 'I suppose you have a nanny who sees to things like that.' Very cross, Fergie snapped back, 'No colic. I look after my baby.'

As Bea was at that moment half the world away it was not strictly true. But it was perhaps an understandable reaction.

Fergie enjoys playing with the children of her father's second marriage, half-brother Andrew and half-sisters Alice and Elizabeth, and she completely won over Paddy McNally's boys, who, missing their mother after her death, were originally very suspicious of their father's new, young girlfriend. Fergie worked hard to win their trust and affection and in the end was very close to them. They called her 'Gingerpuss,' and when their father was away for Grand Prix weekends she would stay at his chalet in Verbier with them. She was in charge. They had a routine of going to the cinema and then out for a hamburger. What little cooking Fergie has done in her life, she did for them. Nothing exotic, just mashed potatoes and shepherd's pies, steak and chips—the easy-to-eat food boys like. But she was not soft with them. She always made sure they were in bed before nine, and they were not allowed to stay up for dinner parties. They couldn't have minded the discipline as both were sad when she and their father broke up. She missed them too and does try to keep in touch.

She now has a family of her own to fill the gaps, and when she was being interviewed for television in France not long after Beatrice's birth, she said happily, 'She's changed our lives. Really she's absolutely unbelievable. I'm very, very fortunate that she is so well and healthy, and she has all the right parts. She's incredibly placid and calm. Sleeps through the night. I don't know where she gets it from . . . probably her father.'

Diana's children never slept through the night when they were small. Both were restless—William from too much energy and Harry because he was prone to small ailments. Diana, like Princess Margaret, was the one who got out of bed to see what was wrong when a cry or a whimper was heard in the night. Her theory was (and still is) that a mother's arms are the most comforting and no doubt she is right. She has always made valiant efforts to keep the children in the forefront of her life and much prefers morning or evening engagements so that she can be with Harry for play and for tea when he comes home from school. They then sit together watching television and Diana supervises bathtime. Both she and her second son miss William now he has gone off to boarding school at Ludgrove Preparatory near Wokingham.

Weekends are always the best days of the week in the Wales family, particularly when the family is united again at school holiday times. At William and Harry's nursery school, as most of the parents had country homes the school shut up shop early on Fridays so that the parents could get away. Diana always went for the boys herself.

There is only Harry to collect now, though the Princess so missed Wills at first that she sneaked him off to Highgrove for one or two weekends.

They drive to the country in Diana's car and the most important event is to check on the health of their pet rabbit. Charles always had a pet rabbit when he was little, and so do they. After that, it's time for a swim in the heated pool—dug by the army as a wedding present. (No, the navy didn't put the water in!) Tea is served in the big, airy kitchen around the kitchen table. Weekends are very family oriented, with Diana cooking the children's lunch and supper and Prince Charles teaching them a bit of gardening (the children have their own vegetable patch) and taking them riding—usually without their mother. Remembering the bad fall from a pony she herself had as a child, Diana is nervous seeing her children riding.

William was the first future King to go to nursery school, which makes Charles the last to have had his first lessons from a governess. Charles loved his governess, Miss Peebles ('Peebie,' as he called her), but the Queen decided to make a break with tradition and at Prince Philip's urging sent her children to school. Miss Peebles was not sent away. She taught the Queen's other children when they were small and remained a loved and honoured member of the family. She died in her own room at the palace many years later. The Queen takes good care of her old retainers.

Whether or not Prince Charles should go to school caused a great deal of discussion. It was something in which the Queen had no experience, having always been taught at home. And it seemed a daring thing to send the heir to the throne into the tough world outside. There were problems to be considered, such as security. Going to school meant a detective would have to go to school every day as well. The Queen worried that her son would not be happy and that other children would be either sycophantic or standoffish. She was well aware that it would not be easy.

Prince Philip had no such fears. He wanted his eldest son to board at his old schools, Cheam and Gordonstoun. He felt it was right that the boy should be taken away from what he thought of as petticoat government. True, Charles was surrounded by women. His mother, granny, governess, and nanny were the biggest influences on him. All four women were uneasy at the idea of school, particularly as Charles was a rather quiet and shy little boy—not at all the extrovert his father had been as a child. Philip won the battle as he always has when it comes to family matters. And his judgment was right. Charles will be the first King with at least some knowledge of the real world. His sister Anne's children will be truly knowledgeable, since they are the first of the family to be sent to an ordinary State school.

Charles's introduction to the world outside the palace was not as dramatic as State school. He went first to Hill House, an expensive day school for rich little children, where he was obviously thoroughly miserable. But as young as he was, he conducted himself with his own innate dignity. His parents must have been proud of him. At the age of nine he was sent to Prince Philip's old prep school, Cheam, and eventually to Gordonstoun, an outward-bound type of establishment with more emphasis on sports than academics.

It was a rotten choice for Charles. His father, a man more into action than abstract thought, had shone there. Prince Charles was unhappy and had fantasies about running away and living in the woods near Balmoral. Eton, where his mother and the Queen Mother would have preferred to send him, would have been a far better choice. He enjoyed his time at university a great deal more, but that was followed by a stint in the navy, which he didn't care for, loathing the lack of privacy. Eventually he did settle down and begin to enjoy it, but at the end of the day Charles is pretty much a homebody.

Diana comes from the kind of family where children are always sent away to school, and she has taken another step forward from the traditional Royal ways by sending her boys to nursery school. There was no question of hiring a governess in Diana's household. She sensibly wanted her boys to have the companionship of other children and for a while was thinking of starting up a palace nursery school herself until it proved impractical.

The Prince and Diana have also swept aside years of Royal tradition by turning their backs on the rugged Gordonstoun where Prince Philip was a student and, in turn, where he sent his three sons. (Charles hated it.)

Instead, Prince William is at Ludgrove, a boarding school within easy reach of home. Diana's own family is Eton-educated and it is significant that Ludgrove is a 'feeder' school for Eton, run by Old Etonians.

Now that Ludgrove is the choice for William it is inevitable that his younger brother, Harry, will follow him there when the time comes. William, a bundle of energy, bossy and a bit of a bully, might well have enjoyed Gordonstoun but it would never be a happy choice for Harry. He would be as miserable there as his father once was.

The issue of a Royal child's education at an ordinary school is a complex one. It is so hard for young Royals to make friends and to know whether they are liked for themselves or for their position. Anne arrived late on her first day at Benenden school in 1963 because she had to stop the Royal limousine to be sick, out of sheer terror. When she and her mother did arrive, three hundred girls in identical uniforms along with the staff of forty were waiting to greet her. A daunting start. But Anne had less difficulty than her older brother. She soon sorted out the sycophants. She has the perfect temperament for a boarding school pupil—unsentimental, quite tough, and capable of finding friends who see things her way. Her own children are now both boarding at Port Regis coeducational prep school, but there was no truck with governesses or expensive private establishments for young gentlemen and ladies previous to that. From the age of four Anne's children went to the local primary school in Minchinhampton along with the butcher's and the baker's kids from the village. The fact there were no fees to pay may have been a bonus!

The Queen's grandchildren have been fortunate in that they have benefited from all the breaks with tradition that she innovated. Early on the Queen decided that her children would not have to bow and curtsey to her as in previous generations; she herself had been taught to curtsey to her father even though he hated the idea of it. She also decreed that up until the age of eighteen her children would be called by their Christian names by family and staff. After their eighteenth birthdays, discreet notes were sent to all the staff telling them that from now on titles would be used, with the Princes addressed as 'Sir' and Anne as 'Ma'am.'

In spite of her heavy work schedule the Queen managed a fair compromise between being the Monarch and being a mother. The long Royal holidays have helped. For ten weeks in the summer and six in the winter, plus a lot of other time as well, the Queen has been able to concentrate on being a family woman. Her State boxes, full of the nation's secrets, still arrive, but throughout the holiday periods they are frequently almost empty. Her influence on the entire family is strong, and she is very much the matriarchal figure. Princess Anne was asked by her biographer, Brian Hoey, if it were difficult to maintain a close relationship with her mother, since her mother is also the Monarch.

'I think you've got it the wrong way round,' Anne said. 'It's much more difficult to remember she is Queen than my mother. After all, I've known her longer as mother than Queen. She has been Queen most of my life but that's not how I think of her—it's the other way round really.'

The Queen has impressed much of her own personality on her children. Though staggeringly rich, she is very aware of the value of money, and this is a trait she has passed on to the children. When as a small boy Charles lost a dog leash in the Buckingham Palace grounds, she made him go find it. Dog leashes cost money, she said firmly. They are all thrifty. Anne, like her mother, goes around turning off electric lights, and she never spent her £2 pocket money when she was at school. It was usually still intact at the end of the week. Charles saves food that would be better thrown away (though Diana is weaning him from this habit). They all think twice about spending money, but it is puzzling to know where this stingy streak comes from, since the Queen Mother is a true happy spender. But then Queen Mary was careful, Queen Alexandra spendthrift, and the most careful of them all was Queen Victoria, who if asked for a loan by one of her relatives, would say reprovingly, 'Pearls do not grow on bushes at Windsor.'

The Queen also created a climate where her family could lead more of a normal life. Anne and her children have benefited from this more than any of the other Windsor children. There has never been a photo call for Peter and Zara. She never mentions them in public. As far as her work is concerned they might not exist. This attempt to seclude her children is a matter of principle as far as Anne is concerned. Like her father, she loathes what she considers any infringement of her privacy and theirs, and she has tried hard to keep them from fully understanding exactly what their position in life is. When Peter asked why someone was photographing him she said sharply, 'It's not you, it's me.'

'They have to be given the chance to grow up reasonably normally,' she said. 'They ought to be judged for themselves.'

Peter and Zara have grown up normally, and Anne is a better mother than she gives herself credit for. She used to sew tiny pockets on her children's pillows to hold teeth when they fell out—the teeth for the fairies. She taught them to ride. Zara had a pony when she was two and a half, and Peter started riding when he was three. When the family stays at friends' homes for the weekend, Anne takes her children down to the kitchen at teatime, makes them a cup of tea and Marmite sandwiches, and sits with them while they eat and drink. She doesn't leave everything to the nanny. She also underrates herself when she says that she doesn't like children much. Anyone seeing the warm, spontaneous hug she gave her son at Zara's christening saw a glimpse of a doting mother. But she doesn't care to be seen as being weak or sentimental in any way. She has always hidden her feelings. It took a lot to make her cry when she was a child, though she was prone to tantrums. One of her worst was when Charles was allowed to go to the Coronation and she was left at home. She was enraged. An awkward child, she was not given to showing affection and never has been. Her weak spot is Zara. Zara gets hugs, and Zara *almost* gets spoiled. The little girl can climb all over her mother as well as wind Anne round her little pinkie.

But if the children are naughty, Anne smacks their bottoms. She caused a bit of an uproar when Peter was seven and Zara was three by smacking both their rear ends at the Badminton Horse Trials, and in full view of a fascinated crowd. Peter wouldn't get down from some dangerous scaffolding, Zara was being noisy, and Anne lost her patience. They got their smacks and were bundled into the car, then taken home to Gatcombe and to bed. Anne, who was chastised herself occasionally when she needed it, believes in a bit of discipline.

She herself could be very naughty. On one Balmoral holiday when she was five or six, she rushed into Prince Richard of Gloucester's room, seized his dagger, and plunged it into the eiderdown right through to the mattress. 'I've always wanted to do that,' she told her cousin and disappeared again. Richard's mother, Princess Alice, was horrified when she saw the damage and wanted Richard to tell the Queen what had happened in case the housekeeper thought that he was responsible. Richard refused to tell on his cousin and never did. In those days Royal children were always brought up to live by the old-fashioned virtues. It was drummed into them that it was wrong and nasty to tell tales. Those nannies had their own warning of what would happen to children who did such a thing:

> Tell-tale-tit,
> Your tongue shall be split,
> And all the little puppy dogs
> Will have a little bit!

Telling tales was quite rightly considered despicable. The late Duke of Gloucester, Prince Henry, had two black Scottish terriers that were not popular with King George V, so they had to be hidden. One day at Sandringham the dogs scampered in as tea was being formally served to most of the family. Both the Duchess of Gloucester and her husband knew that the dogs' presence would annoy the King, and they quickly hid them under the table. It was just bad luck that Princess Margaret, then only age four and not noted for keeping still and quiet, began to run round the room. One of the Scotties jumped out from under the tablecloth and gave her a nasty bite on the leg. Fortunately for the Gloucesters, the King did not notice this assault on his granddaughter, and a very embarrassed Prince Henry pushed the dog back under the table. Little Margaret, knowing the dogs were not meant to be there, did not so much as let out a whimper. She just went rather red and quietly disappeared to have her leg doctored in the nursery, which, said the Duchess of Gloucester with some accuracy, was truly noble of her.

The good, solid, old-fashioned values that were taught in the nursery are perhaps being lost, but it would be expecting too much for the younger generation to stick to the rigid rules that bound their elders. Their elders have had to accept that times change, and that these days it is just as difficult for Royal parents to control their children as it is for any other parents.

In 1988, when Lord Nicholas Windsor, son of the Duke and Duchess of Kent, was eighteen, he was arrested in St. James's Park with another youth. Both were in possession of cannabis. The boys were taken to Bow Street police station (opposite the Opera House) and held for nearly two hours before being released without charges. Lord Nicholas, in spite of his top-drawer Winchester and Harrow education, has a reputation as a rebel. The Queen was not pleased to hear of his arrest, and his mother, who was ill throughout his formative years, must have been heartbroken. Happily, the boy has not been in any trouble since.

The Duke and Duchess of Kent have produced a most attractive daughter, but they have had to live with young Lady Helen's rather coarse nickname—'Melons'—a reference to her voluptuous figure, which she is not averse to flaunting. She flaunted it sunbathing topless on a Mediterranean beach, much to the delight of a hovering photographer. She appears to be unlucky when it comes to photographers. She was snapped hanging out of a boyfriend's window early one morning, perhaps looking for the milkman. Her love affairs are public knowledge. Her parents, no doubt trying to be modern, rented her a villa on Corfu, which she shared quite openly with the boyfriend of the moment. A girl with much sexual allure, she has been described as an innocent in wolf's clothing. Lady Helen is certainly not a bad girl. In fact, she is a perfectly normal one by today's standards. Her problem is being the daughter of Royal parents. Still, they forgive her much, since in the years when her mother was suffering a serious nervous breakdown, Lady Helen gave up her job and became for a while the mother of the family.

Princess Margaret too has every right to be proud of her two children. In spite of her stormy life, they are steady young people, David Linley has made a great success of his own carpentry business creating custom-made furniture, and Sarah is a gentle girl and a talented artist.

Like her mother before her, Lady Sarah's love life has been checkered. Her first boyfriend was stolen from her by cousin Lady Helen Windsor. She then fell in love with Cosmo Fry, a man seven years older than she and who had been previously married. When told this was not a good idea, she sensibly ended the relationship without making any great song and dance about it.

But for some time now she has been the girlfriend of Daniel Chatto, a young painter, who began his career as an actor. His family are comfortably off and stalwartly upper-middle class and there should be no objections to his romance with Lady Sarah. But there is one fly in the ointment.

Chatto is a darkly good-looking man, educated at Westminster School and then New College, Oxford where he read English. His background is show business. His late father, Tom, was an actor and his mother, Ros Chatto, worked for many years as secretary to the late Robin Fox, an impresario who fathered actors Edward and James Fox. According to Robin Fox's wife, Angela, he also fathered Daniel.

Mrs. Fox, who was 78 in 1990, is adamant that her husband had an affair with Mrs. Chatto for ten years and that Daniel was the result. She also says that, among others, Robin Fox had an affair with Princess Marina of Kent, the present Duke of Kent's mother.

Lord Snowdon was dismayed by Angela Fox's claim that his daughter's boyfriend is illegitimate and asked her to withdraw her allegations. Mrs. Fox declined.

And there the matter rests, though if and when Sarah Armstrong-Jones and Daniel Chatto marry—as it is rumoured they will—it seems unlikely that the Royal family will be too concerned about Daniel's parentage. Illegitimacy is not unknown to them and he is a thoroughly nice and presentable young man.

In the past, Sarah, too, like her cousin Helen, has been photographed leaving a boyfriend's flat at seven in the morning, presumably after more than just breakfast. Princess Margaret, like mothers the world over, must look back on the days when she strove so hard to hide her love affair with her daughter's father and marvel at the way times have changed.

ILLUSTRATION ACKNOWLEDGMENTS

The Publishers gratefully acknowledge permission to reproduce the following pictures:

First Plate Section
The Prince and Princess of Wales, 1864—Hulton-Deutsch Collection
The Prince and Princess of Wales, 1864—Vernon Heath
The Duke and Duchess of York, 1893—Downey
The Prince and Princess of Wales and family, 1906—Abergeldie
The Duke and Duchess of York, 1923—Syndication International Ltd
Princess Elizabeth with grandparents, 1935—Hulton-Deutsch Collection
The Duke and Duchess of Kent, 1934—Hulton-Deutsch Collection
The Duke and Duchess of Kent with family, 1942—Hulton-Deutsch Collection
King George VI and family, 1943—Syndication International Ltd
Princess Margaret and Antony Armstrong-Jones, 1960—The Press Association Ltd
Princess Alexandra and family, 1966—Hulton-Deutsch Collection
Anna Wallace, 1981—Syndication International Ltd

Second Plate Section
The following by Alpha Photographic Press Agency, Ltd:
The Queen and family, 1964
The Queen and Prince Philip, 1968
The Queen and Prince Philip, 1970
Princess Anne and Captain Mark Phillips, 1982 (photo: Jim Bennett)
The Prince and Princess of Wales, 1985 (photo: Tim Anderson)
The Duke and Duchess of Kent, 1988 (photo: David Chancellor)
Prince and Princess Michael of Kent, 1989 (photo: David Chancellor)
The Duke and Duchess of York, 1988 (photo: David Chancellor)
Princess Margaret and Roddy Llewelyn, 1989 (photo: David Chancellor)
The Royal Family, 1979—Syndication International Ltd

Third Plate Section
The Prince and Princess of Wales, 1981—*News of the World*
Princess Anne and Mark Phillips—Alpha (photo: J. Appelbee)
Princess Anne and Detective Peter Cross—Rex Features
Paddy McNally and Sarah Ferguson, 1985—Alan Davidson
Princess Anne at Ascot, 1987—Syndication International Ltd
The Queen and Prince Philip—Alpha (photo: J. Appelbee)
Sandringham—Alpha (photo: Paul Webb)
Balmoral—Alpha (photo: Jim Bennett)
Prince and Princess Michael, 1984—Alpha (photo: Jim Bennett)
The Princess of Wales and sons, 1987—Alpha (photo: Jim Bennett)
The Prince and Princess of Wales and sons, 1989—Alpha
The Queen Mother and family, 1989—Alpha
The Duchess of York, 1989—Alpha (photo: David Chancellor)

Index